PRAISE FOR *PROFESSIONAL TROUBLEMAKER*

"As an oft-scared chickenhead who cares too much about what others think, it's so comforting to be guided through my own crippling fear and self-doubt by one of the bravest, most incisively honest, hysterical voices I know. This book was so real and relatable, and so much of it had me belly laughing. This is the essential manual for anybody who is ready to take that leap of faith to bet on the best, uninhibited, whole version of themselves."

—Issa Rae, actor, producer, creator of *Insecure*, and
New York Times bestselling author

"This book is a manual on HOW TO HUMAN. You could spend a lifetime and fortune finding the perfect therapist, mentor, minister, career coach, and girlfriend—or you could just spend a day reading *Professional Troublemaker*. This book—Luvvie Ajayi Jones's most helpful, bold, vulnerable, hilarious, and relevant work yet—is equal parts catharsis and wake-up call, both comforting and galvanizing. I laughed and cried so hard that my family asked me to read in the other room. With her razor-sharp mind, soul on fire, and heart of gold, Luvvie is the writer and artist the world needs right now. This will be my go-to gift for all the beloved troublemakers in my life."

—Glennon Doyle, author of the *#1 New York Times*
bestseller *Untamed* and founder of Together Rising

"There's nobody quite like Luvvie Ajayi Jones. She's a force and a powerhouse, the thunder and the lightning—and *Professional Troublemaker* shows us exactly how she got that way. This is a great book about reaching deep down inside yourself, crushing your fears, unleashing your 'too muchness,' and giving yourself permission to shake the world. In a voice that is funny, wise, bold, and always generous, Luvvie encourages, inspires, and dares us to follow our dreams, fight against injustice, soak up the pleasures of life, and take up all the space in the room. If this book doesn't make you feel bolder and braver by the final page, then you weren't reading it right. I loved every passionate word of it."

—Elizabeth Gilbert, *New York Times*
bestselling author of *Big Magic* and *Eat, Pray, Love*

"Whether you are traversing new territory, bounding back from perceived failure, or learning for the first time how to own the full power of your own voice, Luvvie's Fear-Fighting Manual is the pep talk we all need. Delivered in her singular voice and signature shade, this must read is chock-full of gems that will guide you out of your own way so you can get more out of your life—a life that is more interesting than one lived in fear." —Elaine Welteroth, journalist and *New York Times* bestselling author of *More Than Enough*

"If you've seen her TED talk or read her first bestseller, you know there isn't a smarter or funnier cultural critic alive. This is the eye-opening, soul-nourishing, sidesplitting book you need to replace the anguish of 2020 with the courage to overcome your fears, master your doubts, and make good trouble in 2021."

—Adam Grant, *New York Times* bestselling author of *Think Again* and *Originals*, and host of the TED podcast *WorkLife*

"As if there was ever a reason to think Luvvie Ajayi Jones was simply a powerful voice, *Professional Troublemaker* will remind readers that she is one of the most effective and evocative writers alive."

—Kiese Laymon, *New York Times* bestselling author of *Heavy*

"Some of the greatest pleasures in life come from breaking rules, questioning boundaries, and troublemaking. But to make trouble well—and to bring all the pieces of yourself to life, love, and conflict—is an art. Luvvie Ajayi Jones knows this and shows this as she guides readers to finding their own path to troublemaking with humor, charm, and a whole lot of heart."

—Esther Perel, psychotherapist, podcast host, and *New York Times* bestselling author

"This book is a comfort and a challenge. It inspires, encourages, heartens, and invigorates in equal measure. You should read it."

—Jenny Lawson, *New York Times* bestselling author of *Furiously Happy* and *Let's Pretend This Never Happened*

"Luvvie is authentic power personified. This book has so much depth, ancestral wisdom, and inspiration spoken in the most delightful way. It is an ancient text, wrapped in hilarious observations, charm, and a supportive urging to become more—a blueprint for living with courage and unapologetically standing in your greatness. I legit had my jaw dropped wide-open in so many parts, and I felt God all in this book. There is seriously no one like Luvvie; she is one of one."

—Devi Brown, chief impact officer of Chopra Global

"Tired of the status quo? This book is a MUST read. There is no better time to shake up your life, your work, or your perspective than today. Luvvie pushes you to places you have always wanted to go but never thought you could—until now. If you are a leader, urge your people to read this book. Limiting beliefs will be overcome, empowerment will be at an all-time high, and the term *professional troublemaker* will become standard when it comes to taking people to the next level."

—Mel Robbins, bestselling author of *The 5 Second Rule*

"THIS BOOK. I'm mad Luvvie wrote an even better book than her debut. LIVID in the best way. *Professional Troublemaker* is full of stories that made me laugh until my stomach hurt, advice that made me rearrange my priorities, and so many examples of the highs and lows of living a semi-public creative life. Read this book to be simultaneously entertained and educated. Luvvie Ajayi Jones has a singular writing voice that comes across warm, kind, and just judge-y enough."

—Ashley C. Ford, author of *Somebody's Daughter*

"The three things we need right now are the ability to fight through our fears, the understanding that we can make change in our lives and the world, and the invitation to laugh—hard and often. Luvvie—who is among the most hilarious, passionate women I know—gives us all three in her . . . book, which is chock full of all of the things we all think, but never say. It's the daily vitamin we all need during these times."

—Abby Wambach, Olympic gold medalist and FIFA World Cup champion

"Podcast host Ajayi Jones (*I'm Judging You*) explores how to fight fear in order to speak up for oneself in this witty, insightful guide. . . . Readers needing the extra push to stand up will find Ajayi Jones's advice enlightening and empowering."

—*Publishers Weekly*

PENGUIN LIFE

PROFESSIONAL TROUBLEMAKER

Luvvie Ajayi Jones is an award-winning author, speaker, and podcast host who thrives at the intersection of humor, technology, and justice. She is the author of the *New York Times* bestseller *I'm Judging You: The Do-Better Manual* and runs her own social platform, LuvvNation.

To access Penguin Readers Guides online, visit penguinrandomhouse.com.

PROFESSIONAL TROUBLEMAKER

The Fear-Fighter Manual

LUVVIE AJAYI JONES

life

PENGUIN BOOKS
An imprint of Penguin Random House LLC
penguinrandomhouse.com

First published in the United States of America by Viking,
an imprint of Penguin Random House LLC, 2021
Published with a bonus chapter in Penguin Books 2021

A Penguin Life Book

ISBN 9781984881922 (paperback)

THE LIBRARY OF CONGRESS HAS CATALOGED THE HARDCOVER EDITION AS FOLLOWS:
Names: Ajayi Jones, Luvvie, author.
Title: Professional troublemaker: the fear-fighter manual /
Luvvie Ajayi Jones.
Description: New York: Viking, 2021. |
Identifiers: LCCN 2020043952 (print) | LCCN 2020043953 (ebook) |
ISBN 9781984881908 (hardcover) | ISBN 9781984881915 (ebook) |
ISBN 9780593298770 (international edition) |
Subjects: LCSH: Self-confidence. | Truthfulness and falsehood.
Classification: LCC BF575.S39 A43 2021 (print) | LCC BF575.S39 (ebook) |
DDC 158.1—dc23
LC record available at https://lccn.loc.gov/2020043952
LC ebook record available at https://lccn.loc.gov/2020043953

Printed in the United States of America
1st Printing

BOOK DESIGN BY LUCIA BERNARD

Dedicated to my warrior, my matron saint,
my grandmother, Olúfúnmiláyò Juliana Fáloyin.

Contents

DO

Introduction

I am a professional troublemaker.

What is a professional troublemaker, you ask?

A professional troublemaker is not the person who brings chaos into the midst of any room they are in. That person is a troll. A professional troublemaker is not someone who insists on speaking to hurt feelings. That person is a hater. A professional troublemaker is not someone who wants to disagree with people just because they wanna play devil's advocate. That person is a contrarian, and Satan never told anyone he needed a supervisor, so I'm not sure why so many people volunteer for the position.

A professional troublemaker is someone who critiques the world, the shoddy systems, and the people who refuse to do better. As a writer, a speaker, and a shady Nigerian, I am the person who is giving the side-eye to folks for doing trash things. I am the person who is unable to be quiet when I feel cheated. I am the person who says what you are thinking and feeling but dare not say because you have a job to protect, or you're afraid of how it will land. I even wrote a whole book called *I'm Judging You: The Do-Better Manual.* A book that I TRUST you've read by now. If you haven't, well, I'm judging you. *Clears throat.*

While a professional troublemaker isn't someone who manufactures chaos or crises, they do understand that chaos can come from being honest and authentic and going against the tide. Because in a world that insists on our cooperation even in the face of perpetual turmoil, not standing for it makes you a rebel. Professional troublemakers deal with it because they have a cause. They are often sharp tongued and misunderstood but always golden hearted. A professional troublemaker is committed to speaking the truth and showing up always as themselves, and is almost unable to bow in the face of a world that demands it.

People often ask me how I am confident in who I am, and how I have the nerve to say what I say. I've always shrugged and said I don't remember not being this person. Whenever I got in trouble when I was little, it was usually for my mouth. Being a Naija gal, I come from a culture that prioritizes age when it comes to giving respect, but that never sat well with me. Which is why Little Luvvie got punished usually for telling someone older that she didn't like what they were saying or doing.

But it's also because I come from a long line of professional troublemakers. My grandmother, Olúfúnmiláyọ̀ Fáloyin,* was the one I got to see as I was growing up. When I really give it thought, I realize I got a generation's worth of courage from Grandma.

---

*Pronounced Oh-LOO-foon-me-LAH-yaw FAH-low-YEEN.

My grandma was the chairlady of the board of directors of Team No Chill Enterprises. As an elder Nigerian stateswoman, she was the epitome of Giver of No Dambs.* She was too old to be checked. She knew how to take up the space she was given, and in the times she wasn't given space, she took it. She did all of this with a smile and charm that made her magnetic. She wasn't rude but she was direct. She wasn't hateful, but you would hear her speak her mind. She was open-hearted and open-handed and she prayed with the same fervor that she'd use to lambast you. She could not stand to see people cheated or treated poorly. In her honesty and given the fact that she approached everything with so much heart, she was deeply loved by so many.

This is the crux of what it means to be a professional trouble-maker.

WHEN TROUBLEMAKING MEETS FEAR

My first book, *I'm Judging You: The Do-Better Manual*, asks us all to commit to leaving this world better than we found it. I wrote *Professional Troublemaker: The Fear-Fighter Manual* because in order to do better and be a professional troublemaker, you gotta do some scary shit. This book is the *HOW* to *I'm Judging You*'s *WHAT*. How do we make sure we aren't leaving this third rock from the sun in worse shape than when we showed up? How do we make sure this rotating water sphere doesn't up and quit us? (Well, that answer, I don't know.

---

*Damb: Because it's more fun than "damn." Get used to this.

Mother Earth shoulda definitely kicked us clean off it by now because we've been such dreadful beings.)

There is a lot to fear in this world. In November 2017, I opened the TEDWomen conference with a talk called "Get Comfortable with Being Uncomfortable," which addressed this very subject. When the talk was posted, it was watched more than one million times in a month. At this point, it has received over five million views and continues to climb. Every single day, I get messages from people from all over the world talking about how much impact it had on them. The response lets me know that this idea of living through fear is a major pain point for people. We are afraid of simply showing up in the world, and it affects everything around us as a result.

But here's the thing: We're human. Fear is God's way of making sure we're not being utterly stupid and jumping off mountains without parachutes. God is like, "Let me put something in these beings I'm creating so they aren't constantly coming back here before their time. Because I know their goof-asses need limits." However, the same tool that keeps us from putting our hand in an open fire and leaving it there is the same one keeping us from telling our boss we cannot pay our bills because of how low our pay is, and that we need a raise to be able to live properly.

One of the things I've learned in my journey is how much fear could have stopped me at any moment from doing the thing that changed my life. Or doing that thing that led to me meeting the right person. Or doing the thing that allowed someone else to do the thing that changed their life. We talk about "living our best lives," but how are we gonna do it when we have fear holding our ankles down like some dad sneakers? (I will never understand why them

UGLASS* dad sneakers are a thing. Your feet look like they're embedded in some rocks as you drag those bulky things around all day. Why are people against nice things? Anyway, I digress.)

I don't think we can overcome fear. It's a constant fight and we will get endless opportunities to do scary shit. I'm not going to sit up here and say, "These are the tactics to do away with fear." Some degree of fear will always remain. But even though we're constantly afraid of being burned, not everything is a volcano with molten lava to avoid. Instead, we need to stop expecting fearlessness and acknowledge that we're anxious but we aren't letting fear be our deciding factor.

We have to learn to fight fear like we'd fight the hairstylist who messed up our haircut after we told them we only wanted them to cut two inches for a bob but they went on a trim spree and you ended up with a bowl cut. We gotta fight fear like it called our mama a "bald-headed, trifling bitch." We must fight fear like it drank the last glass of orange juice but left a swig and then put it back in the fridge. Rude AF.

Folks like me, who are committed to speaking truth to power, aren't doing it without fear. We aren't doing it because we are unafraid of consequences or sacrifices we are making because of it. We are doing it because we have to. We know we must still charge forward regardless. We must listen to the wisdom of mother Maya Angelou when she said: "Courage is the most important of all the virtues, because without courage you can't practice any other virtue

---

*Uglass: Ugly + ass. Uglass.

consistently. You can practice any virtue erratically, but nothing consistently without courage."

For the professional troublemaker, the truth, of ourselves and of the things around us, is more important than the fear that stops us from pursuing it. The things we must do are more significant than the things we are afraid to do. It doesn't mean we don't realize there are consequences. It means we acknowledge that they may come but we insist on keeping on.

Professional troublemakers recognize that fear is real, and that it's an everlasting hater, but it must be tackled.

This book is a middle finger up to fear.

Now, I say all this acknowledging that there are systems that make saying "Fuck fear" riskier for some of us. Our marginalized identities compound the effect of wanting to step out of and over our comfort zones. I know that it can be a privilege to be in the position where you feel like you have the choice to be a professional troublemaker. That is why I'm hoping that this book, written by a Black woman, an immigrant who was poor at some point (but didn't know it), somehow allows you to have the gumption to be a troublemaker for yourself.

I think it is important that we know what our problems are, and that we create the solutions for them. We need to create the world we prefer to live in.

That being said, everything I ask of you in this book I ask of myself first, and I ask of myself always. This book is my excuse to tell *ME* to continue to make trouble in the best ways. It is me giving myself permission to not be fearless, because fearlessness doesn't exist. I think the fear will always be there, but what's important is that

I go forward anyway. This isn't a life of sine metu (Latin for "without fear"). It is a life of "I might be afraid but I won't let it stop me."

What I'm sharing in this book is what I would have loved to tell ten-year-old me so that she could always find the confidence to be different. Along with: Don't let them glue that weave in your hair for that college dorm fashion show. It's gonna pull out your hair and sabotage your edges for a couple months. It ain't worth it.

This is also the book I needed when:

- I knew I really didn't want to become a doctor but since it was the dream I'd tied myself to since I was little, I was afraid of choosing something else.

- I didn't call myself a writer even though I'd been writing four times a week for nine years, and my words were reaching people in ways I'd never imagined.

- I was asked to do the biggest talk of my career and I turned it down two times before saying yes because I didn't think I was ready, and I was afraid I'd bomb onstage.

This is also a book I need now, in the times when I'm not feeling so bold. It's a book from me to me that I'm letting other people read. Because even now, I still need the prompts I've put here. Even now, I still need to remind myself to do the scary shit I'm compelled to do and deal with how it falls. Even now, I still stop myself from time to time. This book is for me: the me from yesterday, the me from today, and the me in the future who will need the extra push. It is the book I want to give to my kids one day to embolden them to move through this world unburdened.

In the BE section, I'll be talking about the things we must get right within us before we can do the things that scare us. Because half the battle is with our own self, our own insecurities, and our own baggage. We gotta Harlem Shake it off. (Did I just age myself? I'm fine with it.)

In the SAY section, I'll be pushing us to use our voices for our own greater good, and therefore everyone else's. We're so afraid to say the things that are necessary, and it is part of the reason why we find ourselves constantly fighting a world that doesn't honor us. We've gotta say what is difficult even when our voices shake.

In the DO section, I'll be encouraging us to start putting movement to that voice we're unsilencing. A Ralph Waldo Emerson quote I love is "What you do speaks so loudly that I cannot hear what you say." It is time for our actions to start proving the truth of our words.

Throughout this book, I'm also going to share stories of my grandmother, because her life is truly my biggest lesson on living beyond your fears.

My hope is that the next time you want to do something that takes your breath away as you think about it, you'll find words in this book that tell you, "Yo. You got this. Even if it fails, you will be okay."

So . . . let's get to it.

Me telling on someone to my grandma at her sixtieth birthday party, and her making it seem like what I had to say was the most important thing in the world. One professional troublemaker to another.

PROFESSIONAL
TROUBLEMAKER

BE

We have to make some internal shifts if we wanna fight fear, because what we think is possible is a major part of how far we can go. In the BE section, we're going to talk through the work we gotta do within us, so that even when we're afraid, we're forward-moving.

"FEAR: HALF THE BATTLE
IS WITH OUR OWN SELF,
OUR OWN INSECURITIES,
AND OUR OWN BAGGAGE."

—Luvvie Ajayi Jones

1

KNOW YOURSELF

We fear our full selves.

 We are afraid of who we are, in all our glory (and grit). We're constantly searching for that person. Or forgetting that person. Or repressing that person. Instead of standing strong in who that person is.

Being FULLY ourselves is necessary for us because it serves as a grounding force. I find that's the case for me. There is a lot to be afraid of in this world, because, in general, things can be a wreck out there. And none of us need to be afraid of who we are in our whole personhood, because who has the time?

This standing in your full self isn't about being an immovable person whose beliefs are stuck in a rock. It's not that can't nobody tell you shit, or that you're not able to admit when you're wrong. Instead, it's about having a strong sense of identity. It's about knowing you belong in this world just as much as anyone else. It's about taking up the space you earned simply by being born.

One of my favorite poems is "Desiderata," written by Max Ehrmann. My favorite part is: "You are a child of the universe / no less than the trees and the stars; you have a right to be here. . . ."

"YOU HAVE A RIGHT TO BE HERE." You sure in the hell do.

Oddly enough, knowing this fullness of who you are doesn't make you more stubborn. Instead, it makes you more likely to grow, since you know you have a solid foundation that doesn't change even as you learn new things and new perspectives. This is a step you need to be a professional troublemaker. Because you will GET IN TROUBLE. Guaranteed. What makes you realize it's worth it? This process of knowing the fullness of who you are.

A lot of fear fighting and professional troublemaking is confronting things that will knock us off our square. Things that will slap us into dizziness and make us forget everything we know is real. We need solid feet, rooted in something strong, to continue to stand. Knowing ourselves is important because it provides that foundation for us. It doesn't allow anyone or anything to tell us who we are. Because when people tell us how amazing we are, that's good to absorb. But what about when someone tells us we aren't worthy? Or we don't have value? Or we don't deserve kindness and love? Or that we deserve paper cuts? To know thyself is to not take all the praise to head or take all the shaming to heart. To know ourselves is to write our values in cement even if our goals are in sand.

To know thyself is to know your core, and for me, to know my core is to feel rooted in something outside myself. It is to know not only *who* I am but *whose* I am.

WHOSE WE ARE

Whose I am is not about belonging to someone or being beholden to people. It is about the community you are tied to that holds you accountable. It is about knowing you are part of a tribe that is greater than yourself. It is about feeling deeply connected to someone, and knowing that no matter where you go, you have a base. If we're phones, knowing whose we are is our charging station.

I learned the importance of WHOSE you are growing up. As a Yorùbá girl, I am part of a tribe that prioritizes our people sometimes as much as it prioritizes an individual. Collectivism comes alive for us through the traditional oríkì (OH-ree-kee).

What's an oríkì? It is a Yorùbá word that combines two words to mean "praising your head/mind." *Orí* is "head" and *kì* is "to greet or praise." An oríkì is a greeting that praises you through praising your kinship and speaking life to your destiny. It is your personal hype mantra, and can be spoken or sung.

The original attempts to tell you who you are make up your oríkì. It's used to remind you of your roots and your history. It might include the city your father's from, and where his father is from. It might include the things that make your family name special. It brags on your people. It lets people know who you WERE, who you ARE, and who you WILL BE. It reminds you of those who came before you and blesses those who will come after. It might even include some shade.

Oríkìs are often sung at birthdays and celebrations. They are also sung to see you off into the next life. An oríkì connects you to your ancestors, and it will move even the most stoic to cry because you feel it in your chest. Your tear ducts just give up the ghost and let the water go.

I am the granddaughter of a woman named Olúfúnmiláyọ̀ Juliana Fáloyin, and she's the one who serves as my compass. When Grandma would say her own name, she'd always say it with a smile. Which makes sense, because her name literally means "God gave me joy." It was like her very self and presence brought her joy. When they sang my grandmother's oríkì at her funeral, I got emotional because it was a poetic affirmation of her presence on this earth and a send-off. It was a standing ovation for her spirit.

This is part of my grandma's oríkì:

> Ọmọ Ògbóni Modù lorè, mẹ̀rẹ̀ ní àkún
> Ọmọ Fulani Ìjẹ̀sà a múni má parò oko ọni
> Ọmọ a fi ọsẹ fọsọ kí ómọ Ẹlòmíràn fi eérú fọ ti ẹ
> Ọmọ arúgbìnrin owó bọ̀dìdẹ̀
> Ọmọ Olúmọsẹ atìkùn àyà fọhùn
> Ògbóni gbà mí, Ọ̀dọ̀fin gbà mí
> Ẹ nií tó nií gbà lẹ̀ gbani

What it loosely means (because there are some Yorùbá words that don't exist in English, and it is really tough to give exact meaning) is:

The child of royalty . . .

The child of the Ìjèṣà Fulani who dominates one and
     dominates one's property
The child who brings out soap to wash his/her own
     clothes while someone else's child brings out ashes to
     wash his/hers
The child that springs up money (wealth) in multiples
The child who beats his chest as he speaks (speaks with
     confidence)
Ògbóni, save me. Ọ̀dọ̀fin, save me
It is the one that is prominent enough to save you that
     steps up to do it

It ties her back to those who came before her and gasses her up.

I don't know my oríkì. Many of us don't. Like a lot of traditions,
oríkìs have been de-prioritized as generations pass. I'm out here
oríkì-less AF. But it's okay. I'm fine, really. I'm not mad at all that by
the time I came along, folks were more blasé about it (clearly I'm low-
key salty, but I'll deal with that with my therapist).

However, a lot of what we already do is derivative of oríkìs and we
don't even realize it. The tradition of the oríkì isn't just in Yorùbáland;
it's gone on through the diaspora. You can see it in the way people
rap about themselves. It's in the way people praise God. It's in the
way we say who we are in the moments we feel most proud.

When Christians praise God, we say: King of kings. Lord of
lords. Alpha and Omega. The beginning and the end. The I am. The
Waymaker. That's an oríkì if I ever heard one.

When we think about how people are introduced in something as made-up as the TV show *Game of Thrones*, it tracks. "Daenerys Stormborn of the House Targaryen. First of Her Name. The Unburnt. Queen of the Andals and the First Men. Khaleesi of the Great Grass Sea. Breaker of Chains. Mother of Dragons." THAT IS SUCH AN ORÍKÌ! Didn't you feel gassed up on her behalf anytime they introduced her? I know I did. That's what it is for!

I tend to write ones for people I admire to gas them up as I please. I've done a few in the past.

For Michelle Obama: Michelle LaVaughn of House Obama. First of Her Name. Dame of Dignity. Melanin Magnificence. Chic Chicagoan. Boss Lady of Brilliance. Owner of the Arms of Your Envy. Forever First Lady.

For President Barack Obama: Barack Hussein of House Obama. Second of His Name. Swagnificence in the West Wing. He Who Speaks in Complete Sentences. Shea-Butter-Skinned Leader of the World. Michelle's Boo. 44 for Life.

For Beyoncé: Beyoncé Giselle of House Carter. First of Her Name. Snatcher of Edges. Killer of Stages. Citizen of Creole Wonderland. Legendary Black Girl. Wakandan Council President.

For Oprah: Oprah Gail of House Winfrey. First of Her Name. Changer of the World. Protector of the Realm of Noirpublic. Creator of Paths. Breaker of Chains and Limits.

For Toni Morrison: Toni of House Morrison. First of Her Name. Architect of Words. Acclaimed Author. Shifter of

Culture. Netter of Nobel Prize. Writing Domino. Legendary Laureate.

For Aretha Franklin: Aretha Louise of House Franklin. First of Her Name. Dame of Detroit. Empress of Elevated Sound. Reverberation Royalty. Vocal Victor. Sovereign of Soul. Aural Authority.

For Janelle Monáe: Janelle of House Monáe. First of Her Name. Citizen of the Future. Walker of Tight Ropes. Sprinkler of #NoirPixieDust. Rocker of the Baddest Suits. Giver of No Intergalactic Fucks. Head Android of Wondaland.

So, how do you write a simple *Game of Thrones*–style oríkì for yourself? Here's the formula, and how I come up with the intros.

First Name and Middle Name of House Last Name. Number of Her/His/Their Name (i.e., Juniors are "Second of Their Name").

That's the easy part.

The next part: Throw humility away. The point of this is to give yourself all the credit. I want you to acknowledge the things that make you proud and the things you have accomplished. They don't have to just be professional, but they can be things that feel like your superpower. Feel free to use royal titles for yourself (Queen, King, Earl, Duchess), because why not? (If anyone from the monarchy is reading this, sorry but not sorry for the appropriation.) Get creative with your descriptors if you want. I am also a fan of throwing some alliteration in there for extra pizzazz.

Noun (occupation or descriptor) of Noun (thing).

Luvvie of House Jones. First of Her Name. Assassin of the Alphabet. Bestseller of Books. Conqueror of Copy. Dame of Diction. Critic of Culture. Sorceress of Side-eyes. Eater of Jollof Rice. Rocker of Fierce Shoes. Queen of the Jones Kingdom. Taker of Stages. Nigerian Noble and Chi-Town Creator.

I could keep going, but I'll stop here. You need one of your own and I want you to write it. Now if you have the time. If not, come back to it.

I know you might be thinking, "But those people Luvvie mentioned are famous and extraordinary and hugely dope. I can't even measure up to that." And to that, I say, "Slap yourself." Right now, slap yourself. I want you to leave that kinda talk behind. Because yes, those are some AMAZING people, and they have achieved a lot.

But so have you. By being here on this earth, you have done enough. (We'll deal with impostor syndrome in a few chapters.)

What if you have a complicated relationship with your family members? Or you don't have any familial ties? Or you were adopted so you don't know your biological family history?

For those who might not have blood ties to the people they love most, you are still part of a people who cherish you, adore you, and are glad that you are here on this earth in this space and time. To you, I send love. Not knowing the binds that tie you by blood does not preclude you from belonging to a people or a community or a tribe.

If you are someone who can truly say you don't have an answer to

WHOSE you are, and this book has made it to you and these words are being heard or read by you, then you are truly someone who should laugh at fear. Cackle at it, even. Having no one is not a cause for shame here but one for pride, because it means you have moved through the world, drop-kicking these obstacles by yourself. You are a warrior. Your oríkì can start with ARMY OF ONE. You have battled life by yourself, and even though it might have bruised you and maybe almost drowned you, YOU MADE IT TO LAND! You are still here. High-five yourself. Army of One. Solo Soldier. Fierce Warrior. Rock of Gibraltar has nothing on you.

You might be reading this and saying, "I'm a stay-at-home mom. I don't have professional things to put in my oríkì." Well, being a mom is a whole job that you don't ever retire from, and you are constantly working overtime without pay. TRUST that there are a lot of accomplishments there.

Raiser of Future Leaders. Keeper of Everyone's Shit Together. Master of Calendar. Expert of Efficiency. Queen of the Last Name Dynasty.

Everybody needs an oríkì.

I need you to spend this time bragging on yourself. Type this up, write it up, put it somewhere you will remember. Laminate it, even. You will need this one day—in the moments when you see the worst of yourself or you fall flat on your face. You will need this when you feel like you have failed.

You know those times when you're talking and between every word, you're clapping your disbelief because someone talked to you like you're some useless nonentity? Yeah, those too. In those times, you can read your oríkì and remind yourself who you be (yes, who you be). After you calm down, or to even help you calm down, I want you to have this thing handy, to bring you back to the reality of how dope you are.

Cool? Cool.

WHO WE ARE

Beyond knowing WHOSE we are, there's knowing WHO we are. Outside of our connections to anyone else, we have to know what is important. People often talk about searching for themselves and my simple ass be like, "Where did you go?" But that's me being basic. I know that all too often, we swallow back our impulses, needs, and wants so much that we forget what they tasted like. We lose the appetite to be ourselves because it's been insulted, beaten, trampled, punished, abused, and made fun of out of us. We look up one day and realize we've been performing who we are for so long that we have lost the map.

This uphill battle is no fault of our own. And it is by design that we swallow who we are to fit in. I am always taken aback when people ask me how I am so confident. I am confident because I am constantly doing work to ensure that I do not lose sight of me, so I never have to go looking for me.

When we are sure-footed in who we are, we always have something to come back to. When we know what defines us is not any job or thing we own or professional title we carry, it makes us less likely to lose our way if we lose any of those things.

If I feel like I might wanna lose sight of me or fade, I ask myself the following questions, and then I write the answers down. My fairy godmentor (she doesn't know I've claimed her) Oprah often talks about what we know to be true. Well, these questions have given me clarity to figure that out.

What do you hold dear?

This is what is important to you. Is it family? Is it friends? Is it not losing your edges even though they're weak and wearing a knitted cap that isn't properly lined in the winter might cause your hairline to fall one inch backward?

What are your core values?

Our core values are what we stand for and what guide us. Mine are:

Honesty: This is one of my top values, partly because I'm a bad liar and have a terrible poker face. But mostly because I want to feel trusted by those who know me. It's important that I am one less person others need to doubt.

Authenticity: I am who I am, no matter where I am or who I'm with. Authenticity is close to the honesty core value because it insists that I be honest about myself and how I show up. It doesn't mean I am the same all the time, but it means if I'm quiet, it's because I am allowing myself to observe in the moment. If I'm partying and being the life of the party, in that time I am feeling boisterous.

Benevolence: I think it's important to be kind, and being generous with the things we have is a major part of that, whether it's knowledge or time or money or energy. It means we are less selfish about our lives and think about what we can constantly give to the collective for the greater good.

Shea butter: Yes, shea butter is a core value because I think we'd all be better if we were more moisturized. Get some good body butter in your life and watch your life change. You wake up without rustling your sheets with your extreme ash.

What brings you joy?

What makes your heart smile? Helping people by telling them what I know brings me joy. Having people tell me something I did or said made an impact on them melts my heart. Yes, there's a Captain Save-a-Planet complex there, but I'm working that out with my therapist.

Even on your worst day, what makes you amazing?

At a time when you aren't in the mood to be the best you, what still makes you incredible, just as you are?

What is worth fighting for, even if your arms are too short to box with God?

Let's say you know your uppercut is weak and your jab is rubbish. What will make you lace up your gloves anyway? What do you think you will make the "no violence" exception for? I know I can't fight worth a damb, so I gotta be clear on what will push me to fight if necessary. For me, it's seeing someone who doesn't deserve it be abused or rendered defenseless or voiceless.

What do you want them to say when they're lowering you into the ground?

When it is my time to leave this earth, I want people to say, "The world was better because she was here." I also wanna make sure whoever tries to act like they wanna jump in with me because they're auditioning for Best Mourner of the World, y'all tell them to sit their ass down because this ain't the time for them to be attention whores. I'll be giving them a fierce side-eye from beyond.

All of these questions are things I ask and continue to ask myself, because when I've written the answers down and I go over them, they are the best memento of me. They are my life mission statement. They are my atlas when I find myself off course after a tough encounter or meeting or date or DAY. I look at it when I realize that I, and everyone else, seem to have forgotten who the hell I am (I sure felt it multiple times during wedding planning).

YOUR LIFE MISSION STATEMENT

Write your own life mission statement, your compass. Here's the template. Fill this out.

What's your name?

Who are you proud to be related to?

Even on your worst day, what makes you amazing?

What/who do you hold dear? What do you cherish?

What are your core values? What do they mean?

What brings you joy?

What is worth fighting for, even if your arms are too short to box with God?

What do you want them to say when they're lowering you into the ground?

Here is mine:

I am Ìfẹ́olúwa Luvvie Àjàyí Jones. I am the granddaughter of Fúnmiláyọ̀ Fáloyin and the daughter of Yẹmisí Àjàyí. I am the wife of Carnell Jones. Even on my worst day, I can look in the mirror and be proud of the woman I've become. I have no regrets. My family, both blood and chosen, are who I hold dear. What I cherish is my life, lived happy, whole, and healthy. My core values are honesty, authenticity, benevolence, and shea butter. This means I tell the truth, I'm real to myself and others, I'm generous, and I refuse to be ashy because I should always prioritize being moisturized.*

It brings me joy when I'm able to make someone else's life easier. Also, seeing my enemies upset. Because: petty. I didn't say Jesus was done working on me yet. What I fight for are people who feel like they are powerless or voiceless. When I'm no longer here, I want people so say, "The world was better because she was here."

---

*Yorùbá is a beautiful tonal language whose alphabet uses accents to reflect the sounds. You'll see those accents on the Yorùbá words I have used throughout this book. My name, my grandmother's name, and my mother's name are written here fully accented to honor the traditional language. Moving forward, the accents won't be present on me and my mom's names because we don't use these accents in our everyday lives.

Colloquially and in the world, Yorùbá words, especially names, are often written without accents. When I write my own name, I don't include the accents, and I wanna honor myself in that. I went back and forth about this decision of whether to include them in our names throughout the book, and then I asked my mom for her opinion. She said, "I don't think it's necessary. We are who we are, with or without the accents."

I honor tradition as I honor self.

You can show it to others but you don't need anyone else to read it but you. Above all, it is for you.

This exercise not only lets you know who you are on paper, it also shows you who you aren't. We are often weighed down by other people's projections, preconceptions, and the patterns they expect from us. We are frequently defined by systems, stereotypes, and structures that are larger than us. To know who we are is to insist on knowing we are not what others put on us. We are not the names people call us. We are not our worst moments. So when people try to impose all this agony and trauma on us, we can say, "Nah. That's not my problem." Once you know who you are, it's easier to refute who you aren't.

Do you know who you are? Do you know how much fight it took for you to be wherever you are today? Do you know how many things could have gone wrong to keep you from even being born? Do you know that none of the people you are scared of and none of the situations you're afraid of are bigger than any of that? Do you understand how dope you are, because there are battles you have fought and mountains you have climbed that almost took you out? But they didn't. They did not. You are here now and one thousand motherfuckers shouldn't be able to tell you shit that makes you feel like you don't deserve good things.

Don't let people who can't spell your name right tell you about who you are. Don't let folks who only have courage behind a keyboard define your goodness or your worth as a person. Do not let people who are already rooting for you to falter insist on your value, because they will steer you wrong.

When you are tempted to believe someone's tainted version of you, or believe their projection of who they think you are, reread your mission statement. Remind yourself of who the hell you are before trying to remind anyone else. Because, ultimately, the world will continue to misunderstand us and call us patchy-headed scally-wags with lice. We can't control that. What we can control is our own image of ourselves, and how surely we are worth loving, defending, and redeeming. In all of our messed-up, scared glory.

Your professional troublemaking depends on it.

I hope you feel sufficiently gassed up. I hope this is a chapter you are able to come back to time and time again. I hope in future chapters when I ask you to do things that might be tough, you feel encouraged to know that you are okay. And that you are reminded that you are a legacy of a lot of things going right (even if a lot has gone wrong on the way to this point).

2

BE TOO MUCH

We fear being judged for being different.

 When we talk about people being their full selves and how a lot of people are afraid of it, it's not that people don't want to show up as themselves. It's that they know that when they show up in their full splendor, they will be judged for it. Being ordinary and unremarkable is hardly a life goal, but we are often scared into being that way.

Even though people like to act fake-offended at the idea that they're being judged, we know good and well that we are all judging each other. We just happen to critique each other on the wrong things, like what we look like, who we love, what deity we worship, if any. Instead, we should assess each other on how kind we are, how we're showing up for other humans, and how we're contributing to the world's problems, large or small. (I also like to judge people on whether they drink kombucha, because I don't understand how anyone can appreciate something that tastes like moldy beer, toenail clippings, and bad decisions.)

We judge each other and are judged every single day on who we are and how we are. And oftentimes, people bang their internal gavel on us and decide that we are too much.

TOO (adverb): "to an excessive extent or degree; beyond what is desirable, fitting, or right." (Dictionary.com)

To be TOO something is to do or be something to a level that folks find to be uncouth. It's to be different.

Many of us have been called too loud. Or too aggressive. Or too passionate. Or too intimidating. Or even too quiet. Or too sensitive. Or too tall. Or too short. Or too Black. And when people say we are TOO something, they aren't making a casual observation. They are requesting that we change this thing, that we turn the volume down. Then we feel self-conscious or embarrassed, and turn inwardly to fix something about ourselves that someone else has defined as a problem.

The problem: What we've been told is too much is usually something that is core to who we are, or how we appear, and often it's something we cannot change.

How is someone too tall? Should they hunch over to come down to your level? How is someone too Black? Should they peel their skin off their body to have less melanin? I don't understand the gall that leads people to make some of these judgments. Unfortunately, we internalize these critiques and it leads to us worrying about being different in any way.

As a Black woman who is opinionated, straightforward, and un-apologetic about it, I am secretary of Team Too Much. I even bring the kettle corn to our monthly meetings. I've been considered aggressive or loud or angry for simply being direct. Black women are often on the receiving end of the "too loud," "too brash," "too aggressive" notions, because our very being has become synonymous with too much. I'm convinced it's because people see the divine in us and it is too bright for them to deal with. Meanwhile, they better put their shades on and deal with all this Noir Pixie Dust.*

I especially balk at "too aggressive." When someone says that, did they see us randomly walk up to someone on the street and punch them in the mouth? Did we push someone into a wall for no reason? Did we cuss a nun out? Or is it that we didn't put enough eager exclamation points or emojis in the emails we sent a colleague? Did we ask for what we wanted in straightforward terms? How are we being aggressive? What have we done to earn that title? At least let me earn whatever you accuse me of.

Being accused of TOO MUCHness is to be told to take up less space. Being TOO much is to be excessive. How do you combat that? By being less than you are. And that concept feels like nothing other than self-betrayal. The inverse of too much is too little. I'd rather be too big than too small any day.

Can you imagine if someone walked up to you and said to your face, "I need you to be less"? You'd clutch your pearls and be

---

*Noir Pixie Dust® is what I consider to be the magic of Black people, especially Black women. Yes, I trademarked it. You know people like to steal from us.

offended. But THAT is what they're saying when they say you're too much—they're just saying it in a less accusing and more shaming manner, so you take it to heart. You internalize and absorb it and commit to changing yourself.

All for what? For the whims of people who are more fickle than a ripening avocado. (Seriously, how are avocados okay when you go to bed, and then you wake up to something that looks like a kiwi? Wonders shall never cease.)

Who we are should not be beholden to the moods of the people we are around, their insecurities, or their projections. Because when someone says you are too much, it is more of a statement on them than it is on you.

> You ARE too Black for that white-ass person. Your melanatedness is blinding to the caucasity.
>
> You ARE too tall for that short-ass person. Your height makes their neck hurt, but what's that gotta do with you?
>
> You ARE too aggressive for that complacent-ass person. Your passion irritates their inactivity.
>
> You ARE too quiet for that disruptive-ass person. Your calm makes them agitated.
>
> You ARE too big for that small-ass space. Your vastness chokes their insignificance.

In all of these, your job is not to stop being this person you are accused of being. You aren't supposed to constantly shape-shift to make those around you feel better about their own insecurities or failures. Your job is not to chameleon your way through life to the point where you forget what your true colors are.

If you are too big, then it's a reflection that the place you're in is too small for you. It isn't your job to get smaller to fit there, but to find a place that is bigger than you so you can take up all the space you want and grow infinitely. Anyplace that demands you shrink is a place that will suffocate your spirit and leave you gasping for air. Who wins? Not you. Not anyone, really, because the version of you that they will get is the diet, fake-sugar, stevia version that probably has a bad aftertaste. They might THINK that's a great version because you're so dope that even you at half capacity is more on point than you expect. BUT they don't get the you who is free to show up and be your best, because you are spending time trying to be representative of whatever they think is palatable. And that constant shrinking and dwindling is how giants get locked in cages. You don't belong in a cage simply because it's where others want you to be.

My grandmother was the Queen Mother of Team Too Much International Association of Extra People. Being too much was woven into her spirit. She was too bossy, too confident, too aggressive, too brash, too headstrong, too assertive, too feisty, too strong, too dramatic. Mama Fáloyin, as so many people called her, was the definition of boisterous. Everything she did was big, and I don't think it occurred to her to ever shrink herself.

Let's talk about her theatrics. As an older Nigerian woman, being too dramatic was an obligation of sorts, a set of cultural mores to follow. It was destiny fulfillment. In fact, her entire existence demanded that after she got to a certain age, she had to be melodramatic; otherwise she wasn't doing it right. It made her a joy to be around even when she was upset, because it was often super amusing.

Grandma used to come to the United States once a year and stay with us for a couple of months at a time. She had a tendency to do the most, so of course she and my mom would clash from time to time. One day in particular, they had a major argument and Grandma, in all her feistiness, got extra upset.

This lady suddenly went in her room, threw a few things in a trash bag, put on her shoes, and came into the living room. She had on her house scarf, socks, and sandals. She threw on her coat and grabbed her purse. She looked ridiculous cuz nothing matched or went together, but that was part of the act. We asked her where she was going and she replied with, "I'm leaving. I'm going to go sit at the bus stop and wait for the people who pick up old people to come and get me." I didn't know when the laugh escaped my mouth, but it was too late to catch it. I cackled! She looked at me, all serious, almost offended.

ME: Grandma, who will pick you up?

GRANDMA: I don't know. Someone will take pity on me and come get me.

I wanted to be like, "Lady, stahp it." But I couldn't because I was not about to be the target of her wrath, so I had to fake-beg her to stay. You know she wasn't going anywhere. The trash bag made no sense, because this woman had perfectly good luggage, but she had to do her one-woman show. Also, is there some sort of random old-people pickup service that I haven't heard about? Like a dogcatcher for elders? Like a free Uber service for hysterical geriatrics? Whew! It was hilarious. You might say it was too dramatic, but at least it was amusing.

And TOO EXTRA? Well, she was a pro at that. When my grandmother turned sixty years old in 1991, she decided to do a seven-day celebration to commemorate her life. It was in Ìbàdàn, Nigeria, where she lived and where I grew up. She rented three massive tents and closed off three blocks in front of and surrounding her house for the festivities. No one had to RSVP because everyone was invited. I don't think folks counted, but there had to be about a thousand people who came each day. A cow was killed every day and served in delicious stew for everyone to partake in. The jollof rice was endless. Grandma hired Ebenezer Obey, who was Nigeria's top musician at the time, to come sing and perform from evening to sunup. Literally. He got off the stage at 6 a.m. She threw three major parties in those seven days, and her church choir performed. Come on, holy concert! They showed what an anointed turnup really is. We members of her family wore aṣọ ẹbí* the whole time. Mama Fáloyin herself wore the heaviest of laces, and gold chains so big she'd make

---

*Aṣọ ẹbí (pronounced asho-ehBEE) is Yorùbá for "clothes of kin." It's matching fabric we wear for special occasions, and it signifies to people that those in it are close family and friends of whoever is celebrating.

some rappers jealous. She had two cakes for each day. I especially remember the one that was in the shape of a Bible, because: super Christian. The whole celebration was A LOT. Some might even say it was too much. But why not? How many times do you turn sixty? Once! Do it big, ma'am!

Whether you thought my grandma was TOO anything, you didn't wanna miss that party. This same woman who people thought was too loud was the one people came to, to help them raise a ruckus when they were being treated unfairly or had a problem with some figure of authority. She was loud not only for herself but for people who she thought didn't have a voice to be loud for themselves. I remember plenty of times when we'd get visitors who were looking to her to mediate a conflict they were having with someone who was trying to cheat them. One phone call from her and it would be resolved. Her loudness was not just in service of herself, and people didn't consider her TOO loud when it was in their favor. It is also why she was deeply honored.

I am a proud Nigerian woman. But when I was nine, I moved from Nigeria to the United States and started at a new school, and my confidence in myself was shaken for the first time ever. It was one of the only periods in my life when I felt like I needed to shrink myself because I was too much. I was too different.

(Let the record also show that I didn't know we were moving. I thought we were going on vacation, like we had in the past. Nobody consults the baby or tells them the decisions, I guess. SMDH. What tipped me off that we had moved? When my mom enrolled me in school. I was like, "Wait. We're staying here? But it's cold." We had the nerve to move from balmy-all-year-round Ìbàdàn, Nigeria, to Chicago, USA, where the air makes tears run down your face for eight months out of the year.)

Anyhoo, the first day of school when I walked into my classroom, the teacher asked me to stand in front of all these strange faces and introduce myself. I immediately knew I was different, and I felt self-conscious in a way I never had before. Who I was and where I was from were too off path from what the people in that room were used to. It was my first time walking into a room where not everyone looked like me.

I was sure of nothing. Even the question "What's your name?" felt like a trap. The answer was Ifeoluwa Ajayi,* but right then and there, nine-year-old me knew that the kids (and the teacher herself) wouldn't pronounce it properly, and they'd make it heavy on their tongues, like it was a burden. My name felt like it was too much. It was too foreign. It was too Nigerian. It was too strange. And it wouldn't do.

I wasn't ashamed, because I am truly proud of my name and love it. But I felt like I needed to protect what is a sacred part of me. So in the three seconds after I was asked, I decided to introduce myself as Lovette instead. It was a nickname that one of my aunts would call me from time to time, because Ifeoluwa means "God's Love." (Lovette became Luvvie in college.) Every time afterward, when teachers looked at my original first name on their roll call list and frowned or said, "Whew, okay this one is hard," my decision was

---

*Ifeoluwa Ajayi is pronounced as ee-FEH-oh-LOO-wah ah-jah-YEE, but please don't call me by my first name. It's reserved for the people closest to me. Luvvie will do. (Gotta draw that line. We'll talk more about boundaries in chapter ten.)

affirmed. (They also butchered AJAYI, which is not even a tongue twister but is often turned into one.) The message I kept getting was "This thing about you makes us uncomfortable."

As a Naija girl, I knew the way I spoke was also too strange. The fact that I called a pen "Biro" and cookies "biscuits" weren't my only clues; the first time someone called me an "African booty scratcher" because of how I spoke, I said to myself, "Oh chick. We gotta lose this accent quick, fast, and in a hurry." So I talked less and listened more to how my classmates spoke. By the time I started high school, I had lost most of the telltale sign that I was new: my Nigerian accent.

The one thing I didn't let go of was my food. I still brought jollof rice for lunch. I had briefly tried sandwiches, but I'd be craving spices by the end of lunchtime. So there were times I'd sit in the corner as far from my classmates as possible, to avoid the questions of "What is that smell?" and "What are you eating?" Abeg, face your front and let me enjoy my food in peace.

My heritage, my name, and my mother tongue made me feel too different. And as teenagers, being too distinct from your peers was not cool, so I did my best to not be TOO Nigerian.

Then I got to college, where the best learnings are outside the classroom. It was at the University of Illinois where I reclaimed my Naijaness. It was there that I met others with stories like mine, who also went by new names to keep theirs from being butchered. It was there that I realized that my perspective, which is very much informed by my culture, was one of my superpowers. It was there that I started the blog that led to the life I live now. It is where I stopped hiding the fact that I love switching back and forth between my mother tongue and English, even in a room full of non-Yorùbás.

Who I am in the world today is an unapologetically Nigerian American, Chicagoan, Black woman. As I inhabit all these identities and seamlessly move through them, that thing that was TOO MUCH about me is a major factor in my success. My humor and writing style are tied to all these parts of me.

I hope that a young Black girl or an immigrant who finds themselves in strange lands can see me and know they are not TOO much of who they are. I hope they know they too can let their tongue take them back to their roots without shame. I hope they know their name isn't too distinct. I hope they know they can thrive and build a life that they want, being exactly who they are at their core, even as they come to school smelling like stock fish.

I do not want us to allow people to squelch our TOO MUCHness.

Beyoncé is someone who people frequently say is too much. Her Sasha Fierceness. Her love of glittery onesies. Her out-of-this-world performances. Sometimes people get offended at how she dares to be so BIG, but it's clear she knows that ain't her business. Her job is to take up ALL the space she wants when she wants, and it has made her a living icon. It pays off because that is what has allowed her to be the greatest entertainer alive. After her historic Coachella performance, she cemented that title. She then STAMPED it after her incredible visual album *Black Is King*. LIVING ICON. If you disagree, argue with your step-niece. (This is my book and it's the truth. Bloop.)

I think about how Oprah Winfrey is constantly accused of being TOO MUCH for appearing on the cover of *O, The Oprah Magazine* every single month for twenty years. To run a successful magazine is no small feat, but to do it for two decades is the stuff of legends. Thank God she hasn't let people talk her out of what she's known to work.

Michelle Obama's book tour for *Becoming* was in arenas. People thought that was TOO MUCH too. Meanwhile, our Forever FLOTUS was making a whole documentary in those sold-out appearances. The book became a worldwide bestseller. The vision. The boldness. The guts. I'm so here for all of it.

Imagine if any of these women allowed people to convince them that what they wanted or who they were was TOO MUCH. The brilliance we would all be cheated out of would create a vacuum.

Shout-out to those of us who've been told we are TOO TALKATIVE. Or TOO MOUTHY. Some of us are now able to get paid good money for that as professional speakers. Some of us put the words we have in our heads on paper and write books that allow us to help our parents retire. AMEN! Our TOO MUCHness can really be beneficial. All it takes is time, opportunity, and prowess.

Whatever it is that people think we are TOO much of comes in handy when it benefits others. However, when it stops being of service to folks' lives and starts making them uncomfortable, that is when it becomes something we should stop. This reaction tells me our TOO MUCHness is clearly useful. That thing that we are too much of is our superpower, and we should wield it with pride.

The person who is considered TOO sensitive is probably someone with a high emotional IQ. They're in tune with how people are feeling, allowing them to detect when a situation will have emotional consequences. They're often really thoughtful about how they speak to other people, and they are the calm in storms. On trips, they're the ones who help mediate fights when everyone gets on each other's nerves.

The person who is TOO uptight is probably the one who is great at organizing the group trip. They'll make sure when everyone lands, they'll have transportation to the hotel. They will also make sure the itinerary is set and ready to go. That type A–ness is extra useful for a project manager.

The person who is TOO turnt is the one you end up on adventures with on the trip. Their spontaneous spirit means you will be sure to get into some fun shenanigans that you will never forget. We'll just hope you all don't get arrested while in a foreign country.

You might be wondering, "What if people are right if they say I am TOO something? How do I know I'm not ignoring valid critique?" Good questions.

I ask myself a few questions when it comes to determining what we should consider credible and what we should consider compost.

Is this thing hindering my personal growth?

Is this thing harming someone else?

Is this critique coming from someone who loves and respects me?

If the answer to all three is no, then wipe your shoulders off, pick your head up, and keep it moving. Otherwise, let's dig deeper on those questions.

IS THIS THING HINDERING MY PERSONAL GROWTH?

The thing that people are saying you are TOO much of—does it hinder your personal growth? When the thing actively makes us behave in ways that are contrary to our core values and incongruent with the person we wrote about in our mission statements, it is worth taking seriously. I cannot say I hold benevolence in high regard and then be stingy with my money and time on a regular basis. If I have $100 in my pocket, see someone who is experiencing homelessness and asking for money, and all I reach for are three pennies I find at the bottom of my purse, then I am not honoring who I said I was. THEN I am probably being TOO stingy.

Am I being TOO brash and stern and rigid? Well, do I refuse to evolve my thoughts and ideas because I maintain that my way is the only right way? That can be an obstacle to getting better at humaning. This probably also means people think of me as an immovable person, which means I'm likely to end up with fewer challengers and more YES people. That is how people become unchecked terrors.

Maybe I'm TOO loud, therefore not encouraging others to be heard in a room I'm in, ensuring my voice is the only one that is being amplified, and not allowing a diversity of ideas to be represented. In those moments, we don't need to stop ourselves or think our ideas aren't necessary. But we can remind ourselves to step back. We can be intentional in knowing when to prioritize the collective voice instead of our individual one.

IS THIS THING HARMING SOMEONE ELSE?

Is the thing that I am being critiqued about emotionally, mentally, or physically detrimental to someone else? If so, then yes, I should chill and go work on myself. The person who is called too aggressive might need to get their lives right if it comes with them being abusive to those around them. There absolutely are people who will put hands on other people, even those they say they love. Being physically aggressive mostly comes in handy if you're a professional boxer or an MMA fighter. But a regular human being who is known for constantly throwing 'bows? That is certainly not who I want to be, and that is not someone I want to be close with. Am I enabling their abuse? Will I feel safe around them? Will I be the object of their physical aggression?

Are you being too loud when you visit someone who has a newborn, therefore waking them up? Please take the time to shut up, because you deserve a cuss-out for being inconsiderate. That new mom or new dad has the right to drop-kick you out their house. Relax yourself. You can also definitely be too loud if you're in a movie theater or a library and you need to use your inside voice. (Lord knows I don't have any inside voice. I got an external articulation with my Nigerian ass. I whisper at 50 decibels, but God ain't done working on me yet.)

Does your sensitivity mean you cry anytime you are challenged, therefore using your tears to manipulate others into always giving you your way? There are people who weaponize their tears to avoid accountability. That's not sensitivity but manipulation, and it can breed a lot of resentment in your relationships, both platonic and romantic, because people feel like you invalidate their feelings. That's harmful because it says that they do not matter.

Frankly, sometimes when white women cry, it can literally put Black people in jeopardy. Picture it: A white woman feels challenged or uncomfortable about something a Black person said or did. Instead of using her words, she cries. Instantly, no matter what the initial catalyst of the situation is, she ends up being appeased, pacified, and pampered. We've seen literal white-woman tears shut down conversations, even if she was the instigator of the conflict. The other person? Ends up being scolded. Or fired. Or arrested. Or killed. When Lorelei cries, heads roll.

So yes, times like those can lead to someone else's harm. That is when you check yourself and do better.

Otherwise, we need to be clear about when we are being TOO to a fault.

If whatever you are being accused of is not somehow infringing on somebody else's rights or silencing somebody who has less social access than you, then what is the real accusation? We've all been in rooms with really loud dudes who won't use the shutthefuckup coupon code, and what they do is create disarray with no purpose. But when people accuse you of being loud, is it in the moment when you are trying to make the room better? Is it in the times when you are speaking for somebody who doesn't have a voice? Is it at the times when people would prefer that you not shake the table? In those instances, you aren't being too loud. What you are being is too inconvenient for that room. You've made that room uncomfortable.

IS THIS CRITIQUE COMING FROM SOMEONE WHO LOVES AND RESPECTS ME?

If the "too much" is coming from someone you aren't sure has your best interests at heart or who has been hypercritical of you in the past, then it might not be something you should internalize. I surround myself with people I trust and love and who aren't afraid to pull my card. When THEY, my life's board of directors, call me in and tell me I am being TOO something (like stubborn, stern, thoughtless), I reflect, process what they say, and then figure out how I can do better and show up better next time.

If it's coming from someone who is a troll or a known hater or even someone who might be going through their own trauma in the moment, I have to take it with a grain of salt. This is especially useful in the age of social media, where thousands of people can make judgments on who we are at any given point. Imagine a tweet that goes viral, that has people you will never know and who don't give a shit about you coming at you. As they are telling you you're TOO something, you will need someone close to you to vouch for that thing to be given credence.

But here's the thing. Sometimes the people who tell us we are TOO something are those who love us dearly and want the best for us. They can be people who are closest to us (parents, friends, spouses) and really do adore the ground we walk on. They mean us well, but sometimes we hear "You are TOO _____" from them. It is possible that they are trying to protect us by making that judgment, but they can be projecting their own insecurities, anxieties, and fears onto us in the process.

You have a mother who is more of a quiet type? She might have told you she thinks you need to be more calm or to stop being so brash all the time. We've had family members tell us we're too skinny in an attempt to make sure we are eating as we should be, but it comes across as shaming of our bodies. And shout-out to all the aunties who have greeted someone with "You're putting on too much weight" or "You're getting too fat." They mean well, but the road to hell is paved with good intentions.

Many a kinfolk have created inferiority complexes in people they love with their declarations that we're TOO something. And instead of rejecting their callousness and letting their lack of chill slide off our backs, we take it to heart, blamelessly. Because the people with the ability to hurt us the most are those we love the most.

This third question should not be considered without the first two, because if we do take on what our family and friends say about us ALWAYS, even though the thing they critique does not hinder our personal growth or hurt anyone, we'll be walking replicas of them. Or we'll spend our lives trying to measure up to the person they THINK we should be. We'll be in constant pursuit of their validation, as opposed to constant pursuit of our own growth. And chile, that is exhausting.

Someone called you too tall? Do they not understand that it means they are less likely to need a step stool when you're around? Don't they realize that you can always see above folks at the concert so you can help narrate what's happening onstage? Plus, you probably take amazing group selfies because your arm has reach. Who needs a selfie stick? Not you!

Someone thinks you're too bold? It means you get anyone's attention, and that comes in handy in a crowded room. It means you aren't easy to forget, and that is charisma.

Someone thinks you're too emotional? It means when you're about to get a traffic ticket, you can probably cry on cue and make the cop feel guilty enough to give you a warning.

I'm kidding. Sort of.

So what should you do? BE TOO MUCH. And do not apologize for it. If your TOO MUCHness is not obstructing your personal evolution or actually hurting someone else, stand in it.

Notice I said PERSONAL evolution. Professionally, there is A LOT hanging on us being as un-different from what is expected as possible. We enroll in courses and workshops that teach us how to interview exactly like someone else. We pose for LinkedIn pictures in white button-downs so we can look very standard. If you like leopard as a neutral, you're told not to walk into an office wearing that because it's too odd for a business environment. You like red suits? Nah, we want gray or blue because red is too bold. You want to show your enthusiasm and take charge? You're told to chill, so you can be more of a team player.

We are taught that being TOO different is not welcome, so basing ourselves and our barometer, on our worthiness in our professional worlds, will lead us astray time and time again.

At work, we encounter a lot of people with a lot of feelings. Oftentimes, you are doing your job AND the job of babysitting other adults' feelings, without getting paid overtime for the emotional labor. That in itself is how a great deal of people get convinced that they are TOO MUCH. They are showing up to work in full Technicolor when the business model is all gray scale.

If we base whether we are TOO MUCH on our jobs, we will forever be too much. I wanna take the time to give kudos to those of you who are working and thriving in corporate environments. Those of you who have to go to work and talk to your coworkers in compliment sandwiches so they don't feel like you're being too aggressive. Those of you who learned to bite your tongue even when you wanted to tell that douchebag in the cubicle next to you to go straight to hell. Shout-out to the ones who know their boss is incompetent, yet manage to get work done in spite of them. You have to do your job and theirs, AND perform the politics. I see you. I salute you. I pay my respects to you.

I think about the Black women who have to show up to work after busting their ass to do amazing work, in spite of coworkers with fragile egos who reported them to HR for being "too _____." I see you, woman who knows she's smarter than everyone in that meeting but has to nod and smile so she isn't considered aggressive. I see you, person who shows up with straightened hair so she won't be considered too Black for a place that says they value diversity but the only other person of color is the admin at the front desk. You might have to do what you gotta do to keep these checks coming (until you can find a place where you don't have to wear these types of masks), and I got nothing but respect for it.

To everyone who has been told they are too much, that they are excessive in some way and made to feel like their extraness means they aren't enough, I see you. I feel you. I am you. So what do I do? I insist on being me. The totality of me. And then I add some extra me-ness.

Sometimes I add some extra ME seasoning on myself when I step into a room, because I want people to get used to looking at someone walking in, maybe not in a package they expect, doing good work, and being excellent.

I am often invited to speak at conferences or internally at Fortune 100s, and when I ask what the dress code is, I'm usually told business casual is safest. And check it. I LOVE blazers and oxfords and wing tips. Forty percent of the time, I dress like an old white man from Maine who owns a yacht. My closet is full of the finest in preppy clothes. However, there are times when I will shirk the dress code and defy it on purpose for the sake of being too different. Why? So people know that we belong, in all our forms, in whatever uniform we show up in.

Once, when I arrived at a tech conference I was hosting, the room was full of Chads and Everetts (white nerdy dudes). I was one of two Black people in the room. I showed up the next day wearing a shirt that had Lionel Richie on it, with the words "Hello, is it me you're looking for?" Because the MC they expected probably wasn't me, but there I was anyway. Take that, take that, take that.

I acknowledge that not everyone has the social or professional privilege to always be a rebel with a cause. And I am not here to make you feel some type of way about doing your best. Rather, I want you to keep your head above water in a world that might feel like it is trying to drown you. Do what you can when and where you can. Don't beat yourself up. Lord knows you got enough trees to cut down. You don't need to be your own personal thorn.

I am, however, here to let you know that you aren't alone in being told you are TOO MUCH. And there isn't anything wrong with you. I am encouraging you to examine the times you have downplayed yourself for the comfort of others. I want you to reflect on the times you have been made to feel like you do not belong or you do not measure up or your presence is somehow a nuisance because you are a highlighter in a sea of pencils.

You will always be too much for somebody. You wanna be smaller? Sure, you can try. Some people will still consider your attempt not good enough. You turned your ten down to an eight when they were looking for a four. Why even try? Just give them the full ten. We can bend ourselves till we break trying to conform. And I promise you there will still be someone who is not satisfied.

Your TOO MUCHness is a superpower, and haters don't wanna see you don your cape. So what do you do? Be so much. Be the full totality of you. Add some extra to the you-ness. Be TOO MUCH because no matter what you do and how hard you try, someone somewhere will still think you are TOO something. You #minuswell (might as well) give them real reason to think so. Be the Youest You That Ever Youed.

3

DREAM AUDACIOUSLY

We fear having too much hope.

 We live in a world that often feels like the headquarters of Mayhem Enterprises, breaking our hearts into pieces every single day with chaos and madness. It is too willing to disappoint us with tragedies, horrific news, and bad hair hats. And we have to live in constant suspense, not knowing when these things will happen to us. Pandora's box is forever opening.

So I get why we fear dreaming. It's hard for us to get our hopes up that things will go the way we want them to. Yet, and still, we need to put this worry as far away from our psyches as possible. You might call it madness, but I call it necessary.

When we are afraid of having too much hope, we're actually afraid of being disappointed. We are anxious about expecting the world to gift us and show us grace, because what if we end up on our asses? So we dream small or not at all. Because if we expect nothing or expect something small, we cannot be disappointed when the big things don't happen. We think it's a great defense mechanism, but what it really is is a liability on our lives, because we are constantly bracing for impact. When we are afraid of thinking things can be too good, it can become a self-fulfilling prophecy. We think life, in all its summabitchery, is waiting to punch us in the neck and go, "OH YOU THOUGHT I WAS GONNA BE GOOD TO YOU?" so we don't dream because we don't even wanna give it the satisfaction of pulling the rug from under us.

This shows up in real life when we don't go after jobs we want because we already expect the answer to be no. We might not apply to the school we wanna go to because we think we have no chance in hell of being admitted. But what if we would have met a life helper or the love of our life there, or landed that perfect internship that would have led to the job of our dreams? Basically, we end up living the colorless versions of the lives we truly want, which then confirms that life is shitty.

Here's the thing. Life can absolutely be a filth bucket, even for people who TRY and STRIVE and DREAM. The difference is that those people can go to sleep at night and wake up in the morning knowing that they at least tried. They can take some small solace that they did what they could. Life's shenanigans can be off-the-chart levels for them. But they blame life, not themselves.

Many of us have lost our ability to dream, or we were never allowed to have it in the first place, since we live in a world that makes it really hard if you're not white, male, straight, Christian, able-bodied, and cisgender. We've been bound by oppressive systems that are designed to not give us an inch, even when we earn a mile. We have been shunned and disrespected and erased from the things we are entitled to. We are constantly living in default survival mode, so dreaming is a privilege and an allowance we haven't been able to afford. Imagination is also a benefit that has been yanked from us, because shit ain't fair. Glass ceilings have shown us that all we'll do by wanting more is continue to hit our heads on limits. So we wake up one day having been stripped of the very hope we need if we're gonna have a fighting chance at anything resembling equity in this world.

I want to dream like white men who have never been told there are ceilings for them, let alone caps. I think about the story of Summit and Powder Mountain.* What's Summit, you might ask? It's an invite-only social organization that has its headquarters on the mountain it owns (Powder Mountain). Let me repeat: An organization has property on a mountain that it has spent money on. DID YOU KNOW MOUNTAINS ARE UP FOR SALE??? Because I surely didn't.

Nah, let's talk about THAT. I'll give you the tl;dr (too long; didn't read), simplified version of the story. Summit started because a group of white guys who wanted to change the world for good would invite their friends for weekends in cabins on a mountain they liked in Utah. Then they started going to this mountain more frequently. So

---

*Alyson Shontell, "It's Official: 4 Young Founders Just Bought a $40 Million Mountain to Party On," *Business Insider*, May 7, 2013, https://www.businessinsider.com /what-summit-series-is-and-why-it-bought-40-million-powder-mountain-for -summit-eden-2013-5.

they thought, "Wait, since we're here so often, why don't we buy the mountain and invite more of our friends? Let's make this a thing." And they did just that, buying Powder Mountain for $40 million and getting others to invest in their dream.

I have a few questions that I'd love to ask them:

- How did the conversation about buying the mountain even go?

- Did anyone laugh at the first person who brought up the idea?

- Were they all high, and on what?

- When they reached "Okay let's buy the mountain" consensus, were they afraid of this idea?

- Who do you call when you're looking to buy a mountain? I know there's no yellow pages listing for that. (Meanwhile, I know I just dated myself with that reference.)

The audacity of unshackled white men is massive. The only way I wish to be more like them is by having the lack of oppression that gives me the freedom, gumption, and unmitigated gall to think it's even possible to own a mountain. I want that dauntlessness. The system that white men created, designed, and profit from, that makes the rest of us afraid of our own shadow while they step on our backs, is well done, ain't it? It works so well.

This must be said: It's not that the men of Summit are smarter or even braver than anyone else for thinking about buying a mountain. No. I mean, they are smart, but they (like millions of white men) benefit from being constantly centered, elevated, and catered to, so they have not been programmed to expect less from the world, like the rest of us have. Why would they not think of owning a mountain?

We need the nerve and rashness to dare to think these things are possible too, even when we know that we might need to be four times as good, three times as qualified, and twice as professional to get what they will have handed to them when they walk into a room in their cargo shorts, half asleep. So I say with this caveat and without naïveté: Dreaming big is in itself a privilege. However, I'm asking us to trick ourselves into thinking we have the privilege of dreaming big.

Being audacious enough to dream means discovering the courage to think your life can be bigger than you can even imagine. But often, we don't get there because we are afraid of what happens when hope doesn't pan out. We fear how disappointed or heartbroken we will be.

That is why we have to take the risk and think that what we want to happen is even possible in the first place. Dreaming is a gesture of courage in itself, because to envision our highest timeline is to be bold enough to think someway and somehow, it could come to pass.

On my journey as an accidental writer, author, and speaker, there have been a lot of times I was afraid to dream too big, lest I be let down. But other times, when something happened, I realized it was because I had actually spoken that hope out loud, even if only to myself. Take how my life has changed after writing a vision statement more than ten years ago. In fact, let's rewind to even earlier than that.

Growing up, I knew exactly what I wanted to be: Dr. Luvvie was the dream, because I was bookish and I wanted to help people—you know, the hope of immigrant and first-gen kids everywhere. When we moved to the United States from Nigeria, that dream was one of the few things I brought with me.

Throughout my academic career, I didn't have to try hard to get A's. I would write all my papers the night before they were due or the morning of and get A's. But when I started college at the University of Illinois as a Psychology premed major, Chemistry 101 happened to me.

I attended that class every day and went to office hours with my professor and teacher's aide, but it was an utter struggle. At the end of the semester, I got my grade: a solid D. D for Don't. It was the first of my academic career, and I definitely sobbed like someone had burned my pot of rice.

After having a come-to-Jesus moment with myself—like, "Sis, you don't even like hospitals. You'd be the worst doctor ever!"—I went to my adviser and dropped premed, deciding I'd probably do better pursuing my psychology degree and getting my master's in industrial/organizational psych. I could still help people that way. YAY ME!

(Fun fact: I didn't tell my mom that I had dropped the premed part of my major, so three and a half years later when she came to graduation, she was like, "Okay, so where's the premed graduation?" Me: "See, what had happened was . . . I got this D in chemistry. I dropped that dream very quickly. But hey, I finished college in four years! YAY ME!" I'm an everlasting vagabond. Chei. I think at that point, she was basically thinking since I got out of college and ain't nobody call her about me getting in trouble or acting a complete fool, it was my life. She trusted me with me, which was a gift, because that could have turned out badly. HEY YOUNG PEOPLE READING THIS, DON'T TELL THIS LIE OF OMISSION TO YOUR PARENTS. I will not be held liable for it. Cool? Cool.)

As my doctor dream was ending, another was beginning. My friends peer-pressured me into starting a "weblog." And by "peer-pressured" I'm pretty sure I only needed one suggestion and I was into it. I started my first blog in early 2003; it was titled something emo like *Consider This the Letter I Never Wrote*. In it, I documented my whole college career, writing about exams I wasn't studying for, the D I got, roommate problems. The blog used Comic Sans font, so you know it was a mess. But I loved this new hobby, and my psychology classes too. I did a few marketing internships and realized I was good at marketing too.

When I graduated in 2006, I deleted that undergrad blog and started what is now AwesomelyLuvvie.com. New life, new blog! I'd work my nine-to-five job in marketing, but when I came home, I'd blog. As I wrote about the world and how I saw it, word of my blog spread, and in 2009, I won my first award: Best Humor Blog in the now defunct Black Weblog Awards. I was geeked because here I was getting recognition for my hobby.

Hobby. Yeah, okay.

Get this. I was afraid to call myself a writer. WRITER? WHERE? I was afraid of that title and all the dreams that could come from it that I would be unable to fulfill. Toni Morrison and Maya Angelou and Zora Neale Hurston. Those were writers. I was just a girl who put up blog posts talking about whatever was on my spirit. Writer? "Bish, bye. You can't measure up to that title." That's what I told myself.

I liked my job as a marketing coordinator for a nonprofit that trained organizations in telling their stories in digital media. I was making enough to pay my bills, which weren't many. I was fine. Except I wasn't. I was bored with the job, and I felt restless. But I wasn't going to quit. Nah, son. We don't do that. We will just swallow down the discomfort and keep clocking in every day.

What I should have remembered is that whole honesty-as-my-core-value thing. When I refuse to be honest with myself, the lies I try to tell, even to myself, don't go well. My work ethic is one of my strongest traits, but I started being a shitty employee. I would show up to work and give my some, not my all. I'd update my blog at my desk. And one day, I fell asleep at a staff meeting. Like, full-on eyes closed, head dropped. In a staff meeting of nine people. BRUHHHH. As an employee, I was being increasingly trash.

In April 2010, I was suddenly laid off. They said it was due to budget cuts. I had the nerve to be surprised, y'all. The gall to feel like I'd been blindsided. Sis, you've been a rubbish employee for months! In fact, they did me a favor by laying me off, when they would have been justified in firing me.

That layoff/firing was God and the universe pushing me to take a leap of faith to stand in this writer dream I was too scared to have. But I'm a stubborn goat, so I didn't see it as that. Instead, I was on

Monster.com sending résumés left and right because I needed my biweekly paychecks and insurance! This shoe habit was not going to keep itself up, after all.

Throughout this period, there were times I'd wonder if I needed to stop putting so much time into my blog, but I couldn't quit. Something wouldn't let me. I still didn't consider it anything but my part-time hobby, when all signs were pointing to the fact that my purpose was to use my written words to make people laugh and think critically, and to make the world better.

I was a writer. But I was afraid, because there was no real blueprint for me to follow, and I didn't feel like it was a tangible-enough profession. To make money as I job-hunted, I designed websites and consulted with small businesses and other bloggers to teach them how to tell their stories using social media (my specialty).

After a year and some change of looking for a traditional job (and still blogging), I finally got hired for a full-time position as the social media manager for a global food brand. I went into the office on that first day, decked out in my "I'm serious" business-casual slacks and a button-down. My first task was to create a deck for a campaign, and I was in there knocking it out! Then came 1 p.m. and the walls of that building started closing in on me. Isweartogawd I wanted to slide off my nice ergonomic chair onto the floor and lie there. My spirit was not gelling with this new job. That night, I wrote an email to my new boss. I thanked them for the job and notified them that it was my first day AND my last. Bless it, but I couldn't do it.

In the meantime, other opportunities continued to pour in, all related to my writing. I finally started wondering why I was so afraid of being a writer.

A few months later, I was credentialed to do press coverage on the red carpet and backstage at the Academy Awards (February 2012). I was chosen because a producer who loved my blog thought I should be there. There I was, in my role as Awesomely Luvvie, backstage at the Oscars, eating Wolfgang Puck's shrimp and chocolates, next to journalists from the BBC, CNN, *Entertainment Tonight*! Me. A whole me! WOW.

That experience shifted my world: I was in that room and breathing that air because of my gift, because of my words. How was I NOT a writer? I might not be Toni or Maya, but I was Luvvie, and the fear of the writer title had kept me from truly honoring my purpose. Fear can very concretely keep us from doing and saying the things that are our purpose. But when I made the decision that I was not going to let fear rule my life or dictate what I do, my wildest dreams started coming true.

After college, I had two big dreams that I put down on paper numerous times, through vision statements I'd written or random "life bucket lists" I'd made over the years. One was to write a *New York Times* bestselling book. The other was to help my mom retire one day. As a single mother, Yemi Ajayi has always been one of my prime motivations to soar in this world. The sacrifices she made—moving us to the United States and leaving everything behind, somehow managing to make a dollar out of ten cents—allowed me to dare to dream. And she did it with such grace that I didn't even know that we were one paycheck away from being out on the streets.

I've wanted to make her proud with my life, and I've wanted her last decades on this earth to be as worry-free as possible.

When I turned thirty in 2015, I decided it was going to be my year of "Afraid? Do it anyway." I was going to pursue anything that scared me or that I wouldn't typically do, like Shonda Rhimes's *Year of Yes*. That was the year I went skydiving, when I traveled solo to five countries, and when I wrote my first book. I climbed that personal mountain and poured out seventy-five thousand words that became *I'm Judging You: The Do-Better Manual*. I finally could write that book because I overcame my fear of calling myself a writer. The courage I needed didn't come from a special class I took or some diploma I got. It was literally a shift in how I saw the thing. The monster didn't stop being so big. I just decided to fight it.

The book was published on September 13, 2016, and on September 21, 2016, I got the phone call that it had hit the *New York Times* bestseller list at number five. I was officially in a club that came with special privileges and my life instantly changed. My fees doubled and doors opened for me that I didn't even know existed, which led to my other major dream being realized.

A month later, I called my mother and told her she could stop working because I could now handle the bills for BOTH of us. It was the biggest pleasure of my life to be able to show her that all her work and sacrifices were not in vain. My book hitting the *New York Times* bestseller list allowed me to tell my mom to retire. And that dream led me to the opportunity to write this second book, dedicated to Yẹmí's mother, my grandmother, Fúnmiláyọ̀.

It all began with a blog from a girl who thought she wanted to be a doctor but was really a writer. But she was afraid of that title, and what failing at it could look like. Then God was like, "My hard-headed child, I got plans for you. Trust me. Rest in it." And after my stubborn ass ran out of excuses and dared to use the title that scared me, things began to fall into place in a way that felt divine.

I was afraid because I couldn't find an example of a writer like me, but I became that example for myself. And because of that, I am now that example for other people. We are prone to thinking that if we haven't seen what we want, in the exact form we imagine it in, then it isn't possible. There's a Black girl somewhere who can tell her parents, "I want to be a writer, and I can do it because look at Luv-vie." Oftentimes, when we want something that doesn't come with a manual, we are afraid of it, because we could lose our way since there's no map. Well, maybe WE are supposed to draw the map, so someone who comes behind us won't get lost. Create the map you didn't have. That's what I did. We must give ourselves permission to be who we want to be, even if we don't have the blueprint yet, and that starts with dreaming.

It is truly a blessing to be able to speak my dreams, even if only to myself, and see how they have been realized. I know there's no mag-ical dream fairy that grants wishes. And I don't necessarily claim luck in this either. I think I've seen some of my wildest dreams come true because I've put in a lot of hard work. I also give credit to God's grace, because I know there are people more talented than me or people who work harder than me, whose names we will never know.

But I am always hopeful. While we may voice our wants, we may not always get what we dreamed of, in the exact form we dreamed of it. However, it is important to continue to dream, even in the midst of disappointment, because it opens up our minds and lets us see things bigger.

To many, dreaming is living in a fantasy world where all things are possible and therefore nothing is possible. It's child's play. It's a futile exercise. To some that's inspiring, and to others it's frightening. But when anything is possible and there are no parameters, it actually means more than we know can happen.

The lives we live are full of people's dreams realized. The things we use every day are born from the audacity of someone who thought it was possible. There are many times when I'm traveling and I'm in awe of the fact that I'm in a tin can in the sky. When I'm eye level with clouds and think, "Bruhhhh, whose great-great-great-great-grandparent would have thought this was possible?" that shit feels magical. Science is made up of imaginations that ran wild and dreamed magical things that actually became achievable.

So why don't we operate our lives in this way?

I often think about all that my grandmother overcame to become the fierce woman I ended up knowing, like being orphaned at seventeen and having to start life over. That woman, born in 1931, ended up doing things and creating beings that led to me. Through dreaming that her life could be what she wanted, I am here today, standing on her shoulders. Her existence convinces and coerces me to let my imagination run wild. So I owe it to Fúnmiláyò̩ Fáloyin to think of pies in the sky with my name on them.

She dreamed of raising children who would be God-fearing and good as people. She dreamed of having a family that would never know the suffering she went through. She dreamed of more than what she had in front of her, as a young girl from Lagos, making a way in a world that thought it owned her. Her ferocious spirit knelt for no one, and even as a wife, she maintained her independence. She saw the world and lived loudly.

I've written this book knowing that if she were alive to read it, she would go to everyone she knew and tell them that her granddaughter was a published author, that her name will be known by people far and wide and never forgotten, in a book written by the baby girl of her third child. It would make her do that grin of hers where she'd show every tooth. She'd circle every mention of herself and show each one to everyone she encountered. I think about how proud she would be to be in the center of a book that I am claiming now, in print, will sell millions of copies and inspire people to live their best lives (let's DREAM). She would take cabs and make the drivers stop and read my book with her, as she paid for her fare. She would tell them to buy eight copies for them and their children. She would be the best marketer EVER for this book and anything else I did. I am my grandmother's wildest dream and, honestly, it is the pride of my life. If I accomplish nothing else, I can know I've done that.

When we dream, we're giving others permission to do the same.

When our dreams are big, we're telling the folks who know us that they don't have to be small either.

When our dreams come true, we're expanding the worlds of others because now they know theirs can too.

We must dream and dream boldly and unapologetically.

Sometimes we must dream so big that we make people uncomfortable. That is actually when you know you're doing what you should—when you mention something to someone and they gasp. YES! LOSE YOUR BREATH ON MY BEHALF.

You might be saying, "Wait. I gotta tell people my dreams? What if they jinx it?" No, you don't have to tell everyone all your dreams. I think it's most important that you tell yourself first. Others do not have to know. Not everyone is entitled to your deepest desires. Some people don't deserve the insight into our goals. Our lives aren't about those people. Our dreams can't be stopped by them either.

BUT . . . but . . . keeping our dreams to ourselves doesn't necessarily mean we're on the right track either. There are many times when I mention my goals to someone and they go, "Wait. I think I know someone who could help." There are times when my dreams have been spurred forward by someone I met at the right place when I decided to be bold in my words.

In 2018, I was burned out from traveling so much and working so hard, and I decided that I would take the month of July off. I had the privilege of being able to make that choice, and I recognize that. I made a declaration to myself and even posted it on Instagram, saying, "I'm not going anywhere or getting on any planes unless Beyoncé or Oprah call."

So what happened? I got a call from Yvette Noel-Schure, Beyoncé's longtime publicist, inviting me to the queen's first North America stop of her On the Run II tour. CAN I COME? YES I CAN COME!!! And I hung up and laughed and laughed because my life is weird and I keep saying these weird things out loud and they keep happening.

I've learned that the audacity to speak my dreams out loud, even if only to myself, has taken me far. I marvel at how many times the things I have dared to say have come true. The things I have let myself dream about. I ask, not with entitlement, but with hope, and magical things have happened.

Have the audacity to dream and ask. Sometimes the universe/God amplifies the ask to bigger levels, and that is the best surprise. You have everything to gain, as they add suya seasoning and Maggi cubes to your desires.

If we do not give ourselves permission to dream, how do we give ourselves permission to thrive? So give yourself the allowance to think about that thing that feels too big and too far to touch.

Life's adventures never promised a straight path, and that's often what stops us. But we must dream. All we have, even in the worst moments, are the dreams of better things to come.

4

OWN YOUR DOPENESS

We fear being perceived as arrogant.

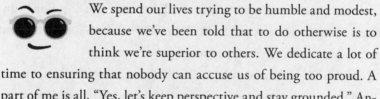 We spend our lives trying to be humble and modest, because we've been told that to do otherwise is to think we're superior to others. We dedicate a lot of time to ensuring that nobody can accuse us of being too proud. A part of me is all, "Yes, let's keep perspective and stay grounded." Another part of me is like, HUMILITY CAN GO TO HELL. LET THESE HOES HAVE IT.

Sometimes you gotta show up, show out, and let people know that you have arrived, so they gotta make room.

There is an oft-posted quote that says, "Carry yourself with the confidence of a mediocre white man." In the previous chapter, I talk about having some of their gumption, but I don't wanna carry myself in the way they do it cuz that confidence is bland AF. It might be ballsy, but it doesn't come with much swag. Instead, I want us to carry ourselves with the confidence of an older West African woman who has been through some things, come through on the other side, and doesn't look like what she's been through. A thousand useless goats can't tell them nothing.

M y grandma was the queen of Smell the Roses While Here. What does that mean? It means that woman was not shy about accepting any and all love sent her way. Growing up with her, I saw what it was like to be unapologetic about how awesome you are. It wasn't that she was arrogant or went around to people declaring how amazing she was. Nah. She didn't have to. But others made sure they told her how incredible she was. And not only did she say thank you, she also sat in the compliment and let it fill her heart up. She didn't run from it, make excuses for it, or diminish herself in an attempt to seem as humble as she was supposed to be.

Mama Fáloyin loved the Lord with all her heart. And like many Black grandmas around the diaspora, she had a main line directly to Jesus and His Holy Posse. So, on Sundays, where would you find her? In church, of course. She was a staunch Christian, and specifically a member of a denomination called Cherubim and Seraphim (C&S). Actually, correction: She was a prophetess at the church. No no. I'm not giving her all the glory yet. Her official title was the Most Senior Mother-in-Israel Prophetess Fáloyin. I want you to read that again. My grandma had a certificate from the church crowning her as THE MOST Senior Mother-in-Israel Prophetess Fáloyin. I laugh about how things and people do the most, but she literally WAS the most. I don't even know what that whole title actually means, but if there's one thing Nigerians love, it is grand titles. The longer, the better. The more grandiose, the better.

Members of the C&S church wore white gowns, prioritized praise and worship, and therefore spent five hours at each church service. My grandma herself contributed to making each service at least thirty minutes longer. Lemme tell you why.

Service started at 10 a.m. Praise and worship went on for about thirty minutes. Then Grandma would show up at around 10:30. (Because why should she be on time? A WHOLE her.) When the pastor and choir learned that she was outside and ready to come in, EVERY-THING stopped. I'm talking record scratch. Stop the presses, and stop the singing. Her presence was then announced to the church as the doors opened, and a whole welcome committee met her by the doors to usher her in.

Then, music started playing and my grandma, like the perpetual holy bride of Christ that she was, made her way down the aisle dancing. As if that wasn't extra enough, Grandma would dance five steps forward but stop to take two steps back, for true peppering and scattering! BRUH! She took her sweet time, and the mini-carnival lasted all the way down the massive church till she took her place at the pew in the first row, at the seat only she could occupy. If doing the most was a sport, that lady was a Hall of Famer. Entrance theme music? Welcome committee? Interruption of services? Dancing for your life? CHECK CHECK CHECK CHECK.

The church insisted on doing this regularly, and Granny, not being shy, protested minimally. She reveled in it. And that in itself is revolutionary behavior, in a world where you are not encouraged to celebrate yourself.

We do not all get a weekly celebration of our very presence via song and dance, but there is something to be said for how we would handle it if it ever came. Many of us don't even know how to accept compliments. Someone tells us our shoes are cute and we're quick to go, "These? Please. I just pulled them out the back of the closet," when a simple "Thank you" could go a long way. People might tell us, "You look amazing," and we go, "Nah, you." There is, of course, nothing wrong with exchanging compliments, but how often do we do it because we are uncomfortable with being praised? How often do WE praise ourselves after doing something great? How often do we sit in the good vibes of someone SEEING us, acknowledging it, and sending some words to prove it? We don't get a gift for being the most self-deprecating in a room. Or being the one who can make fun of ourselves best. We have mastered that. Now I want us to master the art of owning our dopeness.

What I learned from my grandmother is how to allow myself to be truly celebrated. Women, especially, have been told that humility is a required character trait. And somehow, that humility has been turned into perpetual self-deprecation. We've been convinced that the more we downplay our awesomeness, the better the world is. As if knowing we're the shit is somehow a threat to the climate. As if accepting celebration of our wondrous ways makes gas prices go up. As if knowing we wake up and piss excellence is a cause of world hunger.

This permeates everything we do and how we move through the world. When you are not used to owning your dopeness, odds are you're actually covering up how amazing you are. We're not gassing up ourselves like we should, and how does that show up? It means we end up selling ourselves short.

Some of us struggle with telling our friends and family our accomplishments and good news because it seems like we're bragging. But your achievements are factual things. Not speaking about them doesn't mean they didn't happen. And you know what? If speaking about them makes someone feel like you're bragging, so what? AND SO?

You post or send a text about something you've done well. And the person who sees it on social or receives it rolls their eyes at you BECAUSE YOU DID WELL. Or they unfollow you. Or they delete your number. Is that someone you actually want in your life? Is that the person you want to sit next to you every day? Is that the person you want to invite to your home? No? Okay then, why do they matter? Why do their thoughts about you actually make a difference? And then, what if this is someone you actually do not know at all and have never met, and they are mad and call you arrogant because you keep winning? What does this person have to do with you? Should this stranger be the reason you now keep your leveling up to yourself? Is this person the one who will stop you from celebrating yourself?

NO.

Do not let people make you feel bad for being successful, and for being you, and for being amazing, and for being accomplished. If people get upset at you for announcing something you did, those people are not your people. Those people do not deserve your dopeness. And those people serve no important role in your life. Anyone who is upset that I'm doing well is an enemy of progress, and I don't need them around me.

Let's be real. Standing unapologetically in how good you are and how worthy you are will have some people not liking you. Because sometimes we reflect other people's shortcomings. We are a mirror of their failures. And because of that, we will be the target of disdain because people want that confidence and resent it in us. That is perfectly okay. Thankfully, I'm not motivated by others' hate, but if I were, I'd have a trophy shelf where I've collected my naysayers' tears into bottles of various sizes.

Owning your dopeness is not about being liked by others. It's really about being liked by you first. One of my favorite proverbs is "When there is no enemy within, the enemy outside can do you no harm." If you are strong in yourself, the actions of everyone else are less likely to move you.

There are really terrible people who think they're amazing. And people believe them strictly because they've convinced others that they're the shit. Knowing that there are subpar and mediocre-ass people out there who think they deserve all the good in the world and want heaps of praise, when your EXCEPTIONAL ass is questioning yourself at every corner, makes me fight the air. Trust and believe that there are people with far fewer skills than you who cannot be swayed from thinking that a party should be thrown in their honor every day. People who cannot hold a torch to you are out here crowning themselves. Never underestimate the effect of confidence. If you believe you're the dopest thing walking, you might convince people of the same, just because you're so headstrong about it as a fact.

It's time to accept we're incredible specimens. You do not have to wear a T-shirt saying, "I'm the greatest of all time." I'm not saying be arrogant, but I am saying we err on the side of humility to our detriment. Do. Not. Shrink. We've had so much practice shrinking ourselves and trying to make ourselves smaller that when it's time for us to take up space, we don't even know how. Even when we are called, we run. Even when we are celebrated, we tell people it's too much. Even when we're told to speak, we use a whisper. Why? Who are we helping by being muted versions of ourselves?

Some of us not only make ourselves smaller, but we apologize for our very being. We actually say sorry for our presence, as if we exist as some sort of transgression to others. We say sorry when someone passes us on a sidewalk, as if both of us don't have a right to be there at once. We even say sorry for our FACES. I've seen people write on social media about a picture they posted, "Sorry that my face looks like it does." Wait. You are asking people for forgiveness for your visage? HOW? WHY? What did your face do to them?

But I get it. A lot of it is tied to our past traumas, low self-esteem brought on by years of criticism, and other layers of baggage. The world has thrown enough daggers at us that holes remain. This isn't the book that will help you break through those (because that is a book in and of itself). I simply ask that you stop apologizing for your existence and for the things attached to your body. Even if you feel like you should, I am here to tell you that you should not.

And if you don't want to do it for you, do it for the young child in your life who is seeing you apologize for your vitality. Stop saying sorry for yourself, so that the young person can know that they are also not supposed to apologize for who they are. That their existence does not warrant apology but warrants celebration. That the world is better off for them being here.

It makes me so sad that we do this, especially women.

Somewhere along the way, they told us our glitter was ashes. They told us that what we touched turned to dust, not gold. They convinced us that we bled as punishment, not purpose fulfillment. Somewhere along the way, our magic was minimized. They said we were ordinary, not walking proof of miracles. And we started believing them. We did. We let the world tell us we had to apologize for ourselves. We had to be polite but stern, sexy but not too sexual, bosses but not bossy, confident but not cocky, motherly but not matronly. We had to hide the rough edges they created in us and be soft but not fluffy.

And Black women? Well, we've been told we're the mule when we are the mother of all of this. We are jewels. We are the reason for poems to be written, sappy love notes with metaphors that seem hyperbolic but are more grounded in truth than you know.

Somewhere along the way, we were told we weren't enough when we are truly EVERYTHING. We are literally LIFE everlasting. We are God's vessel. Science can't explain us. We are magic. Don't let nobody tell you shit. You're made of pixie dust. They just don't know what to do with it.

Not owning my dopeness almost had me missing out on a major blessing and honor. Lemme tell you that story.

In the beginning of 2016, I was getting ready for the year of *I'm Judging You*. My first book was going to be released in September, so at the top of the year I was focused on that.

In March, I got an email from the OWN team, congratulating me for being chosen as part of Oprah Winfrey's inaugural SuperSoul 100 list. It was a list of one hundred people who Oprah thought were "elevating humanity." I read the email and basically laughed because I just knew it had to be spam. This must be from the same Nigerian prince who said he had $342 million inheritance for me. LMAO. Good one.

Then I got a text from someone who works at an agency that works with the OWN team to tell me to check my email for something important. I was like, "Wait. Was that email real??" I had to go into my spam folder to retrieve it. Sure enough, it was legit. I had been chosen as one of a hundred people who Oprah thought was doing some dope things in this world. BRUHHHHHHHH lemme just lie here in disbelief.

After I managed to close my mouth and call a few people I love while squealing, I finally read the email and saw I was invited to a SuperSoul 100 brunch, just for those who Lady O had chosen.

When I showed up, I was sitting at a table with Sophia Bush. I looked over at the next table and saw Ava DuVernay and Arianna Huffington. Then I looked across the room, which was on the OWN lot, and saw Janet Mock and Zendaya. I was truly floored. In my head, I kept yelling, "How did I get here amongst these giants? HOOOWWWWWW? Was a mistake made?"

No mistake was made. You're dope. You're in the room. Own it. OWN it. Tuck in the impostor syndrome and charge forward. Allow yourself to be celebrated, even among luminaries. You belong.

That is how I finally met Oprah, after being in many rooms with her over the years but never having the courage to introduce myself.

On three previous occasions, I actually said that when I finally met her, she'd have already heard and known my name. Well, this time she chose me to be in the room with her. And I was still shocked by it.

All of it is related, and when you aren't standing in your greatness and you're questioning the grace you find, it is impostor syndrome at work. How often do we let that lack of trust in our amazingness block our blessings? We'll tackle that in the next chapter.

My grandmother always celebrated herself. I still think about how she smiled with her whole face whenever she told us what she was up to or a new thing she'd done. She was earnest in her pride in herself, without diminishing herself or others in the process. And she would not allow others to speak for her. I remember going to a doctor's appointment with her, and the doctor, seeing this older Nigerian woman, assumed she couldn't understand English. He turned to me and said, "What is her birthdate?" Grandma, not missing a beat and smiling widely, said, "Ask me. I was born July 31, 1931." And I sat there like, "You heard the lady."

I want to be like her. If arrogance is the worst thing about me, then I'll be really winning. If thinking highly of myself and being self-affirming is a fault, I want to be the walls of the Grand Canyon.

Speak of yourself and your work with exclamation points, not question marks. When someone asks you who you are and what you do, speak definitively. "I write." Not "Well, I kinda write, sometimes?" If you don't know, they don't know. We must honor ourselves in a world that doesn't want us to, and we will wait for nobody's permission.

And above all, do not question the grace.

5

TRUST WHERE YOU ARE

We fear success.

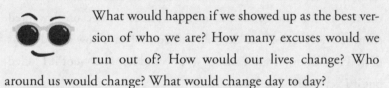What would happen if we showed up as the best version of who we are? How many excuses would we run out of? How would our lives change? Who around us would change? What would change day to day?

We often talk about fear of failure, but fear of success is just as real, if not more so. A lot of times, we know we have exactly what it takes to get what we want or to see our dreams realized, but it scares us to think of how limitless our lives can really be. Maybe we're scared by the possibility of living up to whatever excellence we achieve. Maybe we're unsure that if we taste success, we'll be able to sustain it. Or maybe we worry we can't handle what comes with it. What would it mean for us?

My fear of success is certainly real, because I know that new levels bring new devils. Oftentimes, that's what I'm truly afraid of, even more than the failure part.

A lot of this worry comes from impostor syndrome: questioning whether we deserve whatever the opportunities are, which leads us to talking ourselves out of winning before we even get into the race. Why are we so afraid of what could be that we never give ourselves a chance to soar?

My grandmother didn't finish high school, because when she was eighteen, her parents died and she had to make a way for herself and her little sister. She never got any major degrees, but you couldn't tell that woman she didn't belong in any room she found herself in, whether it was a room where the president of a country was or a room full of taxi drivers. She didn't waste time questioning herself.

That TED Talk I mentioned, which changed my life and has millions of views? I wrote that talk early in the morning, in a taxi on the way to the airport for one of my work trips, because I wanted them to reject it so I wouldn't have to do it. That's how afraid I was of it. That is how afraid I was of what could happen—not if I failed but if I was really good at it.

Back in July 2017, I was invited to speak at TEDWomen by curator Pat Mitchell, the legendary journalist and correspondent. I wanted to say YES because I had wanted to do an official TED Talk for a while! I'd done two TEDx Talks before, but this was an invite to do a talk on the official TED stage. I was already booked for a different conference in a different city that day, so I hit a *wall slide* and declined. These are champagne problems, I'm aware. Still.

Two weeks before TEDWomen (which was happening November 1), I got the schedule for the other conference, and it turned out that the only thing happening the first day was an optional VIP party. I was like, "Wait. Maybe I can drop by TEDWomen in New

Orleans for a day to cheer on my friends and then head to New York." So I hit them up and let them know I'd like to have a day pass to the conference. Upon which they were like, "Why don't you come speak?" And I was like "WAIT WHAT?!?" Pat Mitchell wanted me to take the stage while I was there.

And this is where I panicked and did the thing that is a surefire way to hustle backward: I let fear dictate my decision making.

Here's the thing: TED is really picky about speakers and preparation. People get coaches, talks are vetted, and when you take that stage, you have been prepped extensively for it. Those talks don't soar for no reason. There is a lot of work behind them! So, here I am, two weeks before a TED event, being asked to take the stage. I'm in my head like, WHAT ABOUT MY COACHES? I DON'T EVEN HAVE A TALK YET. OMG TWO WEEKS IS NOTHING.

I did not want to take that stage and bomb. I was not gonna embarrass myself and shame my family name on that big stage. Who did I think I was, to be jumping in last minute? NAWL. So I decided that I was gonna decline (again) and tell Pat I'd be in the audience cheering. I wrote out a three-paragraph email expressing my regret about how I wished I could make it work, but I could not. I was tired after a really full fall of city-hopping for the Together Live tour, and I did not want to bring less than 100 percent to their stage. I was afraid I would fail with drowning colors. Right before I hit Send on the email, I decided to call my girl Eunique Jones Gibson.

ME: Sis. They asked me to do a TED Talk and it's in, like, a week and a half and I think I'll decline because I'm not ready. Everyone else has had months to practice and coaches and here I am sliding in at the eleventh hour.

EUNIQUE: Well, you ain't everybody.

ME: Well, shit.

EUNIQUE: You've been on a stage twice a week for the last six weeks. You've been speaking professionally for almost a decade. Everything you've done up until now has been your coach. Everything has prepared you for this. You're ready.

ME: Whoa.

EUNIQUE: And if they didn't think you could do it, they wouldn't have asked you. You are doing it.

ME: Gahtdamb. Drag me, then! My edges. Here, take them.

EUNIQUE: Aight, get off my phone and go prepare for your TED Talk. Kill it. *Hangs up.*

Bruh, she got me SO TOGETHER. I went in my email and deleted the draft I was going to send Pat. But a part of me was still shook.

The next day, I wrote my talk. While I was in an Uber. On the way to the airport. My one-hour trip to the airport was spent crafting this talk, and I hit Send on it as the car pulled up to O'Hare airport.

I was expecting the TED team to be like, "Luvvie, what is this nonsense? No, never mind. We made a mistake." And I woulda shrugged and said, "Y'all sure did. Whew." I would have been fine because I was looking for any reason to chicken out. But they loved this talk! HOWWW???

Then they told me I needed to be in New Orleans two days before the conference so I could practice, which was required of speakers. I couldn't be in NOLA until the morning of November 1 because I was getting an award in Chicago the day before (brag on yourself, folks!). Again, champagne problems. I was like, "Well, here's the part where they kick me out, which is fine." But instead they were like, "Ah. Well, let's do video rehearsal, then."

Oh and the conference was starting at 6 p.m. on November 1. To make my other conference, I had to take the last flight out, which was at 8 p.m. I let them know, thinking, "Okay, this is the last straw." Pat replied by telling me it was no problem, and they would make sure I was the opening speaker at TEDWomen so I could make that flight.

Every time I thought they'd be like, "This ain't gon' work. Thanks but no thanks," they found a work-around to another one of my (valid) excuses.

At this point, the punk in me wanted to lie out on the ground. I was fresh the hell out of excuses and I REALLY had to do it. I was going on first, after the intro.

I MEAN. Talk about votes of confidence.

The night before the talk, I was at home rehearsing to an audience of one: my husband, Carnell. He was like, "This is pretty good, but I think it's missing something." So I sat down at my computer and read it over and over again, and started changing things. Before I knew it, I'd changed half of the talk, because I wanted it to be the best it possibly could. The new version was one that infused more of my story. It was better. Much better. And over the next two hours, I rehearsed it more times and prayed to God that I would get on that stage and not fail.

The next morning, I hopped on the flight to New Orleans, exhausted because I'd gotten so little sleep from reworking my talk and from being the last-minute packer that I am. I was on that flight looking downtrodden, with tote bags under my eyes. But instead of sleeping, I put my head against the window and repeated my talk to myself over and over again because I had decided to do it from memory, and I still didn't have it memorized.

When I arrived, I kept reading my talk script, and going through it over and over in my head, because I wasn't using any prompts besides the slides that would run behind me. There was no confidence monitor or teleprompter that would help me. I was spooked because this wasn't a talk I had given before.

I don't get too nervous when I'm about to give talks, but for this? I WAS NERVOUS AF. And I was going to be the first speaker! The one thing I wanted to guarantee was that, at least, I'd look good. My yellow blazer, with black blouse, and black jeans, paired with hand-beaded Italian slippers, were my version of a security blanket. Even if I sucked, I wanted folks to be like, "Her speech was trash, but she looked GOODER DINNAMUG." I had my signature red lip, and some drippage in the form of diamond jewelry on. Let's do it!

The time for my talk arrived quicker than I realized it would, since time conspires to embarrass you sometimes. Pat announced me and I walked on the stage, onto the red TED circle, and saw the audience. But before I could say the first word, my mic pack fell off the back of my pants.

Ha! Way to start. So I had to stand on the stage in front of all these people as the sound guy came out to adjust it. Oddly enough, this calmed me *a lot* because hey, shit happens. I took the opportunity to be all "HEY Y'ALL!! How you doing?" It worked some nerves off, because one of the things that were bad that could happen had happened. And I didn't die. It actually wasn't even a big deal.

And then I started my talk. In ten minutes, I dropped more than seventeen hundred words, challenging people to be truth-tellers committed to doing and saying what was difficult because that is necessary for us to move forward. I used myself as the example, how my life changed when I decided to stop being led by fear. I used the idea of being a domino, because the first one to fall causes others to do the same.

Ten minutes and fifty-four seconds straight through. No stops. The TED Talk I gave is the one you can see now.* There is no editing magic. I never paused because I forgot a line. I didn't run backstage to go check my script because I lost my way. My voice did not shake. It poured out of me like I had been doing that very talk for years.

I said my last sentences: "It is our job, it is our obligation, it is our duty to speak truth to power. To be the domino, not just when it's difficult—especially when it's difficult. Thank you."

---

*View the TED Talk at http://go.ted.com/luvvieajayi.

I immediately ran off the stage because I had not forgotten that I had a plane to catch (it was 6:25 p.m. at that point). But before I could leave, the stage manager turned me around and said, "I need you to go back out there and see the standing ovation you're getting right now." And I walked back and saw people on their feet cheering for me.

I was overwhelmed in the best way. I coulda cried, but I didn't have time! I took a bow and ran right back off the stage.

I jumped in the car and made it to the airport by 7:10 p.m. I ran through the airport and made that 8 p.m. flight with thirty minutes to spare. On the flight, I was exhausted but geeked. I was geeked, y'all. I knew I'd killed it. I had done something to be proud of.

A week later, I got an email saying they would like to feature my talk on TED's home page on December 1. I coulda fallen off my chair, because TED doesn't guarantee when talks go up. Some don't see the light of day for six months after they happen, and mine was picked to go up in less than a month.

And surely, when that day came, "Get Comfortable with Being Uncomfortable" was front and center on the TED home page. Within a month, the talk had received one million views. And now, millions have watched it and the number is still growing. Most important, the messages I've been getting from people all over the world who let me know how my talk spurred them to take an action they might not otherwise have taken, have stuck with me.

This talk. This thing I did. In it, I talked about being more conscious of not letting fear lead my decisions, but sometimes I need my own reminder. I let fear of not being ready almost keep me from doing this very thing. Doing the talk was being my own domino, because I thought I wasn't ready. I was proving my own point, even in the process of getting to that stage. It wasn't that I wasn't fearless, it's that I did it anyway. And when we are honoring our gifts, we have to stand in them.

Impostor syndrome is the cousin of fear. Both are boundless bastards.

Impostor syndrome is the feeling of wearing a mask and playing a role that you don't feel at home in. It is present in those moments when you feel like you or your work are a fluke, and that you're a dwarf among giants. Many of us have experienced this, especially when we're in some sort of creative industry. Why? Because we are our own worst enemies and we do not give ourselves enough credit.

I let impostor syndrome trick me into thinking I didn't belong on that TED stage, just like I had when I questioned how Oprah could have chosen me for the SuperSoul 100 list. Let me repeat this. I let impostor syndrome tell me that I was not worthy of where I was being placed and the opportunity that was presented to me. But impostor syndrome lies.

How many times have we let impostor syndrome convince us that we should say NO to YES questions? How many times have we dropped the key to the door we should be opening because we didn't think we were ready? How often have we allowed fear to talk us out of that room that could be life-changing?

How many times has impostor syndrome told us not to write the book, not to audition for that play, not to apply for that job that we are qualified for? How many times have we let impostor syndrome keep us from doing the work we're supposed to do?

We let the voices in our heads spin tales of inadequacy, and we believe them. We look in the mirror and wonder if anyone else realizes that we're just faking it. That voice that is throwing hateration in our confidence dancerie has been allowed to take over, and we sit there thinking we're playing a part we aren't qualified for. We let it convince us that we are not good enough.

Impostor syndrome tells us that we need to be perfect; otherwise we are failing. We need to realize that perfection is the enemy of progress and it does not exist. If you're constantly striving for perfection, you'll be so afraid of failing that you won't create that thing because you'll think it's not good enough. So then you don't let it into the world. Then nobody gets the value of your work, because we never see it because you're too busy constantly trying to perfect it. Take the pressure off.

Impostor syndrome convinces us that what makes us different reduces our worth, when it is truly the opposite. As I said in chapter two, our difference is often our superpower. As a professional speaker who has taken stages all over the world, I find myself in rooms where I am often the ONLY Black woman, and I happen to be the keynote. Instead of letting it OTHER me, I use it to affirm how necessary my work and my voice are.

My Blackness, on those occasions, is an anchor for me. When I walk out of the room, those in it will not forget who I am. You might not remember Scott and Tim, but you're going to remember Luvvie, who came in her fedora, her red lip, and sometimes a pair of crispy

Jordans or wing tips. I must remember that I'm not in there because anyone is doing me a favor. I am there because I bring value to any space I'm in. My opportunities are not from people taking pity on me, but are a result of consistent hard work over a sustained period. To deny that fact is to betray myself and the work I've put in. Impostor syndrome be damned.

My job while in the room is to give value and then try to figure out how I can ensure I am not the ONLY next time. I must recognize my privilege and figure out how to use it so I can leave the door open behind me for someone who looks like me. Because the next time I'm in that room, I don't want to be the ONLY (Black person, woman, person with rhythm, etc.).

Why should I feel out of place? Because I'm not like everyone else in there? Sure. But I am not any less than they are. How did the other folks make it? It's not necessarily because they're smarter. It's not automatically that they know more than I do. It's not because they're more clever. It's that they found the cheat codes or knew somebody who knew somebody.

Impostor syndrome tells us that everyone else is better than us, because they seem to be further ahead or have their shit together more than we do. It tells us that we deserve less than we're worth, because we are replaceable. Impostor syndrome will have us questioning what people say about us that's good. We will ignore the fact that they say we're smart, talented, and gifted, and that the work we do is necessary. But the moment someone tells us something opposite, we take that on as fact. We will, very quickly, believe somebody's negative ideas about us but question five people telling us something positive.

What would happen if we actually took on the positive things people are saying about us, instead of internalizing all the negative? Maybe impostor syndrome wouldn't have such a strong hold on us. Maybe we could use the logic of those numbers to boost us up when we think we aren't ready for a big moment presented to us, or ready to start that business or ask for that promotion.

It lies to us. Impostor syndrome is a liar, and too many of us have accepted it as truth. How do we fight it? How do we kick it out of our heads, or at least turn the volume down?

I remind myself that:

I am not the best. I don't have to be. I am enough. The idea of "best" is temporary. The person who wins a race won it once. The next race, they might no longer be the best. Are they at least in the top three? Did they beat their own time from the last race? We can reach for being the best, but thinking we've lost just because we didn't win is the quickest way to psych ourselves out.

I've worked my ass off. At minimum, that hard work has earned me a ticket in. Even if I am not the best, the fact that I KNOW that I work hard is enough to grant me admittance to that room. My grind got my foot in the door. I can at least give myself that.

Even if I happen to be in the room by accident and by no doing of my own, I AM IN THAT ROOM. It is no longer an accident. Once I'm in there, I am already worthy. How do I make it intentional and purposeful? What is my assignment while I'm breathing in that air? I take the opportunity to learn from the best. I walk away from that room inspired, with a resolve to be a superior version of myself. So next time I AM in the room, I feel at home in it.

I've ended up in spaces with the people I admire most, and each time, I question how I ended up there. EVERY SINGLE TIME. But after I reflect, I go back to some of those reminders. I worked hard for this. I don't have to be the best. I am enough. Since I am here, then it is no accident. I walk away knowing that I need to keep doing what got me in that room, and I need to keep doing it well.

Impostor syndrome does have some redeeming value. It keeps us humble. It keeps us curious. Doubt has purpose sometimes. If we don't think our work is good enough, we strive to do better and be better. Which then makes us greater because practice does just that. It turns us into lifelong climbers who DO end up belonging in any room we end up in, because we've continued to work at our craft.

The folks who are unequivocally confident in their abilities are the ones who do not become better at their craft. They think they're so good that they just need to show up. They are the ones who don't grow, because they're too busy singing their own praises and patting their own backs without the compulsion of evolution.

Practice makes you get better. People who are great at things have committed to something long-term, and done it repeatedly.

M e, in my yellow blazer, black shirt, and red lipstick—I stood on that TED stage and was exactly who I am. I was reminded that my journey was unfolding exactly as it should.

And to think, I almost said NO. When the YES I said changed my life in the best way possible. And what I had to do was trust where I was, and trust that I was ready for it all.

SAY

We need to use our voices. In this section, I ask us to speak up about what we want and need, because our silence doesn't serve anyone. Being quiet about our lives, stories, problems, and lessons does us no favors. When we want to say something and our voice shakes, we should take that to spur us forward, because that is when it is most necessary. Let your voice tremble, but say it anyway.

"WE'VE GOTTA SAY WHAT'S DIFFICULT EVEN WHEN OUR VOICES SHAKE."

—Luvvie Ajayi Jones

6

SPEAK THE TRUTH

We fear the power of honesty.

 We are afraid of the truth. Point-blank period. We don't like hearing it, sharing it, or seeing it. The truth can be the boogeyman. What's wild is that the truth is essential in a well-functioning society, so how are we doing when it isn't welcome, let alone prioritized? We're doing terribly.

We fear honesty because it exposes the rawness of life and our flaws, which we are too willing to ignore. It calls us to the carpet, because once you know, you can't unsee the ugliness of what was exposed. You might even have to do something about it. The truth challenges us to change and be better, and those are all tall orders.

We are also afraid of rocking the boat, which often comes with speaking the truth. We don't want to disrupt harmony in our spaces, and that tends to happen when we challenge what feels comfortable or expected. This is why I believe that one of the biggest forms of courage is being radically honest and transparent.

One of my favorite quotes is "A lie can travel halfway around the world while the truth is putting on its shoes." (Google never knows exactly who said it, as it's attributed to, like, five different dead old white guys, but it's a whole fact!) There was a study done by the University of Massachusetts* that found that in a single ten-minute conversation, most people lied at least once. It's what we do, and we're so used to comfort and harmony that we put those above all else. It's not that we're all lying for the sake of it; we are doing it for self-preservation and to be liked. But oftentimes, it bites us in the ass. It is part of why we are in constant disorder.

Do I lie? For sure. Everyone does. I'm not gonna sit up here and tell you I don't because that would be a lie. But I try really hard not to spew falsities, and I've been that way since I was young. I've known for a long time that I don't know how to lie well because I don't have a poker face at all. My face is a visual outside voice and all my thoughts are loudly written on it. When I'm lying, you can tell.

Growing up, I wasn't the kid who was getting in trouble for climbing trees or touching fire. I was a very self-assured child, so when I got in trouble, it was because of my mouth. I was always defending myself or somebody else. "That's not fair" was one of my favorite phrases as a mini-human. In fact, I'd often get in trouble for saying something that was so direct that it would come across as

---

*University of Massachusetts at Amherst, "UMass Researcher Finds Most People Lie in Everyday Conversation," *Eurekalert!*, https://www.eurekalert.org/pub_releas es/2002-06/uoma-urf061002.php.

rude, then I'd get in further trouble when I'd try to justify what I said. And when I was punished, I didn't understand why I was in trouble for telling the truth.

My very Nigerian mom probably wanted to wring my mouth a few times. I'm actually sure she did. And when she did punish me, I'd tell her that I felt offended and that she owed me an apology. I would write her letters expressing my disappointment in her disappointment and how I felt like I got the short end of the stick. Bruh, I really tried it. Petite and bold.

Even though I'd take whatever punishment came my way, I've known for a long time that truths make people deeply uncomfortable. What did I do, as the professional troublemaker that I am? Made a career out of it. But that was a true accidental happening.

I started my first blog in 2003, as a freshman in college. It was before Facebook, Twitter, Instagram, all of that, back when Myspace was on its last legs. I enjoyed talking about my undergrad life and all the ensuing shenanigans. Writing my thoughts online was a gift to myself, because it allowed me to write in the way that felt most authentic, most real, most truthful.

Blogging was not a career for me then, because it was still considered "playing on the internet." But because I didn't consider it a career, I couldn't fail at it—that was a gift. Since I had no expectations, I didn't doubt my writing or my voice. And when you are writing like nobody's reading, it's going to come out in the truest way possible because there's no agenda. That lack of pretense allowed me to write the things that sometimes made people feel uncomfortable. And as people began to see me as the person writing what they were thinking but didn't dare to say, I gained an audience.

As my blog got bigger and bigger and I got my first awards for it, I realized that people thought my work was extraordinary. I was confused, and not even on some fake-humble shit. Seriously, I was like, "Why? All I'm doing is writing what I think about the world and telling what I see is truth." Then I wondered what everyone else was doing. Were they bullshitting? Were they in these streets not coming correct? It was years before I realized that what made me stand out was the simple act of being straightforward and authentic. I wrote without deceit.

Collectively, we aren't used to truthfulness. It's not because we are bad people, but we shirk honesty so often, even in small instances, that when the big moments come, we don't have the language or capacity for them. If we lie in casual conversations, what happens when we're confronted with important things that really matter or make an impact? We don't have the practice.

I'll give you an example of a small moment. Your friend walks up to you and says, "So I got this new haircut from a new stylist. Do you like it?" You look at your friend and somehow their bangs are cut crooked and this stylist has sabotaged their hair. It's not really curling all the way over.

Your instinct is to instantly say, "Yes, of course I love it." Because right then, you don't want to hurt your friend's feelings or rock the friendship boat. I understand. But then your friend takes a selfie and drops it on Instagram. Now they have a different angle of this haircut and they're like, "Aw hell. That was not what I wanted. This looks really janky!" They come back to you and say, "I just posted my picture on Instagram. Why didn't you tell me my bangs were busted? I asked you if you liked my haircut, and you said you did."

Your friend knows you lied to them. You didn't love their haircut. I know you wanted to make sure you didn't hurt their feelings, but now your friend has a reason to doubt your word. The next time they ask for your opinion, they might be wondering if you're telling them the truth or giving them an answer that appeases, without candor.

In a world that is overflowing with things to side-eye and question, let us not be the type of people who others feel the constant need to distrust. Instead, I want us to be the friends or village members who others count on not only to please them, but to see them at their best. In that way, honesty is a love language. Affirm me with facts. I cannot say I am my sister's or brother's keeper if I'm expected to lie to you constantly. How can I care for you when I can't be open and honest with you?

So how would I deal with that small moment of the haircut gone wrong? Well, two ways. If it's completely messed up AND your dye job is weak, I might have to tell you since you asked me. If it's simply not MY taste, I might reply with something like "What matters is that you like it. If you like it, I'm good with it." Smoothhh. You can't accuse me of lying. Of course I also believe in "Friends don't let friends be raggedy without telling them."

But what about the times when somebody asks us something big or drops a problem at our feet and says, "What do you think?" What about when we are faced with injustice that makes us feel less than, or someone else is doing something that harms us and we have the opportunity to address it? Because we don't want to bring tension, we might let the truth go by the wayside.

I see meetings as a microcosm of the world and how we move through it. You can test out life in a meeting, and *Lord of the Flies* can happen. How many of us have been in meetings where somebody drops an idea that is at worst terrible and at best ill-thought-out? All of us. The answer is all of us. When it happens, often the room goes silent as people try to decide whether they should say something and challenge it. Oftentimes, no challenges ever come. Whenever I see public backlash from a company or brand for airing an insensitive commercial or tone-deaf campaign, I always wonder who was in the room. Who did not tell the truth about the wackness of whatever it was? There is always at least one person there who knows the shit ain't gon' land well. I always wonder, "Why didn't that person speak up?"

> Person 1: They're tired of always being the one to speak up, so they're taking a break.
>
> Person 2: They felt it wasn't their department or charge, so it has nothing to do with them.
>
> Person 3: They felt like it wouldn't be welcome in that room.
>
> Person 4: They felt like they would get punished for challenging it.

All of these are valid reasons.

If you are person 1, I feel you on a spiritual level. You've earned a break, and you are really hoping someone else picks up the trash. I am not even mad at you.

Person 2, I also get it that you want to mind your business. Unfortunately, this is your business. It can affect you if the results of the campaign hit the brand hard and they have to make cuts as a result. It can quickly become your business. We are too willing to absolve ourselves of responsibility about the things that happen in our midst under the guise of minding our business, and it is to all of our detriments. If our neighbor's house is on fire, we cannot take comfort in the fact that it isn't our fire because that smoke can reach our houses next. It is in our best interest to help them put out the fire before it becomes ours, because everyone's well-being should be community business.

Person 3 has detected that the atmosphere is probably one of gaslighting, and they don't feel empowered to speak up. Person 4 has probably seen someone suffer for speaking the truth. Persons 3 and 4, I feel you on a visceral level. You want to preserve self because you've seen others somehow get negative responses. You have all the right to not wield your authenticity because it might very well be weaponized against you. While many people can say they experience this, Black women in particular are put into these situations on a regular basis.

Black women show up to work every day having no room for error and no defenders, especially in crucial moments. In my life, I know I'm SUPPOSED to work for myself. Why? Because after hearing the stories (daily) about what Black people deal with when it comes to their white coworkers who can't handle anything remotely close to the truth, I realize I don't have the tools to work within a corporate environment. They gotta do their jobs AND make sure they are not offending the tender sensibilities of Chad and Becky. It's a lot.

If I worked in an office, I would absolutely get an annual review saying that I was "aggressive," and I would eventually get fired. I know this because I don't have the tools.

I firmly believe that Black women are the adults in the room of the world. We're so often in the role of chaperone, not because we want to be but because we have no other choice. We're thrust to the front of the class because we realize that the whole place will go down in flames if we aren't there. I believe Black women are the moral center of the universe, and can't nobody tell me different. In spite of the fact that we have our heads stepped on, are disrespected constantly, and are treated like we are disposable, we show up. We speak up, show out, and stand up for everyone, even those who don't deserve it. We catch hell for it.

But folks don't listen to us like they should. Things would be so much calmer if the world honored our voices more. There'd be less chaos, more equity, and less suffering if folks understood that Black women got the answers. We're basically part of the largest group project ever, and unfortunately our grade depends on everyone else. We're the ones who refuse to get an F, so we do all the work and everyone benefits from the A that we, and only we, earned.

For us, the compulsion to preserve self is beyond earned, and I salute sistas who are navigating in the best way they know how. I salute those of you who have to deal with the microaggressions, the microappreciations, and the megaprejudice every day. I see you. You are superheroes. So when you still decide to speak up in spite of all this, I know it's a gift. One that we cannot take for granted. Now we need everyone else to step up and speak out.

I won't lie to you and say, "Follow your heart, speak the truth, and nothing bad happens." NAH! Shit can get real and there can be consequences. There is certainly risk to speaking up. However, I would rather risk that than risk regretting my inaction or my silence. I think a lot about the poet Audre Lorde asking, "What are the words you do not yet have? What do you need to say? What are the tyrannies you swallow day by day and attempt to make your own, until you will sicken and die of them, still in silence?" I don't want to hold on to these tyrannies. My disappointment in myself is a much greater consequence to me than other people's disappointment in me.

So how do you find the courage to speak up knowing that there can be fallout? When we are afraid of telling the truth or making a room uncomfortable, the first thing we need to do is figure out the consequence we are afraid of. What is that thing? And then what is the worst-case scenario that comes from that thing? Maybe you'll get written up by human resources (HR), or maybe your client will drop you if you challenge their idea. Or is it that you might get fired if you speak up? What is it that scares you most about telling the truth in this moment?

Now, IF that thing happens, can you figure it out? If you'll be fired and you need that money to eat, by all means, file your nails in that meeting and watch it go to hell. Most Americans are living paycheck to paycheck, so a disruption to their pockets doesn't bode well for how they can live.

My challenge here, however, is to those who are financially secure and not acutely afraid of not having a home if they can't work for two months. On Maslow's hierarchy of needs, if you have the physiological and safety needs handled? This is for you. You have the room to take some risks. Yes, you. We're often so afraid of the consequences that come with speaking up and making rooms uncomfortable that we don't think about the best-case scenario that could happen if we actually do this thing.

If the consequence is you get fired, is that an actual place you want to work? If you can get fired for challenging one idea in one meeting, is that company worth your time and energy? If the consequence is not that you'll be fired or written up, then what is actually on the line if you speak up? Is it that you won't be liked by whoever you challenged?

I've made a career out of being a straight shooter. Not because I walk out the house saying, "YAY TIME TO MAKE PEOPLE UNCOMFORTABLE TODAY," but because I understand that if I'm supposed to show up in the best way possible, I can't be quiet if what's going on around me is not okay. I feel like I have no choice but to be the challenger.

Being a truth-teller is no walk in the park. It is exhausting always feeling like you have to be the adult in the room. It is tiring to be the challenger with no backup. But I also think rooms are elevated when we're in them. If people know you are in the room, then they might be less inclined to bring rubbish in with them because they know you'll throw it out. It means they know they better come as correct as they can so they don't hear your mouth.

Similarly, if you're in the room with the person who's going to ask the questions that matter, the person who's going to say, "Is this idea as fully thought out and as thoughtful as it could be?" you will not present half-baked ideas. If we all exist in a world where we know that everybody's expecting the best of us, that is what we're going to bring into the room.

Challenging people or systems is not easy, even if you've been doing it all your life. It is an intentional decision folks make.

When I turned thirty, I went skydiving because one of my friends asked me to go with him. When he asked, I said YES so quickly that I couldn't take it back. It was such a strong yes that even I was shocked. Being a woman of my word, I stuck to it. So we traveled to some out-of-the-way place on Long Island and signed all types of documents basically saying if we went splat, no one was liable. We got on the plane and went up something like fifteen thousand feet. I was strapped to the professional guy who was jumping with me, and as we were getting closer, he strapped me so tight that I was off my seat. My whole weight was on him, and that actually gave me comfort because I was like, "Well, now you have skin in the game because if I die, you die too. Great, let's do this."

That momentary piece of courage instantly disappeared when we were sitting at the edge of the plane and I was seeing the earth beneath me. I was like, "Oh, this is a bad idea. I've done some stupid things. This is one of them. Why am I doing this on purpose? I'm paying somebody to fall out of a perfectly good plane." Talk about first-world problems.

The moment when we fell out of the plane, I actually forgot how to breathe for three seconds. It was as if my body's reflexes were like, "Nope, nope, we're not good at this. No." Then my body was like, "Remember? Okay, do that using-your-lungs thing." I took a deep breath at some point as we were free falling, and the parachute popped open and we started floating in the sky as my jumper gave me an aerial tour of the New York area. It was stunning, and I was so glad I did this nutty thing! When we landed, I even landed on my feet!

When I want to say something that might feel uncomfortable or difficult or bigger than me, I go back to that time when I jumped out of the plane and lost my breath for three seconds. I think about how when I caught my breath and was able to look at the earth, in wonderment, all I saw was beauty. It was the best thing I could have done. It felt right, even as it was still petrifying.

Even though I've had practice being the truth-teller and the challenger all my life, telling the truth feels scary each time. I say this because a lot of times people believe that being honest comes easy for challengers. They think, "Oh, you've been doing this for a while. You're used to it. You're fine." No, it's never really fine. You just get used to the practice of telling this truth in spite of the fact that it's scary.

If you think about those challengers, the people who constantly make others uncomfortable with their truths, or who show up in the best way they can no matter what room they're in, and you think, "I wish I could do that," I'm here to say you can.

How do you decide when to speak up or challenge?

Being a professional troublemaker is not for the sake of making people uncomfortable, or being a contrarian, or making a room tense. Challenging is about expecting the best of everybody and making sure that they're seeing their blind spots. How do you do this?

Be human. Every single day we have to walk with empathy in the rooms that we're in. We have to see people from where they're at, and we have to recognize their actual humanity. Sometimes when it's really tough to challenge somebody, I say, "Okay, as your fellow global citizen, I feel the obligation to challenge you in this way."

Questions are also a really great way of challenging people. This is what happens in therapy. Your therapist is really asking you a whole bunch of questions, without telling you much, letting you lead yourself to the solution. So sometimes being the challenger is simply asking really good questions. The terrible meeting idea? Reply with "Have you thought about this deeper? What other angles might we look at this from? What are the challenges that might come up if we take this action?" The racist joke someone tells? Ask them, "Can you explain it to me?" so they have to now put words to their prejudice.

We've all met (or been) somebody who's tactless in telling the truth. That's who we conjure up when we think of someone who is a challenger or professional troublemaker. We're thinking about the person who keeps it real in the wrongest way. Don't be that person who is loud and contrarian or cruel for no reason. Be the person who's thoughtful as you do it.

Now, I'm not saying you will not ruffle feathers even if you want to be thoughtful. But if you attempt to be as well informed as possible, you are at least minimizing the risk. That's all you can do. I ask myself three questions before I say something that might shake the table.

Do you mean it? Is this thing something I actually believe?

Can you defend it? Being the challenger, I also have to be okay with being questioned and prodded. My ideas need to be explored deeper. Can I stand in it and justify it? Do I have receipts?

Can you say it thoughtfully or with love? Is my intention good here? I might think I am righteous in my indignation or in my questioning, but am I saying it thoughtfully or with love? No matter how righteous it feels, no matter how true it might feel, if I say this thing in a way that's hateful or that makes people feel demeaned or less than, the message will not land.

Do you mean it? Can you defend it? Can you say it with love? If the answer is yes to all three, I say it and I let the chips fall. Whether I need to present a challenge in a meeting, or to a friend, or to my mom, I run this checklist to keep myself from being completely tactless. It holds me accountable to what I'm really saying and keeps me in check with myself.

It's not a foolproof method, and there are still times I make mistakes or say something I shouldn't. But these questions help you keep your intentions good. Mind you, good intentions might still make for bad impact, but they give you a place to start. Be as thoughtful as you can be. How the challenge lands isn't in your control. Once you have thought about it, you're not being impulsive, you're not being hateful; you're being your solid self, you've done your best.

Each of these questions serves a purpose in ensuring that I stay on solid ground. They are my checkpoints. They are my way of ensuring that even when I'm angry or emotional, I can pause and say, "Wait a minute, is this thing worth saying? Is this the way you want to show up?" It gives me courage to say YES, this is how.

The other thing we need to be aware of when we want to speak the truth is the power we walk with. In my first book, I talked about doing the privilege walk in college. It's an exercise where participants stand in a straight line horizontally in a room. People's hands are resting on the shoulders of the people next to them. The moderator then reads a series of questions, prompting them to either step forward or to step back. For example: "Step forward if you can easily find a Band-Aid in your skin tone in stores." "Step back if your name is frequently mispronounced." "Step forward if you attending college was a foregone conclusion." As you move farther apart, you actually have to break apart from your neighbor. At the end of it, everyone is in different positions. It is a physical representation of power and privilege, and it is incredibly compelling.

Because of my privilege as a straight, Christian, cisgender woman who comes from educated parents, I ended up in the middle. When

I looked back and saw some of my classmates behind me, I remember feeling this visceral sense of responsibility because I wanted them right next to me. The fact that I had to break with them made me feel guilty. I realized then that one of my purposes is to make sure that I don't have to see people behind me. If there are people behind me, I need to find a way to get them by my side.

This is important because when I walk into rooms, I have to recognize the power that I'm walking in with. That realization drives my voice and lets me know that I should say that tough thing. If we leave our power behind, or don't even recognize that we have it, we risk thinking we can't do things that are difficult.

As a professional speaker, I know that when I am onstage in any room, I am the most influential person right then. Why? Because I'm the one with the mic. I can step off the stage and that can instantly change, but in the fifty-five minutes when I hold the mic, I lead. My job is to disrupt what's happening and to use that clout to make sure somebody else who has less authority feels just as significant and seen. Or that someone who doesn't have the mic still feels heard. I am not in the room to make the executives comfortable. I'm there to speak for the intern who couldn't get a word in at the meeting.

One of my friends (who happens to be a brilliant activist and teacher), Brittany Packnett Cunningham, introduced me to the phrase "Spend your privilege." She got it from disability rights advocate Rebecca Cokley. It is the concept that the privilege we have in this world is endless. It doesn't run out. You don't use your voice today and have to re-up the next day. Power is limitless, and using ours for other people does not diminish it. We have to utilize our influence, capabilities, and MONEY for the greater good.

I don't ask people to do the things that I don't ask of myself first. Oftentimes, we need to see somebody else try something risky before we think we can do it. And my career has been a lot of risky moments, but I always use myself as an example. I'm this Black woman who has ended up in some grand rooms, in spite of often being a loudmouth.

I'm not asking the most marginalized people among us to be the ones taking this mantle on. I'm challenging those who are rich, white, straight, and cisgender to do the work. Stop waiting on the rest of the world. And if you decide to wait, make yourself useful.

Let's go back to the meetings. If you are not the truth-teller in the room, you can at least be backup for them. If you aren't going to be the first domino, be the second. If I am typically the person who starts off and asks us to rethink whatever the idea is, having someone chime in with their affirmation of my challenge is refreshing and incredibly helpful. If you believe in the challenge, back it up, because there is strength in numbers. No one wants to be on an island, standing by themselves.

That being said, there are times when I don't always want to be the truth-teller. There are times when I sit and think today's going to be the day when I do not say anything. I'm not challenging. I'm not asking the questions.

We're so often passing the baton to other people, thinking it's their job to tell the truth, but what happens when the challenger decides to take a break? We can't take for granted the person who usually challenges, because it is not just one person's job, it is everyone's jobs. We all need to be the challenger, but everyone is waiting on Superman, when they have red capes too.

For women, this strength in numbers is especially important because we're in spaces where we're constantly being interrupted. Or somebody else will say the exact same thing we just said and get credit for our idea. It's easy to ignore one and it's hard to ignore two. You can't erase three. Strength in troublemaking numbers is necessary!

Instead, many of us are too willing to be quiet when it's needed and dole out empty microappreciations. If after the meeting you walk up to the challenger and say, "OMG I'm so glad you said that," then you're trolling in microappreciation. You're telling me when nobody's listening. The currency I needed is not even usable, and nobody's here to see it. If you cannot back me up in the actual meeting, what is the point? Let's do less of that, and make sure that in the room, we're proverbially taking a stand, not waiting till it's all cleared out. Actually stand next to that person. Use your words to affirm people out loud and give them more credence.

So many people have to deal with that every single day, and I want that to happen less. And that's why I say kudos to people in corporate environments, who have to work with people who are not being courageous or are being silently courageous to them after the fact, which is not courage.

I know I would've been fired a couple of times by now, because if I were on the receiving end of microappreciation, I would've been like, "You know what, keep that." And then somebody would have reported me to HR and then here we are. Because I focus less on the niceties of it all. I want to be kind to you by making sure that I'm showing up for you, by making sure that I'm speaking up when you're afraid to. But what about the moments when I don't want to speak up? Who speaks up for me? Who speaks up for the person who is the challenger?

A lot of people wonder why they are surrounded by people who lie to them. It's because they've proven themselves to be people who cannot be trusted with honesty, lest they weaponize it. If you have an environment where people will be punished for speaking up, then you gotta deal with the consequences of shitty work. If you're the friend who hangs up on their friends anytime they try to tell you about your wack-ass choices, then they'll probably keep quiet as you continue to be secretary of Team Bad Decisions. It's the bed you made, so lie in it.

You want more honesty around you? Ask for it. We have to create spaces that welcome people to feel comfortable to speak and challenge. If there's someone who is usually quiet, seek them out. "Hey, I would love to hear what you have to say. I'd love to hear your feedback and questions. I know a lot of us have been dominating this conversation, but your voice is important. So can you tell us what you think?"

Speak the truth, not only to your Facebook friends, but to your family. What is the use of yelling about racism or homophobia or transphobia or patriarchy to the randoms who hit a button to get our content if we aren't challenging those we know in real life? We sometimes think we're doing work by being loud online, but then we'll be quiet in the rooms we're in, quiet around the people we can touch, quiet in front of the real circle of influence we have. Speak truth to those closest to you, not just the random behind the screen.

A lot of people think they have no platform. You do. Your platform is your kin, squad, colleagues. Do the work close to home so you can have far-reaching consequences. We are most easily moved by the words that come out of the mouths of our loved ones.

I think a lot about the moment when I almost didn't say something because I was told there could be negative consequences. I think about when I was deeply uncomfortable because I could have lost a lot of my livelihood when I spoke out against a conference that was engaging in pay inequality. And I think about the anxiety that I walked into those moments with. But if I only tell the truth when it's easy, what's the point of whatever power or privilege I have? Truth-telling has to be done in the moments when it's really hard. That's when it actually makes the most difference.

And yes, we're afraid of the worst-case scenario happening, but what if the best-case scenario happens? What if we change systems in the rooms that we're in or we change the people we come across because we dare to be people who decided to show up and use our necessary voices?

I say this as a Black woman who is constantly speaking truth to power, who is trying to do it in the most real way she knows how, who sometimes missteps. The greater version of ourselves is the version that is willing to be courageous in the very tough moments. Because those are typically when we need to be most courageous. When it's that scary, when you want to go hide under a blanket, when somebody is telling you that you should be more quiet, do not be more quiet. If you're compelled to do or say this thing, then you're probably supposed to do or say it.

We need to prioritize the truth, because the world is full of things to point out, injustices to fight, systems to dismantle. If we're not starting with honesty, how do we know the problems we need to tackle? You don't fix something you don't know is broken. You don't lie your way to an equitable world or coddle your way to equity. We gotta find our individual integrity and our collective candor for the greater good, and we start by being honest, in whatever space we're in.

A lot of us are risking smaller things than we realize when we choose speaking truth. REAL truth-tellers are the freedom fighters who have been literally beat up, jailed, or killed for daring to challenge the status quo. The Black Panthers we are not, as we sit in glass spaces afraid to simply tell someone, "That's not a good idea." What we are putting on the line is usually not our lives or our freedom.

No one said this would be easy, but the things worth doing are usually not easy. You knew that, though. Truth-telling is a muscle, and like all muscles, it needs practice and exercise to be built. I hate working out, and anyone who says it's fun is a liar and a cheat. Yet I do it because if I don't, it is to my own detriment. I will suffer most for it. Being a gatekeeper of truth takes practice.

When I first started doing public speaking, my voice would shake for the first five to ten minutes I was onstage. I'm not sure if anybody else detected it, but I sure did. And I kept talking, and eventually my voice stopped shaking. I don't know when it happened, but one day I got onstage and I realized my voice wasn't shaking anymore.

I reflect on the words of the world-changing GOOD trouble-maker John Lewis: "When you see something that is not right, not fair, not just, you have a moral obligation to do something, to say something, and not be quiet." We have a moral obligation to tell the truth. Tell the truth, even when our voices shake. Tell the truth even when it might rock the boat. Tell the truth, even when there might be consequences. Because that in itself, makes us more courageous than most people in the world.

Use the three questions, know your voice is necessary, and speak truth to power. Even a whisper of truth makes a difference in an echo chamber of lies.

7

FAIL LOUDLY

We fear failing.

 Failing sucks. We are afraid that people will see our slips showing and find out something about us that will give them ammunition to attack us. We are afraid we will say the wrong thing or do the wrong thing, so to protect ourselves, we say and do nothing of note. Ol' gray-zone-living selves.

If you're living a life of color, of impact, of note, you will make mistakes. You will fuck up. You will show you are an everlasting fool who constantly needs to get their shit together. And that's okay. Because failure is necessary. It's essential for us to live loudly. It is painful, it is usually unexpected, and it can knock us on our asses.

I have failed a lot, and I have failed out loud. It is a rite of passage for your greater good, and we must learn from it.

n 2018, on the day Aretha Franklin died and we all collectively mourned her, the conversation turned to who would do her tribute. What artists could live up to Ms. Franklin's legacy to memorialize her in song? Names were being thrown around online, and someone suggested the name of a beloved R&B artist who was big in the early 1990s.

In my occasional impulsiveness, having not heard the person's name in a long time or noticed them release any new music in at least fifteen years, I tweeted, "Under what rock did they pull that name from?" A few people were like, "That's actually a good suggestion." A lot more people were like, "Yeah I wouldn't have thought of them first in this tribute lineup." The conversation continued as more names were thrown in the pot.

All was well. Or so I thought.

I woke up the next morning to my replies being in utter shambles on Twitter. The conversation had shifted to the fact that since I was not born in the United States, and therefore not African American, I should sit out the conversation.

Thus started the biggest public fail I've ever had.

My friends started hitting me up as they began seeing it all over their own timelines, and I asked them for advice. Should I reply to this? Should I let it ride? Should I speak up for myself? Should I act like I don't see it and tweet other random things?

I chose the "sit this out" route for hours until someone tweeted something that I felt was derogatory about me. That's when my ego took charge and I replied. I responded by saying something about how I noticed that they were trying to other me. I also threw in something about them being so pressed by what I considered to be a simple tweet inquiring about how someone pulled up that particular musician's name.

That was me throwing gasoline on the fire, which caused it to now rage.

And rage it did. My name ended up trending on Twitter. I was the number eight most tweeted-about subject in all of the United States for about an hour. Half the people were calling me everything but a child of God and the other half were wondering why this word *Luvvie* was all up in their timeline. The one who was usually doing the judging was being judged. And very, very loudly.

I logged off. I knew it was bad because I kept getting all types of texts from people checking in on me. "You good? I see what's happening. I'm sorry. Lemme know if you need me."

People were saying I was an entitled Nigerian who didn't know what the hell she was talking about. Folks dug deeper into my tweets, looking for ways to show that I was anti-American and anti–Black American, and anything that could be deemed offensive. Think pieces were written about me, and my name was plastered everywhere, it felt like. Anything I ever said about being Black in America was up for scrutiny. I was dragged.

I felt beat up on and lied about. So I wrote a response in a blog post, explaining myself and talking about how much I was not the person I was being accused of being. Long story short, I didn't approach it well because nowhere in it did I say sorry.

That blog post started a fresh firestorm, with some people becoming deeply invested in my fail and fall. One person went on

Facebook and posted a status about me, saying, "I want to destroy her career." Someone made an anonymous email account where they sent anyone who was a brand partner or any upcoming speaking engagement a message suggesting that clients disassociate from me. One popular anti-Black misogynist sent his audience to target me, bringing a lot of "go back to Africa" and "bitch die" comments onto my platform.

I was in shambles. Whatever tough skin or self-assurance I thought I had? This pierced straight through it. I felt like I was in the Battle of the Bastards, as the troops came at Jon Snow with all sorts of ammunition, and he just looked at them hoping for the best. I was Jon Snow if Jon Snow was lying on his couch crying and hating himself.

I couldn't eat. I refused to eat. My boo even took me to a crab boil, which is one of my faves, and I sat there staring at the delicious goodness of perfectly seasoned seafood and barely touched it. Just like how they say God gets mad if you pass by the color purple without acknowledging it, I bet God is pissed every time you waste a good crab boil. I lost eight pounds in a week. I, who am 120 pounds soaking wet on a gluttonous day when I drink a lot of water, lost eight pounds. So you know I was looking ghastly AF.

And it was my fault. All of it was my fault. I was beating myself up more than anyone else could. It's one thing to disappoint others. That shit sucks. But to disappoint myself was the tougher thing. I felt shame in a way I never have. I was so upset at myself because I made a mistake and said something I shouldn't have. I should have known better. I should have done better. I should have been better.

People went looking for things to be mad at me about, but it was MY fault for giving them things to find. It was my fault that they could say I'd been insensitive. Or said tone-deaf things. Or sometimes was just stupid. Had I not given them anything, they wouldn't have found anything to use to drag me through the mud.

I knew I was wrong. I wasn't a victim of people's meanness as much as I was a victim of my own big-ass mouth, which sometimes isn't as thoughtful as it should be, or maybe makes a joke that isn't a joke because it demeans. My two feet, which were always anchored to the floor, rooted in really liking who I was, felt shaky. I had faced backlash before but not to this level, and not for this long. It felt unrelenting.

So I went dark online. My friends called me to check in, and at the worst moments to remind me of who I really am. They gave me stern talking-tos in the middle of assurance, and they kept me from going deeper into the rabbit hole of shame. My partner said, "You let people steal your light."

I made an appointment with my therapist, because SOS! I was not okay! A few days later when I went in, she told me I was exhibiting symptoms of post-traumatic stress disorder: disrupted sleep, lack of appetite, and an acute sense of being in danger even in innocuous moments.

The incident had knocked me off my square in such a major way. I was drop-kicked off my game and I ran away and hid. I was afraid I would never recover from this thing, and my name was taking an irreparable hit. I legit wanted to quit everything and move to a small town somewhere and be a librarian. Because: dramatic.

The worst part? It made me afraid of my voice. I questioned my judgment. Up until then, I had walked through life rarely doubting my confidence in my voice, the biggest gift God had given me. But after facing this very public backlash, born from using my voice in a careless way, I began second-guessing my gift. I was scared of my own bold shadow: "Shit, if I say this thing, will people get mad?" I felt flutters in the pit of my stomach whenever I'd want to say something, truly afraid and taken right back to the moment when I saw my name on Twitter's trending list. I stopped writing. I stopped speaking up. I hid.

For a year, I didn't write anything on my website besides the TV recaps I was commissioned to write. On Twitter, I was extra cautious about posting anything too strong, lest I ruffle the wrong feathers and start trending again. On other social media, I'd still post about what was on my mind, but I did it with extra "You sure you wanna say this?"

I justified not using my voice as, "Well, maybe I need to evolve out of blogging. Maybe my work needs to look different. Hey, I'm still saying what I need in other ways, through my podcast and whatever."

I was still feeling bruised by the humiliation of it all, so I wanted to leave it behind. That was my ego talking. That was the failure talking. It was fear talking.

My book agent was asking me, "So what's book two gonna be about?" I told her I was still thinking about it. What would I even write about? What did I have to say?

Almost a year to the date, another legendary death rocked the world: Toni Morrison passed away on August 5, 2019. The writer who I quoted on page two of *I'm Judging You: The Do-Better Manual*: "If there's a book that you want to read, but it hasn't been written yet, you must write it." Ms. Toni told us that, and who was I not to listen? Her words had literally been life's instructions for me. She was the woman who made me too shy to call myself a writer because I felt like her words were too great for me to be in the same category with her.

But that woman had left this world, and her death convicted me. I'd never met her, but her permanent absence jolted my spirit awake. It wagged a finger at me because I was choosing to lie down instead of doing what I was put here to do.

I was reminded that writers don't stop because people critique them, no matter how harsh they think it is. They don't abandon their craft because they feel misunderstood or their feelings get hurt. They don't leave their purpose behind because they have loud detractors. They take the mistakes they made and let them spur them to make even better art. God said weapons would form. You do not let them prosper by letting them stop you from using your gift.

The first thing I wrote was a tribute to Toni and what she meant to me, as the favorite teacher I never met. After that, I got the idea for this book. I had spent a year afraid of myself, of my voice and my gift. I could no longer let fear dictate my life.

My journey is truly one of fighting fear constantly.

I failed very loudly, very publicly. But how could I use that for something greater? That sense of defeat was for the greater good of me, and the only way it would be for naught is if I didn't become a better version of me because of it. I asked myself: Why did it happen as it did? How do I move forward? What am I supposed to learn?

So many lessons.

When it comes to failing, we come up with stories about who we are because of it. That is where the shame came in for me. I felt like I got caught with my pants down and my ass all out in the open. I felt exposed and raw, and thought everything I'd achieved was clearly a sham because it was about to get taken away. As people pointed out whatever old problematic thing they didn't like from my raving dumbass twenty-four-year-old self on Twitter, I felt embarrassed.

The lessons were plenty.

THE OLD ME WAS NECESSARY

With therapy, I began to realize the girl from then was necessary because she became the woman from now. And I had to thank her for the work she did and the person she was, because she led me here. Then I had to thank the me now, in her thirties, who is more aware of herself, the strength of her voice, and the world. I couldn't be me without her, so my shame was not needed. I needed to give myself grace and forgive myself for my mistakes.

I had to be kind to that girl from then, the one who was afraid to call herself a writer because she didn't think she could measure up to the title. That girl could've never written this book, could have never confidently showed up in these rooms that I've been in and done her best work. The person who used to talk before she'd think could not be the person with the platform that I have now because I wouldn't use it as responsibly as I do now. I think about how the person who made thirty-five thousand a year could not be the same person who signed a six-figure book deal. I wouldn't even know how to handle the taxes, let alone what to do with the cash.

But that girl had to exist so I could write about her and her mistakes and the things she had to learn through the fire. Luvvie 1.0 had to be here so she could grow into Luvvie 3.0, who could write this book.

NONE OF US BELONG ON PEDESTALS

Not one of us. We are flawed people whose jobs make us seem grander than we are. I know I can be trash and have garbage ways. I am not infallible or smarter than someone just because I have the platform. Nah. I got kicked off my pedestal and I hope people didn't put me back on it, because I don't deserve it. Leave me down here, because I can't live up to the standards folks often ascribe to personalities they follow. I will disappoint you. I will let you down. I will fuck up. But I will hopefully never stop learning how to show up in the best way I know how. I will not stop growing. I will not stop holding myself accountable to who I say I am.

WHEN THESE MOMENTS OF RECKONING HAPPEN, WE NEED TO NOT WASTE THEM

Another lesson for me? The judge will be judged. I often challenge people to do better. This also means I will be challenged to do the same. I will be in the court of public opinion too, because I'm bound to make mistakes. What matters is how I handle it and move forward. That is what I will truly be judged on, and on this, I was held in contempt.

I should have apologized without defending or explaining myself. People want to feel seen and heard when we have done harm. I needed to atone, take accountability, and promise to show up differently next time. I did harm, and I should have copped to it early.

A proper apology woulda been something like:

Hey everyone, today has been distressing, and to see my name in the lights in this way is something I am not proud of. I fucked up and I'm sorry. My words made people upset. My intention, whether good or not, doesn't matter, because we all know intention is not synonymous with impact. I should know better and should be better. I need to make sure that I am being even more thoughtful with how I show up in the world. I have a major platform and with that comes higher expectations. I won't always meet them. In fact, I expect to fall short again. But at least I can aspire to be better than I am. I'm sorry.

That humility could have saved me a lot of trouble, because I was wrong. Not just because of what I said, but how I acted at being challenged. I should have taken the knee and moved forward.

After all this, it also became clear to me that my name was bigger than I realized. I'm not just some random Chicago girl by way of Nigeria, tweeting and cracking jokes with her friends. I am Brand Luvvie, with more than one million total followers on social media. I am representing Company Awe Luv. No matter how much I think of myself as some girl who started writing one day and cool things happened, I am at the helm of massive reach, and it is clear that my responsibilities are greater. My voice carries. My platform is large. I owe the best of me to an audience that's larger than ever before and bigger than I ever imagined. I have to act accordingly.

This doesn't mean I change my voice, but it does mean I have to move slightly differently. I used to be David but now I'm Goliath, and that's a tough pill to swallow. I'm no longer the underdog who can throw bones, but the big dog who gets bones thrown at me. That, for me, is frightening. It means who or what I speak about now has to be different, because my platform is larger.

The whole incident felt like God was grabbing my face and telling me, "You're at new levels. I need you to move different and be more responsible." I mean, did He have to make it so painful? Probably. My stubborn ass probably needed that jolt of reality. Message received, Holiness. I hear You, okay?

I was reminded I should always punch UP, not down. ("Punching up" is when you challenge someone with more power than you. "Punching down" is when you go at someone with less.) Yes, I need to punch up, but who that includes has shifted because I now wield more influence and weight. I can find myself punching down if I'm not cognizant of this dynamic and my stacking privilege. This is why humor is dynamic, and why comedians have to change their routines over the years. The legendary comedian who is doing $50 million Netflix specials can't do the same jokes he did when he was a struggling stand-up comic.

I also learned that I can be proud of my work, but I can't tie my worth to it, because it can be fleeting. While we should own our dopeness, we can't let all the outside praise we get go to our heads. People will love us one day and HATE us the next.

This experience made me more kind, because being at the end of hateful arrows feels harrowing. I've been scathing in the past in my critiques of others, and it was a necessary heart check to chill on that. Growing up looks like being kinder.

Being in the midst of that storm reminded me I need to help other Black women when they find themselves in similar positions. To be a visible Black woman, especially, is to commit to being abused over and over again in hopes that it doesn't pierce your heart too much. I now make it a point to check in on the prominent ladies I know when it becomes their turn in the fire. Hearing from caring voices, even if they aren't super close to you, is helpful.

It also made me wanna vigorously defend Black women who find themselves called out for mistakes that aren't hate-filled. This platform and this voice ain't just for the comfortable times. If people come for me because I've defended someone, I'll deal. I am loved and valued. I deserve to be defended and protected even on my worst days, and so do others.

It takes a lot to be a prominent Black woman. I admire Beyoncé, Serena, and Oprah for more than their work. I deeply respect the grace they show under constant pressure. They're photographed when their expression could be translated to shady and they trend for days, as all types of people make up whole storybooks about their frame of mind. And they keep quiet through it. That is what I don't have yet and I'm trying to learn: the art of shutting the fuck up even as people try to come for you.

One of my mistakes in all this was responding at all to some of the people who were coming for me. I'm the person who usually tells my friends to chill when something similar happens to them. I didn't take my own advice and it blew up spectacularly in my face. I fanned the flame. Yes, I felt hurt, but we ain't gotta attend every fight we're invited to. Next time, I need to ask, "What would Beyoncé do?" Sis wouldn't even act like she saw it. Instead, she'd be somewhere creating amazing art as people talk about her recklessly. It's why I had to start paying my Beyhive memberships. That woman deserves us stanning.

MY PRAYERS NEED TO CHANGE

As I grow and my career grows, I need to say stronger prayers. There's nothing I can really do besides try to always be thoughtful and learn from my mistakes, but I can't say I will never make a mistake again. So if I make the next mistake, does that mean I am now going to be knocked off my square for the next year, because all these arrows decided to point at me?

I'm also going to pray to be fortified in the instances when people call me what I'm not, because it's not going to stop. I can say the sky is blue tomorrow and somebody might be offended by it. Right? If they chose to be offended by it, they will be offended by it.

I have to be fortified, because when the weapons form, may they not prosper. I can't not fulfill God's assignment for me because some people don't like me. I need to learn and get fortified and pray that my armor is stronger than ever, that it gets stronger by the day, that my feet are more solid and planted than ever. I need to pray that as a leader, I'm showing what it looks like to fail and move past it.

I think of my grandmother, whose prayers I know cover me every single day. Those three-hour middle-of-the-night prayers gotta be responsible for some of my success, because I've made it here in spite of and because of myself.

I am a recovering asshole who will use every face-plant as a step stool to be better, smarter, tougher, kinder, and more gracious. I'm thankful for that D I got in chemistry. I'm so glad I got fired/laid off from my marketing job. And trending on Twitter for being reckless with my words was a blessing. Each time I fall on my face, it's a cosmic reboot and redirection that sets me on the path I'm actually supposed to be on. It is a recalibration of my life's GPS. Failure always gets me to higher ground.

I have nothing to regret cuz the falls are necessary for me to learn the things I do not know (and they are plenty). We can fall flat on our faces and rise up in the ashes of our old selves, better than before.

I sleep well at night because I'm at peace with myself and my soul. I wake up in the morning and look at myself in the mirror and really love the woman who looks back at me. She's flawed AF but knows without question that she is better than who she used to be. And she knows her mistakes do not define her; her lessons do.

Similarly, you are not your worst moment or worst mistake. You know who you are (go back to chapter one—that exercise comes in handy when you're in the middle of firestorms). In the midst of your mistakes, it might feel like the world is collapsing or you won't ever recover. But everything, even your worst moments, is temporary. Humiliation is temporary. The acute pain is temporary.

Know that grace and accountability can coexist. Grace makes you forgive yourself for your mistakes and accountability lets you know that the lesson learned must be remembered and those mistakes can't be frequent. It's a dance you must do.

Failure is life's greatest teacher, and the only way we truly fail is to learn nothing from the valleys we experience.

8

ASK FOR MORE

We fear disappointment.

 One of my favorite mantras, which I heard a long time ago and still hold dear, is "It's better to live a life of 'Oh well' than a life of 'What if?'" Many of us are living the what-if life because we do not know how to ask for what we want, what we need, and what we would like. We are constantly leaving things on the table that could be for us because we are afraid of the nos that may come. We don't want to deal with the blow that comes from putting ourselves out there and possibly getting rejected, so we end up being people who never ask.

I wonder what would happen if we were given the permission to constantly ASK FOR MORE, from life and the universe, from relationships, from bosses and colleagues. What might happen when we realize that NO won't kill us but YES could change our lives?

I love this sentiment by the brilliant Paulo Coelho, author of one of my fave books, *The Alchemist*: "The mere possibility of getting what we want fills the soul of the ordinary person with guilt. We look around at all those who have failed to get what they want and feel that we do not deserve to get what we want either. We forget about all the obstacles we overcame, all the suffering we endured, all the things we had to give up in order to get this far."

Our inability to ask for things comes from a lifetime of learning that to ASK is often to be disappointed. It's a well-earned fear. At no point do I think we wake up one day and all of a sudden find ourselves mute when it comes to asking for what we want. Instead, I think we've all had experiences that tell us it is risky to ask people for things. We are Team I Will Figure It Out Myself or Team I Got It, Don't Worry About Me. Why? For a few reasons.

Some of us became these people by necessity. We might have had to raise ourselves because our parents weren't there, physically or emotionally. Or growing up, we didn't have friends to count on. Maybe no one ever provided for us, so we've had to figure out how to do it ourselves. Maybe the only person there for us was us. Perhaps we've had to be this person because no one else has proven loyal, reliable, or stable enough to show up in the way we need.

Or maybe we became this person because we had some painful experiences the times we did ask for something. Maybe it blew up in our face one time too many and now we're afraid of asking. Maybe someone threw something they did for us in our face during a moment of strife, and we've carried that experience around with us as more reason to never ask people for anything.

Whatever your reason is, it's valid and I don't blame you. As someone who has had more than a few "What the hell was that?"

experiences related to me asking for help, I get it. I feel you on a spiritual level. We go together like kettle and corn. That is why I'm here to tell you to ASK FOR MORE anyway.

Unfortunately, the reason doesn't make not asking any less harmful or stunting to your life. When we don't know how to ask for things, for more, we aren't getting everything life can offer us. Does life owe us something? Not really. But life has a whole treasure trove of things we can tap into, which if we don't ask for, we don't get. Like in James 4:2: ". . . we have not, because we ask not." I know it's not as black and white as that, but I still repeat that passage to myself because it is an affirmation of what I'm supposed to be doing and what is in my capacity. I'm less attached to the result knowing that I at least did my part: the asking. Anything else is a bonus.

It took me going to therapy to really understand that I was somebody, in all my boldness, who was afraid to ask for more. Lemme tell you how my therapist, who is a kind middle-aged Black woman (who could be anywhere from thirty-five to sixty-five but I can't tell, because we tend to be ageless and our Black refuses to snap, crackle, or pop), told me about my whole life.

I like going to therapy because I enjoy paying for someone to read me for filth. During certain sessions, I end up word-vomiting about feeling stressed out. I pride myself on being Team I Get Shit Done no matter what, both professionally and personally, and I handle pressure well, but even Atlas shrugged after a while, didn't he?

One day, I was particularly stressed out about work plus home stuff, and my therapist said, "Have you asked your partner for help?"

ME: No, I got it handled. He got things going on too. This is mine to handle.

HER: Why? Don't you think he would want to help you as much as he can?

ME: He would. He's actually asked me what he can help with.

HER: Why don't you tell him to take some things off your plate?

ME: Well, I figured that because I said I got it, I want to stick to my word.

HER: I see why you're stressed out. Your husband sees it too and has asked to help but you aren't letting him help. What do you think that does?

ME: Frustrate me because I need the help and frustrate him because he wants to . . . oh you just tried to get me with my own wisdom!

HER: [Blank stare]

ME: You're right. I'm tripping.

HER: Do you not think you deserve to be helped?

And that is when my head blew off my neck. Do I not think I deserve to be helped? AUNTIE, READ MEEEEE. DRAG MEEEE. SLAYYY ME!

This is how we ended up exploring how I put boulders on my back while other people carry rocks because I would rather shoulder the burden. This is partly because I trust me more to handle it, and partly because I don't think I deserve the help because I tell myself that others need help much more than me. Meanwhile, my back is breaking, all so I can feel like I'm helping others not break theirs.

Did I just read you your life? Yes, I did. Welcome to Club I Got It Even to My Own Detriment. Our meetings are every other Tuesday. Please bring snacks that won't cause heartburn.

Let me break me down for you. I have always been the Responsible One and I feel a deep sense of responsibility for myself, my path, and my actions. I was the seven-year-old who never had to be told to study or do her homework because she was already doing it. I got straight A's and condemned myself for the B's before anyone else could.

I don't want people to worry about me. The world is enough of an unpredictable junkyard. I have never wanted to give those I love or those who I am around another reason to be anxious, upset, or stressed out. If I were a superhero, I'd be SuperIndependent. I don't need anything from anybody. I haven't even asked anyone, my mom included, for money since I was seventeen years old. And I've worn this as a badge of honor for a long time.

As the Responsible One, that same insistence on not being a burden on anyone also came with the self-imposed duty to ensure the people around me were doing okay. Since I was fine, I felt obligated to make sure they were too. This turned me into the Giver Who Never Asks, and that is a problem.

Shout-out to those of us who are GIVERS. We define ourselves by how much we give to others. Our benevolence as a core value is something we are very proud of. (Remember chapter one? Yeah, Auntie Generous over here.) However, GIVERS are usually bad at being TAKERS, which is a liability.

There are so many people who will give you the shirts off their backs but don't know how to receive something as simple as a compliment without feeling like they have to hand it back somehow. I'm a recovering giver, meaning I used to be unable to ask for help or receive gifts without feeling like I owed someone.

We gotta check our motives when all we do is give without knowing how to receive. How can we allow people to fully show us love if we don't allow them to be generous to us? We love the feeling that we get when we're like, "Hey, I just did this thing for somebody." So then why don't we allow others to get the same feeling when they give something to us, whether it's a compliment, a gift, or their time?

When you are only handing out without receiving, you might be unknowingly leading with your ego. Maybe deep down, you love being thanked. Maybe subconsciously, it feeds your ego to always be Captain Here You Go. We love how good it feels to give. Generosity also helps us hide our vulnerability. Always handing out help but never asking for it is ensuring we aren't seen as weak. Or maybe we don't think we deserve moments of service ourselves. We don't want people to think we're taking advantage of them. We don't want to show up as somebody who needs somebody else. It's a problem because we are not being fully honest with ourselves and the people in our lives.

A lot of us will find ourselves in crisis before we say, "I need help." And in those moments of overwhelm, odds are we do not have anything to give, because we're already exerting ourselves to the limit. If we need help, it shouldn't depend on what we can give right back. You don't have to be drowning before you raise your hand and ask for help.

When I began to learn I can receive without being indebted to someone, I began to get freer. I'm still a work in progress on that front. But I now say thank you and mean it. Now I commit myself to giving to someone else, knowing that they don't owe me either.

I have my family and my friends and my village to thank for forcing me to become somebody who got okay with asking for and receiving help. The way the people I love show up for me, give me so much of their time, money, energy, advice, and presence, forced me into TAKING from them. They used love as action to disarm me and to give me help before I could even ask. Their love taught me that when I need something from them, I can ASK.

My village also taught me that there are some acts that are so meaningful that no matter how much I could try to "repay" them, there is no tit for tat because each act of benevolence stands on its own. There's no one thing you can do that's going to feel like an even exchange. Shoot, if someone gives you their kidney, you can't turn around and give them your lungs. That's not how it works.

I have received some large gifts in my life that have stunned me into silence, driving this lesson home. Take, for example, my bachelorette party. Nine of my girlfriends flew me to Anguilla (first class). They bride-napped me and took me on a six-day trip to paradise, taking care of everything. There were no details left untouched. They even made a website to commemorate the trip, and we used the hashtag #BridalLuvv.

The trip was loud, flashy, and expensive AF (we stayed at the Four Seasons villas). Me that just got nice things yesterday. I still remembered, in the past, sharing a bed with friends on trips we insisted on taking, even though we could barely pay our bills. I remembered when the Four Seasons was in my vision statement. Now we were here and it was real life, and I had friends who insisted on giving me this experience.

On that trip, I felt deep gratitude because nine people thought I was deserving of so much of their time, their money, their energy, and their love. I thought back to my therapist saying, "Do you not think you deserve this?" I spent those entire six days in awe because I was like, "Wow, I'm worthy of this?" It made me realize that a lot of the times when we don't know how to receive without feeling like we owe somebody, it is because we might not think we are worthy of that gift, or we might not think we can live up to it.

I couldn't begin to repay it, so I just had to take it all in and be thankful. It was game changing because no one is obligated to do things for us, small or large. But sometimes you will receive gifts and love strictly because you are you, no other reason. When people do that and give to you, receive it. Try not to question it so much. Try not to be like, "Why me?" Why *not* you?

What you can do is continue to be kind and generous. In the process, do not be so quick to turn down help or gifts. Know that you are deserving of the favor because you are here.

In times of frustration, I've lamented how I've ALWAYS done everything myself and this is why I don't need anyone to do anything for me. Meanwhile, I've gone to the ends of the earth for people, even when they didn't ask.

One day, my husband basically channeled my therapist and read the scrolls of my life to me. He said, "You being so openhanded seems to be a function of you not wanting to exert the same pain point on somebody else. I'm going to challenge you to stop saying how much you don't need from someone. I want you to stop saying how much you don't ask for things from people and how much you take care of everything yourself. You say it out loud so often. I ask that of you because what I hear when you say that is you're wearing it as a badge and accomplishment. If this was the Struggle Olympics, that may be okay, but it's not."

You should see the way my edges instantly retracted into my scalp. DID YOU JUST READ ME SO ACCURATELY WITH MY OWN WORDS? You know when someone says something that is so on point that you have no comeback because your brain is doing the "But They're Right" Running Man? That's what happened when he said that to me. The realization that I had come to define myself as someone who did not need anyone. What cookie did I think I was gonna get by running myself into the ground? What martyrdom did I think I was aiming for?

What is the win when we insist on being self-sufficient even in the moments of drowning, when all we need is a hand as we flail in water? Are you saying there's no Lived a Low-Maintenance Life and Needed No One cookie? Well damb. I think about the Brené Brown quote: "I've learned that gasping for air while volunteering to give others CPR is not heroic. It's suffocation by resentment." A WHOLE SERMON.

We are so used to being called strong, especially Black women, that some of us consider it a weakness to need the support of the people we consider community. We cannot base who we are on how little help we need, or how much we are helpful to other people. Because what if there comes a time when we have nothing to GIVE? Does that render us terrible people? Do we lose our compass? Do we feel less than because of it?

When we don't ask, or we don't receive well, we might be blocking our blessings. This goes beyond the times we need help. When we do not know how to ask for what we need or ask for more, we end up receiving less than we should. The truth is, people will give you the absolute minimum if you let them. Sometimes we aren't even "letting" them. We are afraid of being TOO difficult or demanding (hey, chapter two), so we accept the first thing they offer us.

I come from a long line of hagglers, and my grandmother was definitely one. Haggling is an exercise in asking for more until you are satisfied. So why did I come to America and forget my haggling ancestry? I should have been treating job negotiation like a Nigerian market, where the motto is "Always ask for what you want." The first no isn't what they mean. Keep asking, and even if you don't get exactly what you want, you are as close to it as you can get. "At least you tried" is a way of life.

When Mama Fáloyin would come to the United States, she'd ask me to take her to her favorite flea market in Chicago. By me taking her, she meant she needed me to come to be extra hands to hold the plethora of stuff she would be buying. Also, to push the second cart.

My freshman year of high school, K-Swiss shoes were all the rage. My mom, being the coolness blocker that she was (see also: single mother who couldn't afford to buy $75 shoes), wasn't getting me a pair. And since my allowance was, like, $5 a week, the save-up for them would take months.

So me and Grandma went to this large warehouse that honestly instantly overwhelmed me. I had insta-regret the moment we stepped in there because ten thousand square feet of disorganized bins of stuff you have to rummage through is my idea of hell on earth. (That and having to take a Spirit Airlines flight.) I was ready to drop all my sins for sainthood because if real hell was this, I SURELY wasn't tryna go.

After about ninety minutes of rummage fest, I somehow stumbled upon a pair of all-white K-Swisses. They were mid-length, with the five stripes and the white laces. WHAT?!?!? Look at my luck and God! Those shoes were the apple of my eye instantly. (Teenage Luvvie was tacky, doe, so she didn't know them shoes were some UGLASS things and that is why they ended up in a bin in a random warehouse, not in a store on a shelf. All I knew was: OH SNAP I CAN HAVE NAME-BRAND SHOES.) I didn't care that they basically looked like high-top socks with rubber at the bottom or that someone had done a bad job of gluing rubber under some dingy socks (because, mind you, they were white fabric, not even leather).

Grandma saw my excitement (cuz I was probably looking like Eeyore before this) and told me to put them in the cart. I was trying to not get my hopes up, because I knew they weren't gonna make it home with me. They were gonna be too expensive. I just KNEWED it. So we get up to the cashier and the shoes ring up as $25. I'm like, "Well, there goes that. She's gonna drop these." Instead, Grandma goes, "My friend. These are for my granddaughter. Please. Can I have them for ten?" I'm in my head thinking, "This lady is nuts," while also silently mourning the shoes I almost had.

Y'all. When I tell you my grandma somehow got them to agree to selling these shoes to her for $8? WHAT VOODOO SHE DO? And they threw in a mug she saw by the register for free. I was like, "THIS IS ANOINTING." Just bold and manifesting clearances. Gaht-damb superwoman. Ask and you shall receive indeed. Ask boldly, believing the answer is already yes.

I wore those K-Swisses OUT! Those five stripes were probably down to two by the time I was done with them. But the audacity to ask. It was everything. Ask for what you want. The universe might surprise you and say YES.

L emme drop a quick scripture on you right quick. Matthew 7:7: "Ask and it will be given to you; seek and you will find; knock and the door will be opened to you."

What would happen if we all had the sense of entitlement of a Stewart who couldn't even hold a candle to us in a game of Scrabble?

What would happen if we all asked for things with the confidence of a Connor who we'd beat in an IQ test by at least twenty-five points? Can you imagine the game-changing wave of us good, smart, thoughtful people having the nerve of a Garrett who didn't have the sense God gave a goat? My goodness. We might get somewhere!

Or what if we all had the boldness of an older Nigerian woman who believed she can get what she wants through kindness and that smile of hers? Mountains could move!

Do not force yourself to want less to appease other people. Do not dumb down your needs so you won't want to ask for more. You want what you want. Ask for it. A NO will not kill you.

Ask for more, because if the fear of disappointment stops you from going for what you want, then you are choosing failure in advance. It's a self-fulfilling prophecy. If we don't think that we should ask for the thing we want, whether it's a promotion from our boss, or more acts of service from our partner, or more attention from our friends, then we are opting for the NO, instead of trying for a YES. If we get the NO, we are still in the same place we are, losing nothing. But what if we got the YES, which would lead us closer to where we want to be?

When you choose to let fear keep you in your comfort zone, you might think that you're avoiding disappointment when what you're really doing is choosing that path, because you will know that you aren't getting what you want and need. The NO will not kill you, but the YES could save you.

My life changed when I got the courage to ASK for what I want. The courage to ASK people to stop doing things I don't like. The courage to ASK people I work with for what I thought I deserved.

The courage to ASK my partner for what I needed to feel loved. The courage to ASK my friends for their shoulders when I needed to cry. The courage to ASK the universe/God for things I thought were far-fetched.

I know we've heard "Closed mouths don't get fed." It is cliché. But it is true. We close our mouths as people do things to disrespect us. We close our mouths because we do not think we are in the position to ask. We close our mouths because we're afraid of NO. When I learned to open my mouth, my life transformed.

I didn't get smarter or cuter or less loud or less quiet or more interesting. But I was no longer so afraid to be vulnerable and say when I needed help. I was no longer tied to the thing of "I'm the one people don't worry about." I humbled myself and realized that life is not about taking on more than we can stand so someone else can soar on our backs.

You know what happened when I started asking for more? Magic happened. By magic, I mean people gave me more. The love I hoped people felt from me came back infinitely. I felt stronger, knowing that in this world, I didn't walk alone. I felt more loved, because I gave people a chance to show up for me, and to feel just as good as I did when I was leading by giving. And I felt more confident, because things I've dreamt, and some things I never even fathomed, started happening for me.

9

GET YOUR MONEY

We fear being considered greedy.

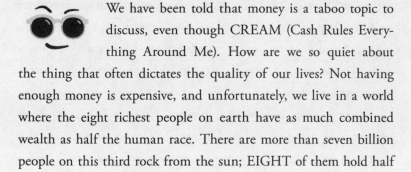 We have been told that money is a taboo topic to discuss, even though CREAM (Cash Rules Everything Around Me). How are we so quiet about the thing that often dictates the quality of our lives? Not having enough money is expensive, and unfortunately, we live in a world where the eight richest people on earth have as much combined wealth as half the human race. There are more than seven billion people on this third rock from the sun; EIGHT of them hold half the wealth. And all of those top eight billionaires have penises, of course.

There is nothing fair about capitalism, and we're all just pawns in it. Butttt I wonder if the pawns can have a little bit more money while we're on the board.

Women are especially discouraged from caring too much about money, because we are supposed to be constantly service-minded, even as others plot how to stack their coins. People assume we want to be in service, and we're pressured to feel obligated to serve. That's why more women over-index in working in nonprofits. According to a project done by the Bayer Center for Nonprofit Management, women make up 74 percent of the nonprofit workforce and are often paid 74 percent or less to do the same job as a man.* We are half of the population but represent three-quarters of those who work in an industry that is all about the greater good. And because nonprofits have fewer resources, historically underpay for labor (because: broke), and are then considered women's work, this love of service we have ends up being an economic justice issue. If women make up 74 percent of the people who work in an industry where the standard and expectation for compensation is low, then, automatically, there is no wage parity for us. Already, we're going to be cheated by the state of affairs.

Doing good in the world is important. It also sucks that it is completely undervalued and debased. Meanwhile, major corporations that lead with profit first, not social good, are printing money! PRINTING! Apple has more than $245 billion in cash. If their CEO went to the ATM, he'd get a receipt that reads $245,000,000,000. CVS receipts everywhere would be jealous. (BTW, why the hell are they so

---

*Peggy Outon, "Women in Nonprofits: Then & Now," *GuideStar*, https://trust .guidestar.org/blog/2015/11/20/women-in-nonprofits-then-now/.

damb long? CVS itself gotta be killing the trees in the Amazon for constantly printing the Dead Sea Scrolls when all you went in there to buy was a pack of Mentos.)

Meanwhile your local nonprofit, which is trying to feed kids from low-income households, has to lie prostrate at the feet of funders, begging like Keith Sweat to fund their $30,000 program. They gotta write two-hundred-page proposals with promises to spend every dollar on the program, not on staff, as if PEOPLE aren't the ones who run the programs. And then IF they are blessed by receiving HALF of what they need to run said program, they gotta send back a hundred-page report that no one got paid to write, because the money can't go to labor. Make it make sense, Fatha Gawd!

Women do that work, with long hours and low pay. In a capitalist society, philanthropy is a burden only we bear, and that has real consequences.

Society does not put the pressure of service on men, so they are able to be capitalists without guilt. You know what pays people a lot? Being an executive in the private sector. Eighty-six percent of Fortune 500 executives are dudes.* Meanwhile, women are made to feel guilty when we want to make adequate (or a lot of) money. Our capitalism comes with a hefty dollop of contrition, because we're afraid to collect our coins, even when the means are clean. We worry that if we care a lot about money or talk about it too much (levels that are super subjective), we are being covetous. Even though we

---

*Kristen Joiner, "Like the Vacuuming, Nonprofit Work Is Women's Work," *Stanford Social Innovation Review*, June 12, 2015, https://ssir.org/articles/entry/like_the_vacuuming_nonprofit_work_is_womens_work.

HAVE to care about money to survive. Everything we get to do is tied to our financial wellness.

This fear is why I feel like women are the ones most likely to do fundraisers ON OUR BIRTHDAYS, asking people to donate money to someone in need. You know those fundraisers on Facebook, where someone's birthday happens and they're asking their friends to give a certain amount to a cause they chose? I *LOOOOVE* our selflessness, but at what cost are we being so giving? It seems like the times we finally do ask for help are solely when it's for someone else's benefit.

I often wonder if the people who are doing fundraisers on their birthdays are behind on their own bills. Are you raising money for breast cancer when you don't know where your rent is coming from, because the job you work so hard at isn't paying you an adequate living wage? Are you selling merchandise from your side hustle and donating proceeds to a local nonprofit when your car note couldn't be paid because you had to choose between that and your child's asthma medication? Sis, you deserve all those coins so you can stand up straight. You do not have to donate anything if you are currently not sure where your next five meals will come from.

Women create and work in nonprofits because, as the nurturers, we say, "We want to help the world." No, help yourself first, sis. And then help the world. Put your mask on first and all that jazz. I preach the gospel of us leaving the world better than we found it, but we also have to be able to leave ourselves better for it, not worse.

We've been told that our goodness in this world is directly tied to how much of ourselves we sacrifice for other people. The pressure to sacrifice ANYTHING is only placed on women. It is OUR jobs to do these fundraisers and to give in excess. To the woman who is making thirty thousand and doing her best but is still struggling to make ends meet, I want you to know that your number one priority is not to save someone else, when you yourself need saving in the moment. But hey, person who is single, has no loans, makes a hundred thousand, maybe you can give more so she won't feel like she has to.

This extends into business especially. We get cheated, particularly as women or as marginalized people. We have been told that people do us a favor by wanting to hire us. All our lives, we have received the jacked-up message that we are less significant and more disposable, and we should yield for everyone else's convenience. So then we internalize it all and wire our mouths shut to protect ourselves.

I do not blame us one bit. The world really has done the job of convincing us that we are liabilities instead of assets, and it's utter bullshit. Some of the fight has been abused out of us, so we are getting deceived left and right, underpaid, overworked, and underappreciated.

The systems of oppression stacked against us devalue us and render us at their mercy. I am VERY clear on that. White men are the measuring stick of it all because they've created it and run it like the unfair well-oiled machine it is.

It is why a white woman makes 79 cents for every dollar Biff makes.

- Latinas make 54 cents for every dollar Chad brings in.

- Native American women make 58 cents for every dollar Trent gets.

- Black women get 62 cents for every dollar Brock takes home.

- Asian women make 90 cents for every dollar Logan secures.

We are systemically hustling backward and it's not okay.

I've talked about how the last time I worked full time for someone else was as the marketing coordinator of a nonprofit that taught other nonprofits how to tell their stories well. At the time, it was my dream job. I remember applying, crossing my fingers, and hoping I'd be so lucky to get an interview. Well, I got the interview and aced it. In September 2008, I received my offer. "Your starting salary will be $35,000." Dang, I'd hoped I could get $40,000, but who was I to be greedy? I instantly replied back to the email and accepted.

I didn't negotiate one thing. Not even the two weeks of paid vacation. Not the 5 percent salary increase I *might* get after a year. I know. Nonprofits are notoriously not gonna pay a lot, but now I know that there is usually more money on the table. Because Me Now knows more. I should have asked for more money.

If you don't take anything else from this book, please absorb this:

ALWAYS NEGOTIATE YOUR JOB OFFERS. It doesn't matter how good the offer is! Always ask for more. A few reasons:

1. Nobody is doing you a favor by hiring you. NOBODY. You are hired to do a job because you have the skill. They need you to do this thing.

b. You are supposed to negotiate. In fact, when you don't negotiate, you are going against standard practice. It's part of the steps of the game of business. You have the right to ALWAYS ask for what you think you are worth. The answer is less your business (you can't control that), but the ASK itself is FULLY your business (you control that). DO IT ALL THE TIME.

iii. The first offer is not the best offer. As in, people always have more money than they first bring to you. The first number thrown at you is NEVER the highest number someone can pay you. They offer you $40,000? Odds are that they have $45,000 in the budget for you. Ask for $7,000 more and they might meet you in the middle. Too many of us opt out because we are afraid. Which leads me to:

4d. You asking for more money (or vacay time or benefits) does not mean they will take back the offer for employment. Just because you say, "I want more," doesn't mean they'll say, "We don't want you anymore." I know it is a major anxiety we have that if we negotiate, they will somehow be offended and take everything off the table. Listen here: Headhunting and hiring and team building are EXPENSIVE for companies! If you are afraid that an offer will be taken off the table the moment you throw a number out, go back to number 1. They are not doing you a favor by offering you a job: They need you too. And HR knows searching for someone else can get expensive and time-consuming. Folks don't want to go back to square one. When they find you, their perfect candidate, they don't want you to walk away. They need you. THEY NEED YOU. So remove the fear that asking for more will mean you lose the job. You won't.

V. Women and people of color haven't been told to negotiate. I've talked to so many HR folks and they always tell me that this makes them face-palm. One of my friends sent a job offer to a candidate. The person accepted immediately. She was like, "SHIT. WHY DIDN'T SHE ASK ME FOR MORE?? I had $15,000 more for her." And before you say, "Why don't people just pay us everything they have? Isn't that what's fair?" Eh. If only business was about fairness. It's not. You have to play the part of the game where you tell them, "This isn't enough. I want more." And then they come back with, "FINE, we found more." I was never given permission or told to ask for more at a job. I found out somewhere along the way.

The number we accept in the beginning of our careers follows us. That $35,000 I accepted without question could have affected every other number I received from that point from that company. A 5 percent raise for $35,000 is $1,750. Sooo that brought me to $36,750 after a year. Imagine if I had negotiated to start at $40,000. Five percent of that is $2,000, which would bring me to $42,000. The same position at the same company could have gotten me over $5,000 MORE in one year if I had simply asked. Not asking for more literally costs us money. It is expensive to be quiet sometimes, and this is one of those instances. We have to ask for more money.

I need us to negotiate ALWAYS. Need. I want us to stop leaving money on the table.

So, my salary of $35,000 from the last full-time job I had? That is now something I've made in one weekend or through one hour of work, and it is WILD to say. How did I get to this point? Well, I built a massive platform, spent ten years building my name, wrote a *New York Times* bestselling book, and proved over and over again that excellence was something I hold dear.

And that number is large. I went from not being able to ask to be paid more than that for a year to asking for it for one event. Let me tell you how I learned to ask: I researched, practiced, and asked for it in spite of the alarms in my head that tried to convince me I was out of line. In spite of the impostor syndrome that gets me from time to time to say, "Who are you to ask for this?" In spite of the guilt of knowing that I've made more in one year than my mother made in one decade of work.

I have negotiated my way to numbers that make me laugh from the discomfort of their enormity.

There are entire books on how to negotiate. Consider picking one of them up. In the meantime, here's my CliffsNotes version:

1. Research the industry. How much are your peers making? How much do people get compensated for comparable work? Know this because it arms you with leverage when you walk into a room. That knowledge is power you can use.

b. Know that you are not being greedy for asking for what you're worth, or asking for more money.

iii. Say the number with an exclamation point, not a question mark, and shut up. What I mean by exclamation point is when you are asked what you want, say, "I'd like $50,000!" Don't say, "Umm . . . I'd like $50,000???" ending with your voice becoming high-pitched so it sounds like you're asking a question. If you're asking the question and not telling, it sounds like you're not sure you're worth the money, so why should they be sure? Say your number with confidence and then say nothing else. Sit there and wait for their response. It is not your time to say more because it will look like you're overexplaining. Before the number comes up, you've already talked about the value you bring, so now is the time for you to kick the ball into their court and wait for them to pick it up.

I've had friends in HR tell me how they have encountered people who said the number they wanted and went silent. And then after five seconds of waiting for the other party to respond, the person jumped back in: "No, it's fine. I can go lower too." NOOOOOOO!!!! Don't do that! I know silence from the other side can be uncomfortable, but do not retract your want! It is valid. The other person is probably processing and doing calculations. Fear kicked in, which is why we sometimes take back what we said we want.

In addition to negotiating for more, we should not stake claims on being cheap hires. Being known as a low-cost hire should not be our value proposition. You are not the Dollar Store and you shouldn't be. I will never be the least expensive option or use that as a rallying cry for someone to want to work with me. Why? Because you get what you pay for, and I know what I bring to the table.

Your value is not how low budget your work is, but how good it is. And people need to be willing to pay for your service. If they cannot afford you, then either they save their money to the point where they can or they go to someone whose services or products are less expensive—but that person doesn't have to be you.

You might have heard of the concept of FAST. GOOD. CHEAP. Pick two out of three when you're looking for a service. You cannot have all three.

If they're FAST and CHEAP, they probably aren't that GOOD. If they're GOOD and CHEAP, they aren't FAST. If they're FAST and GOOD, they are not going to be CHEAP.

People expect all three and I be like, HOW, DOE?? Often, people will pick CHEAP over GOOD. That's how folks end up with

Microsoft clip art logos. If someone is all three, they've undervalued their work, because if they're fast and good, they should not be cheap.

We're often willing to accept less than we want because we're afraid of leaving money on the table. "I cost $100 but they have $20. I should take the $20 because at least $20 is more than $0." Nope. Because now you're saying $20 is the price for you, and next time they want you, they will remember paying the $20 so they probably won't come prepared to pay that $100.

You can, of course, donate your services for causes that are important, or accept lower fees on a case-by-case basis. But as a habit and mantra, success, especially as an entrepreneur, often lies in getting paid what you ask, for the work you do. The people who pay you well for your work give you the freedom to now donate your time to a nonprofit doing good work, or to kids who need what you have to offer. (How often are men expected to donate their time, energy, and services for others? And when they refuse to, who guilts them for it or calls them selfish? How often are men expected to be paid in exposure? Which . . . let me go there . . .)

People LOVE offering us exposure for payment. But exposure is not currency I can use to pay my mortgage or support my shoe habit. I be wanting to say "Expose deez nuts" sometimes. I know I don't have nuts, but the sentiment stands. As someone who started my entrepreneur life as a blogger, I know what it's like to be offered exposure as a serious form of payment from people who didn't know they were being useless.

Every day, a brand that throws millions of dollars to whatever agency creates their simple-ass sans serif logo that conveys "minimalism," even though it's literally their name spelled out in Helvetica font, emails an influencer asking them to do a campaign for "exposure." And every day, an angel loses a string in her harp.

Are they going to make money off this campaign? Odds are, they are. They want us to work for free even though we're making them money, placing them in front of our audience, and doing work that will take us hours (and sometimes days) to complete on their behalf. But they want to pay us with exposure? *Naija accent* Thunda fire you!

Exposure hustling is writing for one of the biggest news outlets on the web and them offering to pay me by tweeting my username on their account so I can get more followers. My mind is always blown by the unmitigated gall. You know what? They can ask, but my answer can always be HELL NO.

I think about a Nicki Minaj story that changed my life and how I look at asking for what I'm worth and my coins. It's all about pickle juice and why we should refuse to drink it.

Why pickle juice? Well, Nicki Minaj was booked for a photo shoot. When she showed up on set, none of the amenities she had asked for were there. She went to catering, and instead of food, there was only a jar of pickles on the table. The clothing options were awful. The whole booking was terrible, so she walked away. Her agent tried to stop her, but she wouldn't accept the situation. She wasn't going to allow pickle juice to be an anchor in future negotiations.

As she said in the MTV documentary *My Time Now*, "I put quality in what I do. . . . So if I turn up to a photo shoot and you got a

$50 clothes budget and some sliced pickles on a motherfuckin' board, you know what? No. I am gonna leave. Is that wrong? Wanting more for myself? Wanting people to treat me with respect? You know what? Next time, they know better. But had I accepted the pickle juice, I would be drinking pickle juice right now."*

It's a great lesson in knowing your worth, standing in it, and demanding it, even in the face of people telling you you're supposed to accept less. She knew her value. DO. NOT. ACCEPT. PICKLE. JUICE. Because again, people will do and give us the minimum that we accept. We'd love to think they will be virtuous, but people are selfish.

The pay gap is so real for women, and it makes me want to fight the air everlasting.

I got an email asking me to speak at a tech conference in Europe, and my lecture agent replied. For every speaking engagement, we ask for my fee, as well as my flight and hotel to be covered. They replied saying they don't really pay speakers and don't pay for travel but "The exposure would be great for you." I remember thinking, "Well, clearly I'm exposed because you found me. Y'all came to me!" And it was a big tech conference that was super dude-bro heavy, so I really doubted that they weren't paying anyone.

I'm part of a group of 250 influential women in business, technology, and media. It's called TheLi.st. We talk to each other about everything from business to personal questions. One thread might

---

*"Nicki Minaj Doesn't Want Your Pickle Juice," *Rap-Up*, https://www.rap-up.com /2010/11/26/nicki-minaj-doesnt-want-your-pickle-juice/.

be about searching for a good investment app, another might be about looking for a nanny for the babies, another might ask who has leads on a chief marketing officer job. It runs the gamut. Every day people are talking and sharing and deepening connections. So I go on TheLi.st and I say, "Hey everyone, I was invited to speak at this conference, which makes more than 15 million euros a year. They're saying that they don't pay anybody."

Within fifteen minutes, women on TheLi.st were like, "Oh, no. One of my guy friends spoke there last year. He was paid, and his books were covered, and his travel was covered." Someone else said they spoke there and their travel was covered.

Because TheLi.st is really diverse, with women of all ethnic backgrounds, I was able to get a useful sense of hierarchy and pattern when it came to how this conference paid people. White men who went to speak were paid, and if it wasn't in cash, the conference bought quantities of their books. Plus their travel was covered. White women typically had their travel paid for. A few Black women who were asked to speak at this conference were told exposure was their compensation.

If NO ONE was paid and it was a policy across the board, then I could make the decision on whether donating my time was worth it. Knowing everyone was treated equally would be okay. But that wasn't the case.

In that moment, I realized I had to be the person who faced her fears head-on and still chugged through. I had to show that I am the person I say I am.

I told my agents that this pattern of pay was not okay and I had a major problem with it. I said I wanted to speak about it publicly. My agents know me well and know I am a truth girl, but they low-key freaked out. They made great points that if I spoke out about it, I might have a harder time booking other engagements from conferences who saw my public pushback and thought I might do the same to them. This could hit my pockets. They were rightfully afraid for me. And honestly, I was afraid for myself.

So I went through my three questions (see chapter six).

I checked in with myself and them: "Okay, I've been speaking for almost a decade; I'm in some pretty influential rooms. I've been on some prestigious stages, and I have a lot of access. I command a pretty big fee. If I can't be the one to speak up about this, who can? Am I expecting the person who just started speaking yesterday? The person who has never gotten paid for a speaking engagement? Am I expecting the person who just got their first speaking engagement last week to now be the one to challenge pay inequality in tech, which is a major industry that is run by dudes who don't look like me? Who am I expecting to do this work, if not me?"

I knew I had the ability to speak up, but I also knew that I was very likely to be punished for using that power. All of those fears were tied to money, being afraid of being greedy and being afraid of the consequences that could come when I, a Black woman, asked loudly to be compensated fairly for work I was expected to do.

Then I thought of my worst-case scenarios: that I would get fewer speaking engagements or none at all. People would stop requesting me, and a big revenue generator for my work would come to a screeching halt. Well, then I'd have to switch up my business model to take on more individual clients. I can always go back to doing consulting focused on marketing. I can always help other small business owners create massive platforms for themselves, like I did for myself. I wouldn't become homeless if I actually made this point and it ruined my speaking career, because if I ran out of my savings, of which I had six months' worth of expenses, I could go lie on my mama's couch till I got back on my feet. I thought through the catastrophic consequences that could happen from speaking out, and even from there, I realized I would still be okay.

After going through all three questions, and the worst-case scenarios, I knew the answers were YES, so I decided to go on Twitter to talk about the situation. It began an hours-long conversation, with others also sharing their stories and frustrations about moments when they were being offered toenail clippings as payment for their work. One woman talked about how she and her brother had been separately invited to speak at a conference in China. They told her they had no budget for speakers. They told him they'd pay him $20,000 and fly him on a private jet to the conference. HER OWN BROTHER. Same work, completely different payments.

Whew shit. Then a *Forbes* writer, Christina Wallace, who also happens to be on TheLi.st, asked me if I'd like to go on record about the situation. Of course, being the glutton for punishment that I am, I said yes. Christina wrote about it with the title "It's Time to End the Pay Gap for Speakers at Tech Conferences."* The caucacious guy who ran the conference ended up sending me and Christina an email full of fucked-up feelings. Because you know what Boris (his actual name) doesn't like? Being challenged and called out by two women,

---

*Christina Wallace, "It's Time to End the Pay Gap for Speakers at Tech Conferences," *Forbes*, March 13, 2017, https://www.forbes.com/sites/christinawallace/2017/03/13/pay-gap-for-speakers-at-tech-conferences/.

one of whom is melanated. This goat said, "When we reply saying 'we don't have a budget for speakers,' the whole unpleasant truth is that we need to prioritize whom we spend our limited budget on, and in this case it's speakers that are perhaps more relevant for our audience, more sought-after. That is far from saying we think Luvvie Ajayi isn't worth paying—we're absolutely sure that for the right audience and in the right city, she easily commands her fee."

Flava Flav voice WOWWWWW the audacity of caucasity is alive and well. The dog whistle, basically saying they're not paying me since Amsterdam ain't Atlanta. Ain't that some shit?? I was facing my front* when y'all came to ME to speak.

Boris blessed us, though, because the piece got updated with his response, further proving my point. He doubled down on the point that the article was making: that they can see me and all my expertise, and the fact that I'm good at what I do, and still not want to pay me what I'm worth, strictly because they don't think I fit the demographic. Basically, I'm too Black to be paid.

The fear I had—that I would lose money after people saw me speaking up against this conference—didn't happen. Quite the opposite, actually. That *Forbes* piece got a lot of attention and ended up getting me more invitations to come speak. That is also the year I did my TED Talk. So, all these really cool things happened from that piece. If I had never spoken up because of fear of repercussions, then the rewards might have never come.

If you're asking me to donate my time, that's one thing. But don't insult my intelligence by telling me the exposure will be worth it.

---

*Facing my front = minding my business.

"We don't have a budget for this campaign, but we will promote you. This will be great exposure."

We're so afraid of charging what we're really worth because we fear that people will walk away. I say good riddance to bad rubbish. People who want to pay us pickle juice for champagne work have to get used to hearing no. Don't come to undergrad with elementary expectations. Don't come to this rice party with a kale dish. I've bent over backward for the opportunity to work with some companies before. I've charged what I knew was less than my value just to "build relationships," and in the end all I felt was cheated. And THAT is the greatest suck of all. When you realize that you were taken advantage of and you let it happen, that's also when you decide you don't want it to happen again.

I firmly believe that people have gotten us to be silent about money in order to take advantage. Our silence is being weaponized against us. We've learned for such a long time that you don't talk money, but it's part of the reason why we get cheated over and over again.

I realize the privilege I have by having a network like TheLi.st, where I can go and ask for radical transparency. I'm able to call a friend and say, "Hey, they want me to do this thing. Here's the fee." Friend will be like, "No. They have double that. Go back and ask for double." I'll hang up. "Yeah, so I'll need this." "Okay." "Sweet." It was that easy? I just had to know y'all had double? Because nobody told me. The value of sharing this type of information cannot be underestimated.

When we think about money, we think about me-me-me. The

worst part is we are doing ourselves a disservice. If I'm walking into any room, I'm not cheap. The problem is, if I don't tell you what my price is, and you tell the same person what your price is and your price is a tenth of mine, that doesn't do me any favors. Why? Because they hear my number and they think, "Oh, she's expensive." I'm not expensive, but I am valuable and I'm asking for what I'm worth. None of us win in this scenario when our work is similar but you're undercutting my prices. The win comes when we can be open and honest and we are both paid fairly.

None of us win when I am up here and you're down here. When we're quiet about our numbers, we're actually cheating each other. But when we share numbers, other people also get used to hearing these big numbers coming from women. "Oh, you don't have enough for my fee in the budget? It's cool. I can't come. Oh, you found it. Thank you."

I want us to stop feeling guilty for dropping a number that we are actually going to earn. Getting paid is not getting a favor. You're gifting them with your work, with the service, with the thing that you studied, the thing that you've put hours into. That is the thing that they're paying for, and they should pay every dime. Do not feel guilty about being a capitalist who wants to do good in the world.

There's a reason why something like 95 percent of billionaires in the world are men. It's not because they're smarter than us or work harder than us. It's more that they have no guilt attached to making buckets of money, and the systems prop them up to allow them to do so. They have no guilt for wanting to be financially prosperous.

You have a right to demand what you're worth. And just because your color might be darker and/or you're a woman does not mean somebody should pay you less. WE have $1 trillion in spending power. So when you show up on our doorstep saying you only have a tiny amount of money to work with, you're insulting me and my skinfolk. Your diversity budget has nothing to do with me.

In the words of Professional Troublemaking Prophetess-at-Large Robyn Rihanna Fenty, "Bitch better have my money."

M y grandma did not play about her money. My aunt told me a story of back in the day when my grandmother was a wigmaker. She learned to make wigs to make ends meet, to supplement my grandfather's income. They did have six kids to raise, after all.

Anyhoo, word of Grandma's wigmaking skills had traveled, and she was hired by the wife of a governor. When Mama Fáloyin delivered the wig to the lady's house, she wasn't there at the time. Grandma realized the lady was trying to shaft her money. NO MA'AM. NO SIR. That's what you're not going to do. So Granny refused to leave until she got her money. At first, they told her the lady wasn't home, so Mama Fáloyin said that was fine, she'd wait for her. And wait she did. After a few hours passed and they realized she wasn't leaving till she got her money, someone finally came outside and handed her what she was owed. THAT'S RIGHT.

Do not be afraid to insist on someone running you your coins. Do not feel like you're being a shark for sending reminder emails on an overdue invoice. Understand that sometimes, you do have to take off your earrings via email and let someone know that the consequence of not paying you means extra fees on top of what they already owe. Collect your coins, without guilt!

We are afraid of talking about money, of admitting that we want more of it, and of insisting that people give us what we have earned. We fear people walking away from us. We fear losing opportunities. We fear getting the reputation of being close-fisted. All valid, but if one of the things people use to disparage me is that I'm serious about being paid, then let it be. In fact, put it on my epitaph: "She came. She saw. She didn't play about her coins."

There are systems in place that are actively working against us in every way. The world is unfair to everyone who is not a straight Christian white dude. It is set up for their triumph, their comfort, their wealth-building. It is designed for the rest of us to be born poor, live poor, and die poor. It is also designed to gaslight us, by teaching us to be afraid of what happens when we want the piece of the pie that belongs to us, but they've hoarded.

I'm not asking for you to ignore the system, nor am I saying it is your job to dismantle that machine. We're disenfranchised in a lot of it. But I am asking you to ask the world for more and get your money.

What happens after we ask is out of our control. We might ask for more money and they still tell us no. But it's important for us to ask so we have a chance to get it. Because not asking is a guaranteed NO, unless we find a saint who says, "I know you didn't ask but here's extra." That doesn't come too often. By asking, we increase our chances of getting something more, even if all we get is 20 cents more. It is still more than we had. It's still more than we were gonna get.

When we ask for more money, we're not breaking up systems or fixing everything, but we are putting ourselves a little bit closer to something that resembles parity. And if we don't do it for ourselves, who is going to do it? I want to think that the world is benevolent and people are really kind and would go out of their way constantly to ensure justice and equity, but it's not how it goes. A lot of this will fall on us; we have to roll massive boulders uphill because we don't have any other choice.

So ask for more, get your money, and do it without guilt. And then when you get money and you have abundance, pass some of that on to someone else, and we can have a circle of giving. But we cannot be of service to others if we can't be of service to ourselves first.

10

DRAW YOUR LINES

We fear not being considered nice.

People can be some no-personal-space-respecting goats, all up in our faces and spaces when we don't want them. That's why it's so important for us to be serious about boundaries. And as I get older and my grays disrespect my edges more, one of the facts of life that I hold dear is knowing that we have to teach people what we expect from them and how we want to be treated. If we do not, we'll constantly have people getting on our nerves, and life is too short for side-eye-induced high blood pressure.

Boundaries are some of my favorite things to draw. They became so when I realized that I had an obligation to let people know when they do something I don't like. As the professional cantankerous auntie that I've been since I could talk, I am not the most patient person at times. That's because I have some firm lines I don't want people to cross, and when they do, it instantly grinds my gears. Since

I have zero poker face, my annoyance is usually written all over it, because as I mentioned earlier, my face is basically an outside voice.

For me, drawing boundaries is a matter of social grace. If I don't, I'm probably looking like someone stole my last cookie, and no one wants that. We must create and vocalize our boundaries, no matter how much it might be jarring to others.

Having boundaries and drawing our lines is not about playing keep-away with people, and it isn't about preventing people from getting close to us (well, sometimes physically it is). It is about establishing the standards and the treatment we expect and deserve.

People often feel entitled to our lives, energy, time, space, and platforms. Usually, it's not from malice but from habit, and we are not used to creating and standing in boundaries. We tend to move freely. We touch, kiss, and move other people's bodies. We manage other people's time. We infringe upon other people's platforms. It is how we operate as a society. What's wild is MOST people are annoyed by someone crossing their boundaries.

So why are boundaries so difficult to establish? Why do we have such a hard time telling people to stop that thing we don't like them doing when it pertains to us? Because we are concerned about ostracizing people and making them feel uncomfortable. We fear disrupting harmony, hurting feelings, and seeming difficult.

As I'm moving through the world, of course I must consider other people (I'm not a sociopath). But like the flight attendants tell us as we post our last Facebook message before takeoff, we must put our oxygen masks on first before we do it for others. I need to feel as comfortable and as assured as I can. I am not obligated to use my time, body, space, or energy in ways that don't suit me.

However, while everyone else isn't necessarily responsible for my comfort, they also might be culpable in my discomfort. Lemme explain. When I walk into a room, the people in it do not have to make sure I'm feeling tended to and perfectly at home. HOWEVER, if the folks in the room start throwing insults my way, then they are liable for my uneasiness. That being said, my boundaries are my responsibility to voice, because what happens when people don't realize I've drawn lines in invisible ink? They're not culpable if they don't know. We often get mad at someone crossing boundaries we didn't establish, and we have to ask ourselves how the person could have known to do better by us or to do something different.

Yes, there are some universal boundaries we should all honor, like consent should come before sex. A person should be able to walk down the street butt-nekkid wearing nothing but socks and a smile, and no one should touch them, unless they have a sign that says, "Touch me freely." Even then, I might still ask.

Besides those, we cannot assume anything else of anyone. Do we realize how much we go through life letting people talk to us any kinda way and doing things to us that we don't like? What do we do about it? A lot of times, we roll our eyes. Or we deep-sigh. Or we hope they magically stop doing that thing we don't like. But people will bring trash to you if you are a willing receptacle.

We cannot assume everyone is operating from the same understanding. We do not operate from the same mind frame. This is why we have to be intentional about speaking our boundaries out loud. We gotta speak up about the things or space we need from people. That is our responsibility. Whether or not people honor it is theirs.

Personal, professional, emotional, and physical boundaries are all important. We think we can't afford to tell people our boundaries for fear of ostracizing them. But really, we cannot afford NOT to tell people our boundaries, because when we are silent, we betray ourselves. And we must betray ourselves less.

One of my grandmother's biggest boundaries was being spoken to in a loud voice in the middle of conflict. Here's the thing: Nigerians do not have an inside voice at all. Come around my family during the holidays and it sounds like a hundred people are in the room, even if it's only twenty. Yelling as we speak to each other is a love language. Even now, when we get on the phone, we act like 5G cell phone service is not a thing, and that our phones are tin cans connected by string. We are SO LOUD. We use whatever the "unnecessarily loud" decibel measurement is. I remember when I used to make fun of my elders for doing it. Now I'm an elder and I do it.

Even with those cultural mores, Mama Fáloyin did not suffer fools when it came to how she wanted to be respected at all times. Yes, you might yell her name in glee when you saw her and to hype her up (in church and anywhere else). But if she was talking to you sternly and you raised your voice? There was hell to pay. By hell, I mean dramatics.

GRANDMA: Did you finish your homework?

YOU, slightly frustrated and with a slight tilt up in your voice: Grandma, yes. I said I finished it thirty minutes ago.

GRANDMA: Ehh so you're yelling. Óyá come and beat me.

Sis, how did it escalate so quickly? How did my slight annoyance become "In fact, go get a belt and beat me"? It was hilarious when you weren't the person on the other end of it. I swear, she would sometimes respond to situations as if she were in her own personal *All My Children* episode. (Which was her favorite soap opera, by the way. That was her shit! Maybe it's because the theatrics were right up her alley. When Susan Lucci kept getting nominated for a Daytime Emmy but not winning, I think Grandma went to Jesus to intervene. Next thing you know, Susan is standing on that stage holding her award. Amen, saints.)

So Grandma would also pull the "Your own mother wouldn't talk to me like that," which would instantly shame you for the unearned brazenness you showed. Your ego would be knocked down to size.

This line that my grandma drew was known by adults and kids alike. What you not gon' do in the presence of Fúnmi Fáloyin is raise your voice at her in discontent. She'd straight up ask you, "You and who?" It's a question with no real answer, because it's one of those "Lemme make sure you know who you're dealing with" things. And I saw it over and over again, how the most blunt and surly people honored that line of hers. I saw how Nigerian police, who often give no fucks about decorum, would yell at someone in one sentence and speak to my grandmother with such deference and warm tones the next.

It let me know that people are capable of acting like they have sense. They just wield that based on who is in front of them, and what that person has allowed them to get away with. Although it is not our fault when people abuse or disrespect us, how others treat us can be a reflection of our allowances.

At the core of setting boundaries is trying to minimize self-betrayal as we exist in this world. The person who I need to make sure is okay at the end of the day/life is me, because I'm the one I have to answer to and I'm a critical child of God. Whew! I'm tough, more so on myself than anyone else. And if I gotta tell ME that I somehow bent myself out of shape for someone else, I'ma be mad as hell at myself. I've been mad as hell at me plenty of times before, and I find it really hard to forgive myself. That alone has made me insist on getting better and better about being clear to others about my limits.

I'm usually leery of people who don't have any clear boundaries. Why? Because their lack of boundaries means they are less likely to understand the paint-thick lines that I draw. They might have a hard time with me speaking my limits, seeing it as an act of hostility instead of an act of self-preservation. Plus, they might take my strong boundaries as lack of transparency and vulnerability. They will have a hard time honoring mine. There is an African proverb that says, "Be careful when a naked person offers you a shirt." My structure will make your free-willingness look like austerity.

One of my biggest boundaries is that I don't like hugging people

I don't know. I'm not anti-hugs, because I don't mind waist-bumping folks I know (who also like to be hugged by folks they know)! What I am not a huge fan of is squeezing the body of someone whose name I am not familiar with. This is a tough boundary to have. Why? Because people love to hug! It is a sign of kinship, friendliness, and sometimes kindness. And I, as someone who has a book and is somewhat visible and relatively approachable (when I don't have Resting Side-Eye Face), look pretty huggable. So the fact that I don't really like hugs from non-friends and -family can make me seem aloof when people meet me and I decline. And because of that, I find myself letting strangers hug me way more often than I'd like, and then feeling some type of way after.

How it happens: Someone sees me in public (like in the airport) and they're excited and I'm honored! They go, "I'm a hugger!" I wanna respond with "I'm a Capricorn!" since we're shouting out random attributes. I see their smiles and it makes it that much more difficult to say, "I'd prefer to fist bump." (After COVID-19 and learning how few people wash their hands, I don't even wanna shake hands anymore.) But a lot of times, I'm not even given the choice in the hug. My reflexes are slower than I'd like, and before I can say anything, I'm face-deep in the bosom of a woman who loves my work. I'm both honored and slightly taken aback. I walk away feeling a bit surly.

In that case, when meeting someone who really likes me, I'm afraid to disappoint them or hurt their feelings. The easier choice is to accept the hug. But easier for who? Not me. If it's a day when I'm at a conference speaking, I could be doing that two hundred more times. One paper cut isn't bad, but two hundred might hurt like hell. I'm not comparing hugs from strangers to paper cuts. OR AM I?

Hugs feel very personal to me. This is why I'm not giving them to everyone I meet. This is also why they're such a tough boundary. People take it personally because it probably feels like a personal rejection. I fully understand how someone could feel slighted by being told that their gesture isn't welcome. However, it's one of those "it's not you, it's me" situations. As an experienced introvert, I find my energy sapped by people. Peopling makes me tired and I usually have to recharge after doing it a lot. Hugs are Super Saiyan levels of peopling when they go into the hundreds. Protect your space and energy in the decent ways you know how.

I've asked people what the best way to decline a hug is. A large number have advised me to say, "Oh, I have a cold." Or "I'm not feeling well." Soooo the answer to telling people about what I want is to lie? Nah. Why do we need to betray ourselves in that way, by creating a false moment in order to receive the response? Who does it serve? The person who wants the hug? Okay. Meanwhile, now you're having to fake sniffles. All for what? To prevent the discomfort of someone who feels like they should receive a body squeeze from you. I don't even think the means justifies the end.

Others have advised me to make sure I'm holding something in both hands. Or that I do a quick *Matrix* backbend to avoid people's grasps. So I gotta be flexible, doing yoga and training with Mr. Miyagi at home to practice and get quicker reflexes to avoid folks' arms around me. Won't it be easier to be able to say, "Hey, I'd prefer not to do that, person whose name I don't know"?

Even the hugging expectation is super gendered. Men's personal space is often respected. Women are supposed to be the nurturers and our bodies seem to be community property, so we're expected to wanna hug folks at will. NAWL.

Many of us were not allowed to draw our boundaries growing up, especially with family. We've all seen it, or had it done to us, when we were little: A family member would visit and we'd be forced to hug them. In those moments, we learned that being related dominates our agency and we started thinking that we do not have the right to make choices for our comfort. These small moments have far-reaching impact on how we move through the world.

We normalize constant betrayal of our needs and ourselves and others around us when we do not take boundaries seriously. We say that everyone has access that is irrevocable, no matter how terribly they treat us or show up. It is not necessarily our fault, but it is our problem.

While drawing strong lines in person can be hard, even electronically we are very hesitant to create the boundaries we need. Because again, we prioritize everyone else's harmony over justice.

Social media is the land of crossed boundaries, because there is something about being behind a keyboard that makes people forget all their home training. Folks stay acting out on there.

Since boundaries are my favorite things, right under wing tip shoes and red velvet cupcakes, I have a lot of them regarding how people should interact with me online. And I very quickly realized that in order for me to not have my entire nerves be tapped on by people and their good intent, it was important for me to make loud PSAs about what my lines were.

There are a few things that really grind my gears and cross my virtual boundaries.

- When people tag me in photos I'm not in to get my attention—this is the virtual version of cold-calling me to tell me about your event.

- When people tag me in photos I'm not in to get my audience's attention—this taps on the shoulders of those who follow me. It's like putting a billboard on my lawn.

- When people direct message (DM) me to ask for a favor when they've never messaged me before—this is like walking up to a random stranger on the street and asking them to buy the T-shirt you're selling. Can you at least say hi first and introduce yourself? It always feels like some sort of invasion when the ask is money. I've had someone ask me to pay for their tuition before, and it felt like someone reached directly into my pocket rummaging for cash.

All of this is not to say don't talk to me. Rather, it is to say treat me like a person you want to build a relationship with, not someone to take advantage of. Asking for help or a favor is not the problem. The problem is doing it without regard for creating real rapport.

What happens on social media is both a gift and a curse. Because we are all now two degrees separated at most, we feel like everyone is accessible. At its best, this allows us to forge deep connections with people we might never have known otherwise. At its worst, it makes us forget that behind the names and profile pictures are real people. If we kept in mind that we are not entitled to anyone's space, time, or energy, we'd act like we have broughtupsy.

As an early adopter of social platforms, I've been cognizant of the importance of curating the space I want for years, because our experience on these mediums is wholly dependent on who we let into our eHouses. The people we friend, follow, and like determine the quality of the time we spend scrolling. You might look up one day and find that logging into Facebook stresses you out, because half your timeline is touting janky-ass conspiracy theories and the other half are pro-troglodytes. If your eyes bulge out your face and you want to drop-kick everyone in the face, you should know that it is time to make a purge.

Facebook, for example, allows you to have five thousand friends. Just because that is the maximum doesn't mean that is the number you should have. Just because your house can safely fit one hundred people in it doesn't mean that is the number you should invite for dinner today. We don't control a lot in life, but we can manage who we let into our physical and virtual spaces.

So you know I got rules for how I accept social media connections.

FACEBOOK

Treat this as the summer picnic of social media. Ask yourself: Have I met you in real life? Do I actually know you by face, and if I see you walking and a road is between us, will I make it a point to cross the street to come greet you, or will I duck behind cars so you won't see me? Why is this important? Well, if I don't want to cheerfully acknowledge you in person and would rather do calisthenics to avoid you, then why do I need to see your posts in my timeline? A lot of people blanket-friend everyone they went to high school and college with. That is how they end up getting upset that the dude who was the first-string quarterback is now a raving Tea Party guy who you think is also running a local cult. UNFRIEND, SIS. No one needs that energy.

TWITTER

Twitter is the equivalent of a happy hour on social media. Ask yourself: Would I maintain more than a five-minute conversation with you if we met at a mixer? At this place, where everyone is talking and I'm moving from conversation to conversation, would I sustain a conversation with you because I find you fascinating? This is relevant, as it's a space where we're sharing thoughts, opinions, news. I want my timeline to be useful, funny, timely, and interesting. This is also where you might wanna avoid the person who believes the world is flat.

LINKEDIN

Treat LinkedIn like it's a professional conference. Ask yourself: Does our work overlap in some way career-wise? Would we end up at the same professional event? As we all put on our white button-downs and show up as the most industry versions of ourselves, will your posts be relevant to me in business? Can we actually network? This is where I must avoid the multilevel marketing schemers. No, I don't wanna promote your weight-loss tea, and I certainly don't wanna sell your fake-ass Lisa Frank leggings.

INSTAGRAM

Instagram is the house party of social media. Ask yourself: Would I sit through a slideshow of your last vacation pictures? I'm on Instagram to let my hair down, be a little bit more open about my day-to-day, and share the highlights of my world and thoughts. Sometimes the highlights include lowlights too. It's a platform that allows us to be both professional and personal. The folks I wanna follow there have to be intriguing to me on some level.

There are people I know in real life who I would not add on LinkedIn. There are people I don't even know and have never met who I follow on Instagram. There are folks who I wouldn't necessarily break bread with whose tweets are my must-reads. Our social media choices can be personal, even when we say they aren't. I can like you as a person but hide you in my feed if your work tires me out or saps my energy.

Across the board, I don't typically follow or friend complete strangers. In the times when I do hit "Follow" on someone I've never met, it's because I feel connected to them in some way. I saw their work, and I liked it. Or they left a comment or two that made me laugh. We often say there are no strangers in the world. I agree when people make themselves organically familiar. This doesn't include the trolls who comment under every picture you post saying, "Follow me." You already know I ain't for that. Block block block.

With the strong criteria I have for how I let folks into my eLife, you might be saying, "Wait, but won't that create an echo chamber?" It absolutely can if the only people I follow are thirty-five-year-old Nigerian Americans with short hair who grew up exactly as I did. But somehow, I still don't think all I have are people who think exactly like me! We can disagree, but what everyone who I let in has in common is that they care about humankind and on a basic level are decent human beings. I find them to be mostly kind, smart, and funny.

The people who are racist, sexist homophobes who are transphobic aren't the ones I allow in. And when they slip through, I fix that quickly by removing our connection. If, in an attempt to not create an echo chamber, we let these folks live in our electronic villages, we're almost vouching for their fuckshit.

I also do not let hate or slurs fly in my eSpaces. One of the things I'm most proud of is my audience (shout-out to LuvvNation) and the energy of my platforms. While the rest of the internet can often be a dumpster fire, my comments section and my blog are the opposite. It is something that I speak about often, because the people who read my work tout it. The community I've built over the years of writing online knows that if my name is attached to a space, I expect you to show up correct. That means being thoughtful and not a hateful shrew. People say half the fun of my work is my words, and the other half is the comments in response.

In the moments when something I write goes viral, and it's shared on troll pages and I see my space overrun by the type of people who make you lose faith in humans, my audience handles it before I even have a chance. Seeing how protective they are of the safety of the space lets me know I've done something right.

This is also why I am not shy about deleting foolishness that people bring to my space online. My social media is a dictatorship, not a democracy. I block, report as spam, and mute as needed. I am not obligated to receive or consume debris that someone drops at my feet. I take it out the back and throw it in the ether. I'm not the United States government, so speech that I deem daft does not have freedom to live on my platforms.

We spend a lot of our time, online and in real life, having our boundaries crossed. And we say nothing. Why not? Because we might think we're making a big deal out of nothing. Or we question whether we're being crotchety. Or we wonder if it will make us less likable since we will be asking someone to do something different.

Well, if it's getting on your nerves, why shouldn't you say it? It is for the betterment of you and whoever is on the other end. When someone crosses my boundaries the first time, I assume it's because they didn't know. So then I tell them. If they do it over and over again after they have been told, I assume they don't care. At that point, my action to remove them from my life is blameless. I done told you, but you ain't listen. When people don't respect your boundaries after you've told them, block them without guilt. They don't get access to you anymore.

People will not like it when you start establishing and enforcing your drawn lines. They will feel like you built a gate to keep THEM out, instead of seeing it as a gate to keep anything that doesn't serve you out. They might take it personally, and there's gonna be very little you can do about that.

I remember receiving a note from someone who was mad that she couldn't comment on my Facebook personal page. She felt like I was "keeping people at bay." I replied back with "I have a public fan page, a Twitter account, an Instagram account. And I cannot keep some semblance of privacy on my personal page? That is a lot of access. Can't help that you feel that way. It is what it is."

These things aren't only online occurrences. I was at a friend's personal event, stuffing my face with food, when someone came up to me to ask for a hug and a selfie. And I said I'd do it once I finished eating. She got offended and let a mutual friend know that I wasn't nice. Maybe I should have dapped her up and kept it moving, but I thought I was being "nice" by saying I'd do it after I finished chewing food. But nah, she still got upset. That lesson is: Don't be afraid of not being nice, because people will take from an interaction whatever they want. It is out of your control, good intentions and all.

When you draw boundaries, people might say you've changed and you think you're somehow better than them. They might say you are not nice. Let them. In fact, they will be saying it from afar because it won't be to your face since your drawn lines are so good, they won't be able to reach you. Preserve your sanity, because even if you try to bend yourself backward for folks, they'll still say you didn't do enough. You don't OWE anyone your time, energy, or platform. Do not feel guilty about being protective of any of those things.

Before I got married, my VERY strong boundary was not to speak about my relationship or whether I was even in one. As a result, folks who were nosy created stories about my love life, my sexual orientation, and whatever else they wanted to fill in the gap on. All I asked of folks was that whoever they thought I was dating (he/she/them) be a bad bitch, and I would be satisfied. PLEASE start a rumor that I had an affair with Rihanna. That'd be lit!

When I got engaged, I posted a picture of me and my boo (now husband) on social. The post went up five days after it happened, because I wanted to take my time and not rush breaking boundaries I wasn't even fully comfortable with. Before I posted, I asked myself, "Shit. Now do people have to know?" But I said yes because my ring was gonna tell on me so lemme tell on myself. When the post went up, it got SO MUCH ATTENTION. I got 54,000 likes and 8,800 comments. I have done a lot in my life and accomplished a lot. The engagement post is the one that garnered the most likes and comments EVER for me. It was overwhelming. I remember people being like, "OMG I didn't even know she was dating someone." It's possible to be visible and still keep some of our spaces to ourselves.

Don't be out here clocking my womb. I've already had people be like, "OMG you posted a random piece about babies. You tryna tell us something?" I'm still a tithing member of Real G's Move in Silence like Gnomes Church. Just cuz you know I'm married doesn't mean I'm gonna be live-posting everything. Ain't gon' be no peeing on a stick on Instagram Live happening.

I've found weddings are the event of the world where people will most test your boundaries. If you are not used to drawing lines, you might not be ready to have a wedding. Consider going to a courthouse and calling it a day, because people will TRY YOU during weddings. I don't know what it is about folks and that day. All types of randoms allasudden feel entitled to everything in your life. From the folks asking if they're invited (if you have to ask, odds are the answer is a swift NOPE) to the kinfolk who wanna bring plus-four. You got plus-four money? WHO IS PAYING FOR ALL THEM PLATES?!?

(Low-key, I know if my grandmother were alive when I got married, she'd have wanted to bring a whole posse of the village plus ten. And I'd have given it to her. I thought about her on my wedding day. She would have had an amazing time. She would have had her own entrance moment, like her church one. She would have worn ALL GOLD EVERYTHING with matching shoes and bag and dripping in at least five gold chains. She would have loved the man I married.)

Remember: Your life is not a carnival and not everyone should get a ticket to it. I see my own life as a highly exclusive club (where there are beds and the rice flows and no one has to wear heels or uncomfortable clothes), and the ones who come in are on the guest list. They are the people I know are a good time and won't start a fight. The cool thing is, if someone rowdy comes in, I can kick 'em out at anytime. Remember: Not everyone gets a ticket to your life. This is YOUR club, so you have the right to have whoever you want in there.

Draw lines, even if the person is family. Honestly, it's especially important to know you can have boundaries with the people you love. These are the folks we feel most obligated to bend till we break for. These are the ones who can manipulate us to erase the boundaries that are most important to our well-being. These are the ones who early on teach us that our feelings aren't worth protecting because we are erroneously obligated through blood connection.

Do not get to the point where you give everyone everything you have, in terms of energy and time and brain power and money and even your presence. Because what will happen is you will be left with nothing and they will still have everything that you gave them.

Know that you have the right to have your preferences, your borders, your boundaries. Tell people outright that you prefer another type of behavior. Wear a T-shirt. Make PSAs. Use a hashtag. Feel no guilt about it. Prevent riffraffery and the enemies of progress from constantly piercing your territory. Build a wall to keep tomfoolery out.

Draw your lines without guilt.

DO

We can't be all talk with no action. In this DO section,
let's start doing the things that might seem scary.

"GROW ANYWAY.

DO WHAT'S HARD ANYWAY.

CHANGE ANYWAY."

—Luvvie Ajayi Jones

11

GROW WILDLY

We fear change.

 Change is scary because we fear the unknown and the new territories it takes us into. We like what is familiar because that is what is comfortable and what we know intimately.

I come to you, as Change Averse Club president, because I love control and I love knowing things. The mystery that comes with future things is my kryptonite. You'd think a lifetime of not being psychic would have gotten me used to it by now. But I've been forced to deal with it because I have the nerve to want better things, and I realize how old habits, old ways, and old thoughts won't get me those things.

Let's face it: I am a mess. I mean that in the most self-aware, not-put-downy way possible. Like how Forky from *Toy Story 4* declared, "I am trash!" because he knew it was fact, since he was made up of literal garbage. As humans, by default, we are walking compost heaps who are constantly trying God's patience and daring Him/Her/Them to activate another flood. As a species, we're lazy, selfish, self-serving, money-obsessed, climate-killing atomic fragments. The fact that Jesus hasn't come to get us yet, dragging us by our soiled hoodies, is a testimony of praise.

And I am a fool who has put her foot in her mouth more than a couple of times, with a stubborn streak and a perfectionism problem that sometimes requires me to be told to go occupy a seat because I'm doing too much. I'm a piece of work in progress. Can't nobody tell me my flaws because I'll read that tome of a list to you in a hot second.

Humans are sentient sewage sometimes. It is what it is. What we can do is attempt to not be as scummy as we used to be. If we at least try, we can be better and assure ourselves that we're not complete litter. It's the least we can do, honestly. This is why one of my life's goals is to not be the same type of trash I was last decade, last year, or last week. I'm probably the same fool I was yesterday and that's okay. I'll give myself that grace. But tomorrow? I should be better.

What happens when you commit to not being as terrible as you used to be? It means you are going to change. It means you are constantly going to be different from who you used to be, even if only in small ways. It means the only thing that will stay the same is your perpetual evolution. It's that quote from an old dead Greek dude, Heraclitus of Ephesus, come to life: "Change is the only constant in life." Nobody has proven this wrong yet.

What I know is that who we are right this moment is not who we're going to end up being. Not only should we want to change, it is our duty to change. It is our duty to constantly look to be better than we are. And you know what that is? Growth. Growth is an obligation, and we gotta give ourselves permission to grow wildly, like my cuticles after a month of neglect.

Permission is one thing; execution is another.

Once you know you gotta get doper and better, now comes the part where the ground you stand on will be shaken up. When folks talk about "growing pains," they mean it literally. Change is not fun. Growth is not sunshine and rainbows, because it means our comfort zones are going to be pulled away from us. It means what's convenient is not going to be what prevails. Shit is hard, and that's why it is scary.

This is also why change often happens by force, not by choice. We don't wake up one day and say, "I feel really comfortable and things are great. I should make a change." That's not typically how it happens. Usually there's a catalyst that coerces us into shifting.

Sometimes it's something external, like losing our job unexpectedly or getting sick outta nowhere or finding out we're pregnant or losing someone we love. OR GETTING MARRIED *coughs*

Other times, the force is internal—not a major external moment but our conscience, our spirit. We're feeling bored or we're feeling like we're not in the right place. Or we're feeling unexcited to wake up in the morning because we have to clock in somewhere we don't want to go. Or we're feeling like we are gasping our way through life. Whatever the impetus, internal or external, change can throw us off our feet.

In my life, the moments I've been called to change have been very clear, like moving to the United States when I was nine and having to become the new girl for the first time ever in my life.

Or like the time I got to college, took Chemistry 101, and got the first D of my academic career (see chapter three). That was when I dropped my premed major and my lifelong dream of being a doctor, and through a series of domino moments became a writer, which led me to this book.

There's the moment when I received major backlash online and learned that I needed to be better as a thinker, as a human, as an intellectual, as somebody with a platform (see chapter seven).

There's me getting married and realizing that I have to be less selfish and less me-me-me, and that I also have to work through my own trauma to make sure I'm not passing it on and projecting it onto my partner.

Each one of these cataclysmic moments was deeply uncomfortable, agonizing, with tears (snot bubbles included), and shrouded by struggle. They had me doubting everything I knew to be true. I could feel my emotional bones stretching, and the growing pains felt physical at times.

But each one of these incidents also led me to becoming the person that I am now. Even if I didn't understand it in the moment, change always leads me to something greater. My life is a testimony to the instances when I've been forced to change, and the lessons that I've learned have always been greater than anything I could have imagined. And those lessons were stairs to the person I am now, and who I am now is another step to the person I'm going to be.

There's an Igbo proverb that goes, "A palm nut that wants to become palm oil must pass through fire." "Diamonds are formed under pressure" is another good reminder. YES. To become who you must be, you gotta go through some things!

Growing wildly is sometimes not a choice but a need, because life will give you no other slot. In these moments, we have to know change is as much a part of life as breathing is.

I think about my grandmother. Mama Fáloyin might have once been a chill, patient, soft-spoken person, but I wouldn't know. There's no point in even speculating, because her life was filled with so many abrupt occasions that insisted she change from moment to moment. All of that contributed to the woman who I knew to be tough, fierce, take-no-shit, and loving with all her heart.

Fúnmiláyọ̀ Fáloyin was born in Lagos as Fúnmiláyọ̀ Láṣórè, to David and Celina Láṣórè. David was an educated man, a teacher by trade, while Celina kept the home running. They had five children, and Fúnmi was kid number three. Fọlọ́unshọ́* followed her. Their last-born died at a young age.

When my grandma was about sixteen or seventeen years old, her life changed completely. Her paternal grandmother was next in line to rule Ọ̀rún Èkìtì,† a town in Èkìtì state, Nigeria. Their lineage had come up in the succession of the throne, and because her grandmother was a woman, she couldn't become king. She thought about her son,

---

*Pronounced Faw-LAW-oon-SHAW
†Pronounced Ay-Kee-Tee

David, and chose him to take her place, since he had the knowledge and the preferred gender of royalty in a patriarchy (yup). Often you are left with very little choice when strong traditions like this call, so my grandmother's parents uprooted their family from the hustle and bustle of Lagos to the rurality of the rituals of Ọrún Èkìtì.

I cannot even imagine what such a disruption to your life would feel like. Overnight, Fúnmiláyọ̀ became a princess, along with her younger sister, Fọlọ́unshọ́. At that point, she was the oldest child still at home, because her two older brothers were out in the world.

Within a year of ascending the throne, my grandmother's father, David, died suddenly. Because life can be a summabitch sometimes, her mother, Celina, passed away not long after that.

In less than eighteen months, my grandmother's life turned upside down. She went from being a city girl, in a household with both of her parents, to moving to a town and becoming royalty, to becoming an orphan. She had to grow up very quickly from that point because LIFE DOESN'T OFTEN WARN US THAT IT'S ABOUT TO DROPKICK US IN THE FACE.

As the oldest heir who was traceable, my grandmother was made a regent of Ọrún Èkìtì. A regent is someone who is appointed to rule in the interim as they find a king. She stayed regent for a few months, until they finally found a new king. Can you imagine how an eighteen-year-old who had lost the people most important to her might feel, and then to be told to handle the business of a city? Bruh!

After that, she was moved to Iléṣà, under the charge of her uncle, her dad's younger brother, who happened to be a cartoon villain. His legend precedes him as a man who wasn't only tough but was also cruel. This uncle then sold all of her father's property and heirlooms, because nothing enables greed as much as death. Instead of these things coming to my grandma and the remaining siblings, it all went to him. Plus, he set fire to David's house. It's why we don't have any pictures of the Láṣórès. So much burned down with that house.

So Fúnmiláyọ̀, at eighteen, takes on parenting her younger sibling, thirteen-year-old Fọlọ́unshọ́, while under the control of a man who stole everything that she was entitled to.

Going from having a family of four to only two of you remaining in so little time had to feel like heartbreak whiplash. How could she have even grieved? Did she smile at all in those days? Did she ever think hope was a useless emotion? Did she ever want to give up on everything and wither away? Did she feel equipped to carry on when so much of what and who she knew as her grounding was gone?

She didn't seem to be the giving-up type, because after all those curveballs, her uncle decided to throw her another one: an arranged marriage. Fúnmiláyọ̀ was informed that she was being betrothed to some older man, so at eighteen, she would be forced to start a family with some stranger.

Since she wasn't given any other option, she created one herself: to run away.

My grandmother took her only remaining sibling and fled Iléṣà to Ìbàdàn, two hours away, to start life over, rather than be tied to a man she never knew by a man she probably wished she didn't know. She chose the road that felt freer: Start with nothing. This was 1950, a time when women were still supposed to be YESSIR-ing men who claimed authority over their lives. This teenager, who had been to hell on earth and could have stayed there, decided to trade that hell for another in a city where she didn't really have roots.

In Ìbàdàn, she met my grandfather, Emmanuel Ọládiípọ̀ Fáloyin. It is there that she started the legacy I hail from. It is there that she birthed my mom, Olúyẹmisí (her third child). It is there that I was born. It is in the family house that she and my grandfather built where I learned that family was my safe harbor. It is there where I became the first version of myself.

Mama Fáloyin's life was full of moments when the old her wouldn't serve her or keep her safe. Her life was full of times when she had to choose to change where she physically was. Her early life was tumultuous enough that she might never even have survived long enough to give birth to the woman who would give me life and allow me to be here.

She HAD to change. Fúnmiláyọ̀ at fifteen, living in Lagos, was not the same person at seventeen in Ọrún Èkìtì. That person at eighteen in Iléṣà was not the same person who then showed up in Ìbàdàn. She wouldn't have survived in Ìbàdàn, so she had to be done away with. But all of those people had to exist to become the sixty-year-old who threw a seven-day party to celebrate six decades of not breaking even when life tried to snap her in half. Her joy was in knowing what she had to weather to get to where she was. Like Miss Sofia from *The Color Purple*, all her life she had to fight. But she was always victorious.

I think about another set of wise words from Miss Angelou: "You may not control all the events that happen to you, but you can decide not to be reduced by them." Change sometimes shocks us into learning maturity, resilience, and discernment. These are all things we need, but sometimes the reason we're afraid of change is because we're scared of what other people will say. Imagine if my grandma had stayed in Iléṣà because of what people would say about her if she didn't become Random Old Man's wife? Chile, we must DO it anyway. My grandmother was not reduced by those struggles, even as they changed her.

As we are going through life, and people who know one version of us see us grow, we might hear them say, "You've changed." Sometimes, it will hurt our feelings to hear, because that's the intention behind the statement. They're saying that we are no longer the old us and that they don't recognize who we are. But what they're really saying is THEY haven't changed. They might be thinking we aren't on the same level as them anymore and are projecting that onto us. And yeah, it's really easy to be offended by it. We might be tempted to make somebody else feel better and say, "No, I haven't changed. I'm still the same person." We are wrong. We did change. We tried something new. We got new results. We changed our worlds. Maybe we're not on the same level anymore, and that's okay. It doesn't mean I'm better than you. It only means I'm different.

Not changing is a detriment. What if we are supposed to spur positive change in everyone else? What if we are supposed to push everyone else out of their box?

Instead of taking affront to the notion that we've changed, we should simply say, "Thank you for noticing. I've been working hard at being better." Because to change is to adapt to challenges we've faced. It means we are adjusting to what life has thrown us and doing things differently. If the change they see is us being more cruel, hateful, and thoughtless, then maybe we can say, "Hmmm . . . I should adjust." Otherwise, NAH.

They see that you are not exactly like you used to be, but why is that an insult? Why would you want to be exactly who you used to be? That means you aren't doing your job as a person. It means you're not doing what's necessary. Change is necessary. To be the same person you were last year or last decade means you've learned nothing new and you're doing things the same way and at the same level you used to. It means that you're not growing, and what's not growing is dying. To be the same person you used to be means you're not getting new tools to handle what life throws at you. It means you're insisting on talking the same way, thinking the same way. It means you're not pushing back on what you think is true. Things are constantly changing around you, so why would you stay the same?

I can't stop growing just because it's going to make somebody more comfortable. My job in the world is not to make other people comfortable. And if they somehow take my evolution, my adjustments, my choices as an affront to their lack of evolution, then I guess I am doing it right. We should all want to change. We should all want to be better. We should all feel like we're more prepared to handle some of the curveballs that are thrown our way. And to be quite honest, a lot of times the things that we have to do, the people we have to be, the places that we have to go will require us to change. We can't be sorry about it.

Your change and your choices aren't about anyone else. They are about you. What is best for you might offend other people because once you start making choices that are truly yours, others might project their failure to do the same on you and resent you for it. That is not your fault, nor is it your business. Grow anyway. Do what's hard anyway. Change anyway.

magine this: You and another person both start on the first floor in a climb to the top. You are taking big steps and quickly find yourself on the seventh floor. But when you look down, the other person is only on floor three. Sure, it warrants comparison because you started at the same place. The distance is more clear. The thing is, though, we don't go up the stairs at the same pace. Our journeys are different. The dragons we each have to slay are different. Instead of comparing, our job should be to cheer each other on and tell each other to keep going. Maybe we even warn them of the dragons that await and share how we beat ours. But instead we take other people's growth as an affront.

When someone calls you "funny acting," it might mean they aren't used to the new you, whatever they perceive that to be. You're someone who is known to be quiet and now you've been using your voice more? Funny acting. You used to go to all the parties and now refuse to be at the club? Funny acting.

You used to be the go-to for "I need to borrow some money," but now you've insisted the bank is closed? Funny acting. You used to constantly be the organizer of events, parties, and friend get-togethers, but you stopped because you need to focus more on building your dreams? Funny acting.

You know what I say? BE FUNNY ACTING THEN! If me looking like I'm trying to get my life together is me being funny acting, then call me a clown if you want!

People might think you've changed because they would change if they were in your position. But what's actually changed is their behavior toward you. Often, it is completely outside us. It happens.

What people see as you changing is really you doing what is necessary to meet your goals. It is you doing what is needed to honor your own boundaries. It is actually you trying to ensure that you aren't placing everyone's needs over your own like you used to.

As you evolve, you should not let people weaponize the old you against the new you. There are those who will hate your growth so much that they will remind you of your past in an attempt to piss on your future.

When people want to judge you from four versions of you ago, there's not much you can do. You just gotta keep being this version and accept that they never received the software update cuz their device can't handle the tech upgrade (iPhone 2S faces). You can't come and break your neck trying to get people to see you now when they don't want to.

I'm telling you, people will try it. "Remember when you used to . . . ?"

"Sis, remember when your eyebrows looked like sperm over your eyes, with the super thin tail? Whew, 1998 was rough for you. But look at you now! You changed that shape. Why can't I change?"

Every auntie in life is good for this. "OMG I remember when you used to pee in the bed." Ma'am, that was literally thirty years ago and I was four. Can you not?

When people remind you of your past selves, tell them yes, you remember her/him/them and you're glad they existed, because who you are now is so much better and you're thankful for it. Further pepper them by saying how proud you are that you, with all your flaws, keep doing the work to make sure you are never that person again. Then smile widely and tell them you wish they'd grow up too. (Okay, maybe don't add that part. I'm still petty. I ain't grown out of that yet.)

We fear change and then attach the guilt of what we could lose to it, further making it harder to welcome with open arms. I want us to give ourselves permission to grow and change, without guilt.

When my first book came out and instantly hit the *New York Times* bestseller list, my life changed immediately. I went from being a girl who blogs to being an author in an elite club. I was already traveling a lot, but my inquiries tripled and my fees doubled. I basically lived on planes, in between speaking engagements.

What that meant was I stopped being able to write three times a week like I had been doing. As the side-eye sorceress of pop culture happenings, reacting to what was happening in the world with my commentary was what had built my career, and suddenly I didn't have time for it. Why? Because I barely knew what city I was in at any moment from the rapid pace I was on. And I carried a lot of guilt about it. As my audience asked, "Ooo I wonder what Luvvie will say about this," on news that was happening, I'd be running (late) to catch another flight, and I'd feel these pangs of fault, not being able to do my job.

What I didn't realize was my job had changed, and that was okay. My job was no longer to be the person sitting at home every day in her pajamas, reacting to the news of the day. My job now was to take stages, telling people about my lessons, my mistakes, and my triumphs. My job was to make sure the book I had written, a manifesto of my thoughts about life, had the furthest reach it could have. My job was to ensure that a Black woman like myself could also get these doors opened for her.

It was change I didn't readily accept, because I was stuck in a cycle of guilt and fear that my audience would think I'd left them behind. That thing that got me to where I was? Turns out it needed to be left behind to get me to where I needed to go.

What I didn't realize is that the people who were upset that I'd "changed" and didn't blog anymore weren't the people I should have been speaking to. The ones who saw my posts on Facebook, Instagram, and Twitter and cheered these new adventures on were the ones who mattered. The ones who said, "I miss your blog posts but I LOVE this new season in your life" were the ones who fed my spirit.

I was no longer the girl with the blog updating every day. I had evolved into the bestselling author, the international keynote speaker, the CEO of a media company. I had grown, and that was exactly what was needed, because it allowed my work to have more impact. It also ushered in more attention and scrutiny on my words, and even though that sometimes led to egg on my face, it also led me to being so much more thoughtful than I was.

What happens when we're given permission early enough to change, to grow? When we are told, "Listen, I already know you're going to have to be different from who you are today and that's okay. Don't feel guilty about it." How much does that free us, when we know that this isn't something to run away from, but to look forward to? When the people in our lives can say, "I know you have a book tour coming and you'll be MIA. I'll be here when you get back. Because the new life that you're leading is calling for you to be gone more often and I support you"? Whewww! The freedom.

As I've leveled up in my career, I've had to be less accessible at certain points in time to people I love. Sometimes I'm so useless that I need my assistant to be the one booking brunch time with my friends. I could have been hit with the "Oh, now I gotta go through someone to see you?" And I have been. But the friends I am closest to are the ones who go, "I've already asked your team about your availability. See you in a week." Same goes for when I was writing this book and my husband said, "You're on deadline. Let me know if you need to disappear somewhere for a week to get it done."

Imagine waking up in the morning and not feeling shame because your friend knows change looks like us not having the same time we used to have on the phone together, or it means we might have to schedule the next time we see each other. Imagine not being worried about who we are offending with the change that is required of us. It gives us wings. We can now do the best work of our lives. We can be the best people possible without constantly being afraid of what we're leaving behind, who we're leaving behind, or who's feeling small as we're trying to be big. When the changes that I need to make aren't met with eye rolls of inconvenience but are met with affirmations of understanding, I have the room to stretch as I need.

We have to learn how to change and how to grow without guilt. Once we do that, we'll be freer in general for it because the fear of change will start to go away a little bit. We begin to learn it's a part of life and something we have to do. We know it might be uncomfortable, but we realize the most uncomfortable things are usually the most necessary things. It can be good to be in our comfort zones, but sometimes the comfort zones insulate us and keep us from doing what we're actually supposed to do.

Give yourself permission to grow wildly. To transform. To change your opinions. To change your surroundings. To change three times a day while on vacation because you've had all these outfits just waiting to see the sun. You ALWAYS have a right to be different from how or who you were, if that is what is in your heart. You have a right to change your mind about your beliefs. You have a right to change political parties after learning more. You have a right to change the color of the bathroom, so don't let that be the reason you don't buy that house (*side-eyes all the shoppers on HGTV's House Hunters*).

Change: It's not optional. It's life's necessary and perpetual go-to that can break our hearts, make us scream, thrill us. It will challenge us and sometimes make us wonder if we can make it past the pains of it all. I think about young Fúnmiláyọ̀ and how many times life stretched her till she almost snapped. I wonder how she made it through constant change, and how many times she was afraid of taking the road less traveled but did it anyway. I think about one of her favorite scriptures, Psalm 61: "When my heart is overwhelmed: lead me to the rock that is higher than I." That is what I chant to myself in the times I'm called to grow beyond what feels feasible. I always end up on those high rocks, and I'm thankful.

12

FIRE YOURSELF

We fear losing control.

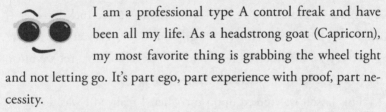 I am a professional type A control freak and have been all my life. As a headstrong goat (Capricorn), my most favorite thing is grabbing the wheel tight and not letting go. It's part ego, part experience with proof, part necessity.

As I've mentioned, my kryptonite is feeling like I am not in charge of situations, and that outcomes could depend on someone else's whims. It makes me uneasy.

Needless to say, this is not ideal when you live in a world with other people. Life is one giant group project, and our grade is largely dependent on other people's actions, since we're trapped in this giant web of other beings with two legs, two arms, and a brain. So I double down by insisting on driving every single thing I think I can. I bear-hug my responsibilities, afraid to be loose and lose. Kahlil Gibran said, "Our anxiety does not come from thinking about the future but from wanting to control it." A WHOLE WORD.

The fear of not being in control is real and normal. It's also a liability, truly. I got to that conclusion when I realized that I was adding to my own suffering by not accepting the fact that I am truly not in control of a lot of things. None of us are. It is a tough Achilles' heel to have, because life is a series of things that happen that we didn't see coming. God is the ultimate organizer, humans have free will, and even when we do our personal best, things can still go to hell in a handbasket.

As you know, people can be abominable. Pure walking compost. We can be shallow, fickle, and trifling. We give fellow humans plenty of reasons to not trust us. And if you are already someone who is cynical or prone to give side-eyes, when you see fuckshit everywhere you look, you tighten your grip on the things you care about. There is a lot of reason to be afraid of lack of control. Yet we must try to fight that fear. Because it is necessary.

This lesson was forced upon me when I realized I was doing so much that I constantly operated in a mode of exhaustion. But it wasn't a lesson I learned and then absorbed and stuck to. I've had to fire myself. I have to fire myself. I will have to fire myself. It is a constant struggle, like many of the lessons in this book.

There are three people I trust above all else in this world: me, myself, and I. I've spent a lifetime depending on myself, getting things done no matter what, and making the impossible seem easy. And it ain't just my story. You're probably reading this right now and nodding your head. I see you. I get you. I am you. I know that if something is in my hands, it will get handled. Olivia Pope is my mentor. Black women are my lucky charms and guiding lights. WE DOES THIS. That trust I have in myself has led to so many wins that my faith in myself is massive. It's why I'm harder on me than anyone else can ever be. It's why I think I could climb mountains if I really focused. It's why I wrote this book. I trust me so hard. That's ego.

But it can be a detriment. Self-reliance, just like anything else, can be a problem when there's too much of it. What we call independence and self-sufficiency is often us operating from a place of fearing chaos. What happens when we depend on other people and they let us down? What happens if we put something in someone else's hands and they drop the ball? What happens when we lose something because we trusted it to someone else? We run that scenario over and over again and find ourselves doing everything ourselves. But what is the consequence? What do we lose as we hold and juggle ten balls at once?

We can lose a lot. When we take on too much because we trust and depend on ourselves for a lot, we get overextended. We look at our plate and it looks tall. We look at our to-do lists and they look endless. We look at our lives and feel overwhelmed. Being a card-carrying member of Team Everything Falls on Me is exhausting. EGG-ZOS-TEEN.

You wake up one day and realize the dark circles under your eyes have claimed eminent domain, and that headache you used to get sometimes is now knocking all the time. You're stressed out, burned out, and tapped out. And you're cussing out the people closest to you for doing the smallest thing because every gahtdamb person is tap-dancing on your very last nerves. Oh just me? Fine.

But really. What are the consequences of us living life carrying responsibilities purely on our backs? Plainly, we tire ourselves out. The truly bad part is when being tired is so much our default that we no longer think of it as a negative thing. We think it just is. We deal because exhaustion in the rat-race world is normalized!

In our everyday lives, trying to control everything not only guarantees that we will ABSOLUTELY miss some things, but it can actually cost us more. We cannot do it all by ourselves, no matter how many planners we have or time-management apps we use. When we take on too much, no one thing can receive our full attention and things are bound to fall through the cracks, cracks we might not even know exist. We're running constant checklists in our heads and it's keeping our shoulders by our necks.

On occasions like these, life can sometimes force us to fire ourselves through circumstances beyond our control (yup), like aging, or accidents, or health issues. What happens then? We, Team I Do It All, find ourselves in a place that feels so foreign it might as well be Mars. A place where we are unable to do for ourselves. A place where we HAVE to depend on others, even for the most basic things.

I think about my grandmother. Mama Fáloyin was as self-reliant as they come. Fire herself? NEVER. Who? A whole her. No. She even used to tell my grandfather that she didn't need him, to remind him that she could handle whatever with or without his help. Grandpa was a man of few words, so he'd just blank-stare her till she tired herself out from ranting.

My grandmother became a widow in December 1991, four months after that epic sixtieth birthday bash. Life can be an insufferable bastard sometimes. As she got older, she began to rely more and more on her kids and grandkids. She got diagnosed with diabetes when she turned sixty-four, and had to start taking medication for the first time. The years went by and age made her shrink a bit physically, and she couldn't move around freely like she used to. A few years later, she had a stroke, and one of my aunts had to go to Nigeria to bring her to the United States to get treatment. The woman who used to hop on a plane to head anywhere, whenever she wanted, was now unable to even speak, let alone travel unaccompanied.

I remember visiting her in the hospital one day and being taken aback by how helpless and fragile she seemed. The fierce dynamo I was so accustomed to couldn't even feed herself. The tears came before I could stop them.

The doctor told us that she might never talk again, and I think my grandma took it as a dare. A couple months later, her speech was back to 100 percent. The stroke she wasn't supposed to recover from seemed like an extended hiccup. She walked a bit slower, but other than that, she was okay. But after that, my grandmother started letting people do things for her in a way she hadn't previously. It must have been a jarring thing for her to experience.

After she recovered here for a year, she wanted to be back at her own house doing her thing, so she returned to Nigeria. She had house help staying there with her, had other people running errands for her, and seemed less intense about controlling day-to-day things. My mom would call her and ask her what she was eating and if she was taking her meds. Before, Grandma might have been annoyed about being fussed over in that way, but by then, she realized it was a show of love.

It was another twelve years before we lost her. But whenever Mama Fáloyin was in the United States, she'd come and stay with us, even though we lived in a small apartment. My mom would regulate her food, meal planning for her to make sure she wasn't snacking as she liked—her sugar intake had to be leveled. Grandma couldn't go on her random shopping trips for hours like she used to (this was before everyone had cell phones, so we didn't want anything to happen and she couldn't reach us). When she got cataracts in both her eyes and couldn't get surgery on them until they matured, she needed my mom to help her arrange her pillbox.

I remember one day, she came to me and said, "Tell your mom I said thank you. She takes really good care of me. God will continue to bless her." It was with so much appreciation. I'm a useless somebody, though. I'm not sure I relayed the message. But my mother knew her mother's gratitude, because she heard it herself. This lifelong soldier had dropped the reins and allowed herself to be fully in the hands of someone else. It was a show of strength, in her moment of weakness, to surrender herself to someone she knew would not let her fall.

If love is a verb, is there a greater show of love than to abdicate your very being to the person you raised well enough to hold you up? What is pride when we can have love shown to us instead?

I hope that one day we are surrounded by people who we trust enough that we can let go of our control. I pray that I'll have lived a life that's so good, I'll be blessed with people who are a reflection of it. And those people, if needed, can be entrusted with my very life. I aspire to live in a way that I attract that favor.

On the professional side, we say we're chasing success when what we're really doing is chasing money. On the personal side, we think we're chasing happiness when what we're really doing is trying to fulfill other people's happiness, not ours. I had to redefine success for myself. A successful life is one lived on my own terms, not one where I end every day more tired than the last. And if everyone else around me is happy but I'm empty, then I have betrayed myself.

Empires of one do not exist, in business or in our intimate lives. Businesses aren't built with just one person. A family doesn't exist if only one person is in it. We cannot do any of this life thing alone, so we gotta learn how to let go quicker than we realize.

For years, I was a solo entrepreneur. (The only people I was paying on a regular basis were the IRS, and they came for 30 percent of my little coins every year without fail.) I was blogging on my site, freelance-writing for outlets, doing social media consulting, brand ambassadorships, event hosting. I was my own assistant, manager, publicist, accounts payable/receivable, editor, graphic designer, social media manager, chief operating officer. And of course I was CEO. "Tired" was my middle name but I called myself "grinding."

Then in 2015, I went on a vacation to Kenya with a group of my friends. Seven days of gallivanting with my girls was the plan, but I still managed to throw some work in the mix. I had a meetup with the Bloggers Association of Kenya one of the days and it was incredible. It was a sold-out event where I got to meet and talk to one hundred of my longtime readers in Nairobi.

The other piece of work I had to do was to write a recap of the TV show *Scandal* for *Vulture*. Around that time, my *Scandal* recaps were hugely popular, because my three-thousand-word synopses of each episode filled you in on everything you needed to know about the show, even if you didn't watch it. They were one of the most thorough on these interwebs, which is why they got much praise, even from Shonda Rhimes herself.

I told my editor that I would make it happen come hell or high water (heh). At 5 a.m. Kenya time, as everyone else slept, I was watching a feed of *Scandal* as it aired live in the United States. I needed to make my deadline.

At 8 a.m. as my crew woke up to get ready to go to the elephant orphanage, I told them they might have to go without me. My recaps took an average of three hours to write, and I was only halfway through at that point.

My friends decided to wait for me, even though the elephant orphanage closed at noon and I got my work done by 9:30 a.m. (**fist pumps**). After getting dressed and commuting, we got there at 11 a.m. I still hadn't slept BUT ELEPHANTS! However, I was exhausted. I was on vacation but I still couldn't afford to relax, because if I wasn't working, I wasn't making money. Being solo got old right then and there. I was almost too tired to enjoy this thing that I was so excited to do in a country I was seeing for the first time, because I had gotten no sleep. I knew I had to change things up.

That night when I watched my friends sleeping soundly, I was like, "Daaaang I'm jealous." Work-life balance is already a scam, but

I had none. It was all work cuz I was motivated by the ability to pay bills and buy shoes. The only way I could do that was to be on the clock, even while on the other side of the world.

One of the consequences of being a one-woman team? The inability to relax when it is needed. We can't be fully present at any moment because we're running checklists of things undone and remembering emails we didn't answer and projects we haven't pitched.

So what do we need to do? We need to fire ourselves from being the Responsible One. Firing yourself isn't about letting go of everything you do and letting everyone run through wildly. After all, you know I'm a fan of boundaries. Firing yourself is about finding people who you can rely on to do what they need to do.

So how do you do it?

CREATE SYSTEMS THAT CAN, AT LEAST, SIFT OUT THE OVERTLY BOGUS PEOPLE

When you fire yourself, learning to ask people for help when you need it is a good start (see chapter eight). But more important, know who to ask by paying attention to the people who show up for you over and over again. See who asks nothing much of you. Who offers to help you when you need it, not looking for payback? Who doesn't care whether you're Jenny from the Block or J.Lo?

There are people who have earned our trust and deserve to be allowed to show us love by doing acts of service for us. They are around us, waiting to be tapped in. But we're often so busy trying to get things done that we don't see them.

Professionally, have a hiring process that tries to sift out incompetence and laziness. Hiring is not a science but an art, and it is hard as shit. People have learned to interview well, so some folks will talk a good game. But focus on finding people who are passionate about the work you're doing, are willing to work hard, take initiative, and are forever students.

This part is tough if you're new to this, so . . .

BE OKAY WITH SUCKING AT THIS

I don't like not being good at things I do. And as much as I trust myself, I'm not good at everything, which really annoys me and my ego. So firing myself was hard and messy and is hard and messy and I'm still learning how to do it better.

One of the first things I did was get an assistant to handle emails for me. She was with me for four years and then she moved on. And then I went through five assistants in a year. Why? Because I still wasn't that good at delegating. My previous assistant was really good at finding things to do and filling the gaps I needed filled. But when it came time for me to have someone who wasn't so self-starting or intuitive, I bombed. I SUCKED at being a boss who gave expectations, deadlines, and whatnot. So I kept having people fail at their jobs, since I still was in "It's easier if I do it myself" mode. It was so frustrating.

We can all fall into the trap of "It's easier for me to do it than to teach someone else." Buuuut you can spend one hour a day doing something (accounting for five hours of your week every week) or you can spend five hours (one time) teaching someone what you need done, and now you have saved twenty hours' of work per month.

Accept that handing the reins over is not going to be easy. You might even feel like you're shirking your responsibility. "I should be the one doing this." Why should you? Is it only YOU who has the skills to do it? Check your ego. Unless the task is literally requiring your brain, someone else can do it, so it doesn't HAVE to be your responsibility.

As you let go, you will probably get on folks' nerves micromanaging, since you have an EXACT way you want it done. You might still try to exert control by dictating everything to a T, since that fear doesn't automatically go away just because you're doing something about it.

Do you want it done or do you want it perfect? Also, what is perfect anyway?

Note here: I am LITERALLY reading myself for filth right now. This whole section is for ME to reread because I gotta get my shit together regarding this. I'm a work in progress. Let's work on this together.

ACCEPT THAT PEOPLE WILL DROP THE BALL

The other thing you have to do is accept that people will disappoint you and mess up in some way. Your husband might forget to pick up the dry cleaning. Your assistant might spell someone's name wrong in an email. Your kid might not wash the dishes squeaky clean. People WILL do janky things on your behalf. This is inevitable and there's very little you can do to avoid it. Why? Because you do not control anyone else, even if you pay them or birthed them or decided to marry them. Even if your instructions were impeccable. It's probably gonna drive you up the wall when it happens.

Your job is not to automatically take the reins back when this occurs. You either decide to give grace because this person is otherwise reliable and this was a solitary mistake, or you reassign the task or job to someone else. If people make mistakes over and over again on your behalf, then yes, fire them from that thing. But instead of being the one to replace them at the helm, find someone else. Has this person made a massive mistake before? Is this a pattern or an exceptional moment that isn't common?

FORGIVE. RETRAIN. FIRE.

Those are your options. None of them are "Just do it yourself." On deadline? Sure, do it yourself this time. But after that, don't take it on! You don't have time! Let someone do it even if they won't do it as well as you would. Maybe doing it long enough gives them practice. Basically, give people a chance to fail instead of failing them before giving them that chance.

Besides, every mistake is not catastrophic. Every mistake is not going to erase all you've worked for. Every mistake does not hold equal weight. When they drop the ball, what was the real consequence? Did you lose money? An amazing opportunity? A chance to do terribly nasty and amazing things with Idris Elba? What did you lose?

Ask yourself if you can recover from it or if the damage was irreparable. And then determine if the person is holding themselves accountable and taking it seriously. Are they learning the lesson they need to learn so it doesn't happen again?

REMOVE THE GUILT

One of the hardest things to do is overcome the guilt we might feel when we realize we cannot do it all. We feel guilty because sometimes we make judgments about who we are and what we are worth based on what we can do for folks. But we're not being fair to ourselves when we do this. Yes, you need help. That's okay. No, you shouldn't be able to do it yourself. Yes, you are still supermom in whatever shape you find yourself today. You don't have to be the person with five arms who can vacuum, cook dinner, help with homework, and entertain all at once. Oh your mom was? Well, ask her how many times she wanted to jump out of a first-floor window onto soft grass and just lie there. That doesn't have to be your story.

Yes, you are still a boss if you aren't the person doing ALL the day-to-day work of operating the company. Actually, I think you are even more of a boss if you have a functional team.

Also, someone else's failure or lack of success or even lack of action should not lead to instant admonishment of ourselves. They messed up. Okay, was there a part we played in it? Did we not give the right instructions? Did we not prioritize it correctly? It doesn't matter. We gotta learn to let go of the need for control by understanding we don't control outcomes, even if we give the best training, the best love, the best cheat codes.

I think about the times when I've trusted someone to do something and they didn't. It's served as positive reinforcement of the habit of doing it all myself. "SEE?? I gave someone the chance and they let me down. I should have done it myself." Then I'll beat myself up because I shouldn't have even been in the situation. Then I get mad at me that I should have done it myself and stopped being lazy. When how the hell can I even think I'm lazy? Sis, who do you think you are, Storm? You're not an X-Man. You're not being lazy. You happen to have a lot of things to do, ma'am. Guilt will have you stuck on what you should have done instead of how to move forward, and it's not worth it.

TRUST THE COSMIC DESIGN

Above all, trust life. Yes, it's a raving douchecanoe at times. But trust the universe/God. Sometimes I think half my reason for believing in a deity is so I don't lose hope and think life is a random mixture of arbitrary instances and none of it has any structure. That might drive me mad. I choose to believe in a higher being as an anchor and a grounding. I don't think I have a choice but to have a deep belief that it will work out. It lets me get out of bed even when I'm feeling low.

If control is a mirage, trust that God will order your steps. Have faith that Allah will place the right people in your path: the helpers.

One of my favorite prayers when I'm about to walk into a new room is: "Please let my helper find me. Let me not miss the right connection I am supposed to make. Let me not miss the reason I am here."

Trust that the mistakes or hiccups or learnings are all to prepare you for the path you're walking. I believe that even when I've made hiring decisions that didn't work out, they were for the best. Each time made me look within and ask myself, "How can I be a better leader for the next person?" As a result, I'm a much more astute boss. Falling on my face over and over again in a revolving door of folks who didn't work out as I tried to fire myself was a mirror. I realized that I hadn't had the practice at this, but to build the empire I want and the impactful company I desire, I would have to develop skill sets I didn't have before.

ANNND if you're bad at firing yourself, hire someone who can help you do just that. There are all types of consultants who specialize in this. Fire yourself from firing yourself!

You can do all of this and it might still be hard. You might still wanna do it yourself. People will still disappoint you. You might trust the wrong person. None of this means you have to do it yourself. Get off that hamster wheel. Keep looking for the right person. They exist. The person who can assist you without fucking up basic calendar details is out there. The accountant who can file your taxes without getting you audited exists. The housekeeper who can come and clean, even if your apartment is just one bedroom, and leave your space so perfectly tidy that you wanna buy her a short set and matching bucket hat is in the world. The partner who will let you nap and take care of the kids so they don't destroy the house is somewhere. The babysitter who could tutor them in math, because common core is clearly an alien language, exists.

Firing ourselves doesn't mean we hand over our keys to the next random person we find and let them drive us into a wall. It means we move over, find people who are better suited to do what we need them to do, and we let them do it. Because right now, we're on hour thirty-two of the road trip, and we're still driving all by ourselves. We might have only stopped once to pee but dassit. Meanwhile, our eyes are bloodshot and our shoulders are by our necks and our stomachs are grumbling because we haven't had time to eat.

When we fire ourselves, it means we've pulled over to the parking lot of someone who is a really good and safe driver. We scoot over to the passenger's side as they get in. They drive and we catch up on sleep for a bit. We wake up, all is well, and our job is to keep the snacks coming and the music bopping. We end up at the place we wanted to go, well rested and ready for adventures. Plus, we enjoyed the journey and the open road and were able to appreciate all we took in.

Fire yourself. Move over. Let the wheel go.

One of the things that has gotten me to this point in my career has been my consistency and my grind. I have pushed through and delivered time and time again with my writing, especially on my main website. But now? I'm clear that I can't do that anymore. I can't put life on pause to meet certain deadlines anymore. I'm pulling my

OG card and firing myself from the expectation of always being on call. I have paid my dues and now I am building a team of folks around me to help manage it all. This empire of ONE is done, personally and professionally.

I need help. And that's okay. You need help? That's okay. You don't think you need help? Get help anyway.

Maybe you have to be a team of one by necessity. Maybe it's because every dime you make, you try to magically stretch it to a dollar to live, pay your necessary bills, and maybe have some left over to buy a pair of shoes every six months or something. Maybe you want to fire yourself but don't have the means. I see you and I was you. And I hope one day, in this unfair capitalist nightmare we find ourselves in, you happen to make enough to get you the help you need. In the meantime, I hope you shed the guilt of not being able to get everything done all the time. I hope you are gentle on yourself when you drop a ball. I hope you give yourself grace when you cannot handle everything facing you.

Fire yourself from the expectation that you should be Superwoman or Thor.

Fire yourself from the mom guilt that says you have to somehow create magic every day for your little broke best friends.

Fire yourself from the scolding you usually give yourself when you look at your bank account and see it isn't where you want it to be.

I see the quote that folks use to "inspire" others to do more: "Beyoncé has the same 24 hours a day as you." No, she doesn't. Even Beyoncé wouldn't tell you that. She might have 240 hours in her day because she has ten people doing various things for her life to run smoothly.

Do not let social media highlight reels make you feel bad for being a tired and fed-up team of one. Don't let folks guilt you for not getting to items 3 to 10 on your to-do list because you spent the day juggling allthethings and ran out of time. Do not think your job is to become more productive in a world that makes it really hard to get things done if you aren't part of the 1 percent.

I've been writing online and professionally for almost twenty years. I've been working for myself full-time for eleven years. The time I spent being a team of one has taught me a lot, made sure I can juggle seven balls at once, AND has been my proof that I CAN do this. But there can no longer be just me. I need to sleep more. The "sleep when I die" mantra is not cute. No, I need to sleep NOW.

We have to be vulnerable and know that we are always risking being heartbroken or burned. Yet and still, we must charge forward. We have a finite amount of time in our days and lives. We simply need more people. We have to drop the ball and give other people the chance to gift us with their time and services.

FIRE YOURSELF. Outsource some of your life. Because you know what won't be cute on a tombstone? "Her grind was impeccable and she did it all by herself." We have no one to prove anything to. Especially those of us who have established ourselves for over a decade. What other receipts do we need to show? We have to fire ourselves from being all things to all people today so we can have room to become the kickass future people we gotta be.

It is time. Build your team. Find your helpers. Get some more sleep.

13

TAKE NO SHIT

We fear ruffling feathers.

We are afraid of being ostracized in any way by the people around us, and we fear coming across as difficult, because at our core, we want community. We want to be liked and we want people to think we are nice. Whether we're kids or full grown, acceptance by other humans is a need, because it is how we are hardwired. So we try our best to do what others will consider palatable or cordial or amiable.

As a result, we swallow our words and our feelings down while plastering a smile on our face, even when we want to scream. We acquiesce to people and then spend our lives being constantly devalued and disrespected. In our need for acceptance, forced niceness ends up doing us a major disservice, as we prioritize others' wants above ours.

When I wrote *I'm Judging You*, some people said: "You wrote a book admitting that you're judging people?" And I said, "Yes, because I am." We're all actually judging each other. The problem is we're judging each other on the things that make no sense: what we look like, who we love, the religion we practice, the color of our skin, the gender we say we are.

Instead, we should be judging on other things: Are we showing up in the world in the best way possible? Are we being kind? Are we making sure that we're holding ourselves accountable for other people too? When I say I'm judging you, I'm not judging you because of what you look like; I'm judging you by who you actually are.

I think that we are often wasting our time trying to be nice. Why? Because humans are fickle beings. People are consistently inconsistent about what they want, so when we base our actions on the end goal, which is to be considered nice or anything else, it can be for naught. There is no way you can guarantee that somebody will like you. In the words of Elyana Rausa, "You are not required to set yourself on fire to keep other people warm." So what's the point of trying so hard?

When we go out of our way to people-please, it feels like a trauma response. It's as if we are placing our value on being as agreeable as we can be in order to be loved or accepted. It is often self-betrayal.

There is nothing wrong with wanting to be "nice," but I don't think that should be our goal. Granted, I'm not saying walk around with the intent of being an asshole. Nah. But being seen as cordial should not be the main motivator of our behavior.

Instead, I think we should aspire to be kind. To be kind is to be generous, fair, honest, helpful, altruistic, gracious, tolerant, understanding, humble, giving, vulnerable, magnanimous, service-driven. To be nice is to smile a lot and be chatty with random strangers. Nice is talking about the weather. Kind is caring about whether someone has an umbrella in case it rains.

People have niceness and kindness mixed up. Niceness might mean saying positive things. But kindness is doing positive things: being thoughtful and considerate, prioritizing people's humanity over everything else.

I don't exist in this world for someone to describe me only as "nice" when I'm not in the room. Nice can be empty and shallow and passive. Nice tells me nothing about someone when that is the only thing that is used to describe them. If I ask someone about you and their strongest statement is "She's nice," then I'll assume you're a walking doormat. Or you're someone who is always smiling, even in the moments of strife, which feels dishonest. It says to me that I might need to question you more on how you're really feeling. It tells me nothing of note. Nice is the saltine cracker of adjectives; it's bland.

When we're always trying to be nice, we take a lot of shit and deal with a lot of people's awful behavior, and we don't hold them accountable. We end up being at the other end of unjust things more than we should, because in our politeness, we relegate our own feelings to the bottom of the barrel.

We don't have to do any of that to be loved. We don't have to bend ourselves backward to have the people who matter see us and cherish us. Even if you're cantankerous, you can still find folks who will stan you!

Mama Fáloyin was one of the kindest people I've ever met. She was also super feisty and took no shit, and people knew that. If anyone tried her, she'd get all Queen Bee on them and sting. But her heart was huge and to her, everyone was a neighbor she was responsible for. If people were in a bind, they'd knock on her door, and she would listen to them, help if she could, and send them off with a Tupperware of food and a truly meant prayer of "God bless you, ọmọ mi" (my child).

When she died, she died loved by droves of people. There were all sorts of dignitaries and people who had known her closely for decades paying their respects. Granny was Team No Chill, and she was adored. She wasn't a woman who felt the need to placate others if that wasn't her real thought in the moment.

Some of the stories I've heard about her are legendary, especially from when she was younger, before I was even born. When my mom was in elementary school, her teacher took some scissors to her hair, as punishment for her not having her homework done. My grandma flipped out! The next day, she took my mom to school herself, while holding scissors. She got there and asked for the teacher. Why was Grandma there with scissors? Because she said since the lady cut her child's hair, she was there to cut the teacher's hair too. She was dead-ass serious. It took ten people kneeling down in front of Grandma, begging her and invoking God's mercy, for her to abandon the mission and go back home. That teacher never tried anything else with any of the Fáloyin kids again.

My grandma could have let it slide, but you know what would have happened if she had? The teacher would have thought it was okay to keep doing extreme things like this. This is why I push back against the constant encouragement to take the high road when we are harmed. I think some high roads need to stay under construction.

Let's talk about taking the high road, because it is definitely a thing people tell us we should do to somehow be the better person. You know the one time I disagreed with my fave Michelle Obama was when she said, "When they go low, we go high." Honestly, when people go low, sometimes we have to meet them there. If you go low, I might go gutter.

I am not a fan of asking folks to turn the other cheek in situations where they shouldn't feel obligated to do so. On certain occasions, the insistence on taking the high road is actually harming us more than it's helping. Putting harmony over justice and civility over amends is a harmful practice if we are telling people to constantly bypass defending themselves or standing against what is awry. I'm not for the kumbaya of it all. People read that Jesus told us to turn the other cheek and love our neighbors, but that is the SAME person who also flipped tables in a temple when folks did too much.

The need for niceness permeates how we move through the world, address those in our daily lives, and even combat systems that don't serve us. We are always trying to be "civil" above all else.

In June 2018, America's forty-fifth president (and the first walking Cheeto in the White House) signed an executive order that led to the separation of migrant children and their parents at the United States border. The people's champ and forever truth-teller, Maxine Waters, was very vocal in her rightful critique about it, saying: "We don't know what damage has been done to these children. All that we know is they're in cages. They're in prisons. They're in jails. I don't care what they call it, that's where they are and Mr. President, we will see you every day, every hour of the day, everywhere that we are to let you know you cannot get away with this."* NO LIES TOLD. The next day, her own party called her comments "divisive." If the truth is divisive, then what it is pointing out must be what is especially repugnant. Chuck Schumer said, "We all have to remember to treat our fellow Americans, all of our fellow Americans, with the kind of civility and respect we expect will be afforded to us." Sir, those kids in cages aren't being treated with ANY type of civility, so please have a fucking seat.

When will people realize that niceness and taking the high road are not going to save us? You don't make change by being civil to the people who are not looking at other people as full humans. Being nicer about how you're talking about Trump is not doing anything. There's a thin line between being nice and enabling bullshit.

If we can't put justice over niceness, what are we doing as a people? Where are we going to end up if we continue to turn the other cheek when somebody harms us? The people who harm us are not being told to be civil or nice or to take the high road. It's always the person who's been victimized in some way who is told to make that choice. Does that serve us? We're going to be civil and we're going to nice our way into bondage.

Here's the thing about villains and people who harm us. Usually when somebody does something to you that is not just disrespectful but harmful to you as a person, you're already past the point of civility. This person isn't looking at you as a full human being. You can't change their behavior or affect the outcome by being really nice

---

*Jamie Ehrlich, "Maxine Waters Encourages Supporters to Harass Trump Administration Officials," CNN, June 25, 2018, https://www.cnn.com/2018/06/25/politics/maxine-waters-trump-officials/index.html.

about it. This is why people who insist on politeness miss the point. All this "We should be nicer" gets us nowhere, because if people wanna take offense to our words, they will find a reason. Nah, I'm not nice. Yes, I will challenge your bullshit.

Why do people prioritize civility over justice? Justice does not come just because you're begging for it. Justice does not come because you're being nice about the other person who's not giving you justice. So I don't understand the insistence on this high road.

When you are in a fight for your life, when you're in a fight for the world, when you're in a fight against something like white supremacy, how sweet your tone is won't be a factor in getting basic rights. You don't civil your way to justice.

And when we talk about folks protesting in the streets, people get mad because "Well it's not orderly how people protest." When half of the country is wishing for immigrants to be separated from their family members and we're being told to be civil about it, what is civility doing for us? What is this niceness doing? We're prioritizing the wrong thing.

Someone (some thing, some system, some power structure) convinced us that if we were more civil or respectable or dressed nicer, we'd be more worthy of justice or love or good things. We are worthy of all those things TODAY. Now. Even when we cuss and swear and we don't form our sentences perfectly. Even if we aren't buttoned up. Even if we mess up sometimes.

I want us to push past the idea that civility or niceness is the key. Fights are not about politeness. I'm not saying we have to be assholes to everybody. I'm not saying we have to walk around being angry. I'm saying that when it's time for us to challenge systems and people, how we say it should not nullify the message. We can still be kind, but we do not have to be nice. And our needs and wants are valid even if we don't express them neatly.

We need to TAKE NO SHIT, and if you need permission to do that, consider this that.

This doesn't mean you address everyone who brings trash to you or says something about you. You don't have that kind of time. It also doesn't mean you accept every invitation to fight. Nah. It means in the times when it's called for, and you will know those times, do not feel bad for meeting someone in the basement. This doesn't mean you're a bad person or you're immature. It means you made a decision to engage with someone as they asked for it. Sometimes a good "BITCH WHO DO YOU THINK YOU'RE TALKING TO?" is warranted. Sometimes you gotta remind people that messing with you comes with a cost. It be like that, and folks gotta deal. And sometimes, taking no shit might even look like silence to the person who is trying to force you to pay attention to them.

We've spent so much time telling people to be nice and civil that we feel like we have no room to defend ourselves in a world that's constantly at war with us. You don't owe anyone civility if they have traumatized you. Nor do you owe them a hello, even in person. They can take this full side-eye.

I am calling on us to challenge ourselves to be more truthful, to be more outspoken. Be kinder, speak louder. Use your voice and don't let people silence you or make you feel bad because they don't see what you're doing as civil or nice. Fight for people who are not you. Insist on being uncomfortable and taking yourself outside your usual space to fight for other people who might not have the right to fight, or the voice, or the money, or the stature, or the positioning. That's kindness.

I aspire to be kind, and I hope my actions are kind. I hope when I'm gone, someone somewhere describes me as such, because my life is a journey in giving as much as I've received. Kind is compassionate. And we can be kind and generous, but we need to take no shit. The first person we need to be kind to is ourselves.

Grandma was Team Take No Shit. When she was younger, there was a time when she was taking a seminar at her church to go up in the ranks. She was the first woman allowed to even take it, so it was a big deal! When she completed all the requirements for it and called the church to say she was coming for her plaque, the pastor said he wasn't going to give it to her. The moment Grandma heard that, she hulked up, put on some pants, and rode to that church. See, Mama Fáloyin didn't wear pants often. She was usually in a dress or caftan. She only wore pants for two reasons: Because she was cold. Or because she needed to fight.

Well, when she showed up at the church in her fighting pants, the pastor didn't want the smoke, so he went into his office and locked the door. Who born him to say NO to her getting what she had earned?

What did Mama Fáloyin do? She stood in front of his office door and refused to leave. "You can be in there all day but I'll be out here waiting. I'm not going anywhere until he gives me my certificate."

My grandfather, who was usually the peacekeeper, backed her up and said, "You better give it to her. She will be here all day and I will be right here behind her." I STAN a supportive bae! Long story short, she walked out of that church with what she came for. The pastor, who wasn't used to any of that, learned on that day that Fúnmiláyọ̀ Ọmọ Láṣórè is not one to trifle with.

They cherished her at that church. If she was missing from church for too many weeks in a row, they'd send a contingent to go visit her to see if she was doing okay or check on whether they'd somehow offended her. But really, they loved her dearly.

When my grandmother died in 2011 in Nigeria, the high-ranking women in her church insisted on being the ones to dress her, instead of the morticians. They wanted her to have the utmost care as she was prepared. They wanted to send her off with love.

We traveled to Nigeria as a family to give her a proper send-off. I was in the room as Mama Fáloyin got her last bath. I remember trying to take in everything that was happening, because I didn't want to miss anything about it. I was acutely aware of the fact that I was bearing witness to a sacred space and ritual. Even as the chemicals in the room made it hard to breathe, I dared not move. The tears that streamed down my face weren't just from the formaldehyde—they were also my grief and gratitude.

I remember staring at the body of the person who was the prototype of womanhood for me. As they dressed her, they prayed over her. It was done with such care, too, putting her in one of the white gowns she wore for church (a sutana) that my aunt picked out. They draped one of her favorite purple sashes over her with sanctity. My heart throbbed because it was the utmost display of love. My goodness. To be cherished and respected like that, having lived openly, freely, totally. I was affirmed by it because it was the pinnacle of a life well lived.

She did it on her own terms, even when she was painted into corners. She did it joyfully and genuinely, fiery and full of moxie.

A life well lived is not one where you made sure the rooms you were in didn't have friction. A life well lived isn't about plastering a fake smile on your face. A life well lived is not about how many people you did not upset. A life well lived is one where you commit to being kind. Where you connect your humanity to that of others, and it shows in the way you move through the world. And that's what we gotta do.

We will ruffle feathers. We might be the villains in a few people's stories. We might even blow up a few bridges. But our worth is not based on how much we acquiesced to the people we knew. The goal is to betray ourselves less.

So, be kind but take no shit.

14

BUILD A SQUAD

We fear betrayal.

 Although we spend our lives looking for the approval of others, we are also afraid of building community outside of our families. I have come across a lot of people who hail the fact that they are movements of one and don't roll with a squad. We know those people. Sometimes, we ARE those people.

But the thing is, we NEED people.

Humans are not meant to do life alone. Even the most introverted and crotchety of us are not meant to be recluses, living life away from everyone with no one to turn to. When people are imprisoned, there is a reason why the biggest punishment is solitary confinement. To lock a person away from all human contact is to torture them.

We need people to cheer for us, encourage us, challenge us, scold us, love us, be there for us. But we are afraid to need people. We are afraid of community. What are we afraid of when we don't embrace this need?

We are afraid of being deceived or double-crossed. We do not want to be betrayed, and the fear of that hurt often keeps us from squadding up in the way we need to. We are also afraid of being rejected, and that's a form of betrayal, ain't it? We are afraid of giving people the power to punch us in the proverbial chest because we've let them get close. Some of us have parents who have beat it into our heads to "trust no one." We carry their traumas as ours. We wear their fears as ours before we can even understand the world in its most basic ways.

To squad up is to form community with people who aren't our blood. It is to create bonds and friendships and acquaintanceships with others, allowing them access to us. That access is tied by nothing but free will, and it can be revoked at will. THAT scares us. Our family? Well, they're kinda obligated to stick around through our bullshit, but no one else is. That means we're beholden to the whims of other humans who we've grown attached to.

Like a lot of our other fears, this one is valid and earned. Humans can be dishonest, selfish, self-centered, and all that other jazz. They give us many reasons to wanna lock ourselves in dark rooms and say nothing to anyone ever again. So I totally understand why someone could be of the team "no new friends." Or "no friends at all." Sometimes the drama that people bring into our lives tempts us into thinking, "Fuck everyone. I'ma just be by myself." I get it.

Yet, we can't surrender to this temptation. We absolutely need to squad up, and we need to do it outside our bloodlines. It's a crapshoot, and some of us luck out while others end up with the worst guides ever. Since we don't get to choose our original kin, those we choose to become our family are key guides in this life journey.

The communities we belong to are an important part of our identity. They TEACH us what is acceptable, respectable, or tolerable, from the way we dress to the music we listen to, to the things we consider our core beliefs. None of your friends smoke? Well, you'll be less likely to. None of your friends have a master's degree? Where do you even start if you want to get yours? All your friends dress like members of the Addams Family? Then your seersucker shorts will probably seem out of place.

Our lives are one big group decision, try as we may to seem utterly unmoved by others' whims. It's a chicken or the egg syndrome. Do we select who we hang out with based on who we are, or do we become who we are based on who our friends are? Although it might be scary to think about others having this much control over us, I say we accept it and use it to our benefit.

My grandma was an alpha woman in every way. She got married by choice, and didn't lose herself in the identity of "wife of Emmanuel." In a period when women being hit by their husbands wasn't just okay but the norm, that wasn't her experience. I don't think my grandfather was that dude, but if he had any temptation to be that dude, I'm sure he was out of it. Grandma could BOX. She came from a family of fighters. She was Nigerian Miss Sofia, and according to stories I've heard, my grandpa used to shake his head and say he just got out of her way when she was upset.

Once in Nigeria, she was in the car as my uncle drove and one of my aunts was in the front seat. They got cut off by a driver, and instead of him being apologetic, he started cussing at them. My uncle pulled over and got out. You'd think my grandmother would have been the peacekeeper. NOPE. This woman jumped out the car herself, grabbed the driver by his shirt, and threatened to slap him and the person who was in the car with him. At the end of it all, the driver and his passenger ended up prostrating themselves at her feet to apologize for disrespecting her.

How did she become this chick? Well, having to fend for herself since the age of eighteen probably made her grow some seriously tough skin. And somewhere along the way, she curated a squad of other tough-ass, take-no-shit Nigerian women. Married or not, these women LIVED. They didn't discourage her from taking up space. In fact, her crew of fellow professional troublemakers hyped her up and affirmed her in the times when she had to put on pants and let someone have it! At her sixtieth birthday, they were right next to her, in their own specific fabric, looking like the proud, territorial friends we all want. I think they all coordinated their "sunglasses even though it's nighttime" look.

Bold women rock with other bold women because we create space for each other and affirm identities society is usually so quick to denounce. We normalize each other's bravado, which allows us to step into the world with confidence. It's almost to the point where if you don't stand up with your head tall, you'll feel slightly out of place. The badassery of my friends usually reminds me who the hell I am and why I need to keep my chin square, and that is a gift I've gratefully received and will continue to.

The people we are surrounded by really do affirm our lives and our decisions. They can peer-pressure us into being and doing better, because seeing them up close can inspire us to know what's possible.

I hate working out because it feels like trash during and especially after, and, like I said earlier, anyone who says it feels good is a liar and a cheat. Even with that core belief, sometimes I work out strictly because my friends are working out. Sure, I could do it because it is good for my heart health and yada yada, but sometimes I don't want to be left out and that's what gets me to do those thousand jump ropes.

You also need a strong village to hold you up in the times when you can't. If people demean you or make you feel like you aren't worth loving or defending, your squad will remind you of who you are. If you doubt everything you know about you, they bring you back to what you stand for. The real ones don't go running after you fall on your ass. Who is there taking your hand and pulling you back on your feet? Remember them.

My accomplishments might be half because of my drive and the other half because I don't come from half-stepping people. The people who I love do amazing shit, so that's also my job. If they were slackers, maybe I'd feel less pressure to always GO. Without competition or envy, we can compare ourselves to them with the lens of "Well if it's possible for her, it's possible for me." My crew normalizes winning.

As I discussed in chapter one, it is integral that we know whose we are. Who do we come from? Who do we claim? Who do we belong to? This WHO isn't just about the last names we carry or the legacy of our lineage. I firmly affirm the fact that I belong to a crew of dope-ass friends too.

Entrepreneur Jim Rohn made popular the idea of "You are the

sum of the five closest people to you." This rings true to me. Even if that number isn't five, I am the sum of the villages of people who have surrounded me throughout my life. How far I've been able to go has been directly tied to those people. How smooth or rocky my journey has been is because of those people. How big I dream has been because of their confidence.

Even beyond the gassing up of each other, I find so much value in how my friends are my greatest challengers. We take "my sister's keeper" and "my brother's keeper" literally. Part of the reason is because we are representations of the people we claim. We represent WHOSE we are.

We challenge each other because if I'm your keeper, your under-skirt can't be showing on my watch. Your mistake can't go unchecked; otherwise I'm leaving your back wide-open, when I said I got it. It's about holding each other accountable and calling each other in (not out) when we fall on our faces. If you're making piss-poor decisions, your friends should be able to pull you by your collar and tell you to get your shit together. A friend group that does that is a gift, and will always ensure that we are being the version of ourselves that we'll be proud of. Otherwise, we'll have to answer to them, and we don't want that smoke.

There are so many rewards to building a proper village that the accompanying fear isn't worth it. Throughout my life, I've felt betrayed and abandoned and rejected by people who I let into my life. We've all felt it. It's knocked me on my ass a few times. But I also think about what others have done for me or said to me that has lifted me up or pushed me forward. Those moments beat any of the betrayals. Those times attest to the need to never harden myself completely.

When I say "build a squad," I don't mean "make everyone your best friend." We can have multiple squads, all with different purposes and proximity. I have multiple groups of friends who I've met in different times of my life, in different spaces, who serve different purposes. Some people might exist in multiple squads. That's okay too.

Part of the reason why people struggle with friendships (and relationships, for that matter) is that they expect everyone in their lives to fulfill all their needs. We expect friends to mentor us, play hard with us, challenge us, be our shoulders to cry on. Yes, our friends are supposed to do that, but no one or two people can do or be all of that for you. You have to spread that responsibility around.

We are less likely to experience the deep betrayals and the rejections if we understand that people serve certain purposes and not everyone can be in the same role with the same expectations.

I think there are five types of squads that we all need.

1. THE DAY ONES

The Day Ones are the friends you've had since you were younger, before the glow up or whatever it is that people know you for now. They are the ones who can pull out embarrassing pics of you at any time, since they have ample. They remember when you had the snaggleteeth and can humble you in a hot second. Remember when you had chicken pox in the eighth grade? They do! They have the proof. They also might call you by a nickname that no one else knows now. Y'all went to elementary or high school together or grew up in the same neighborhood. These are the people who knew you when none of you had agendas and when all of you were a mess, and they couldn't care less what you do now.

Why is it important to have these people? Because they're a mirror of who you were. They give you perspective, and as you're going to conferences or meeting new people or getting promotions, they are a reminder of how far you've come, and of the person you used to be when you were still dreaming of who you are today. No matter how successful your Day Ones get, the fact that you can reminisce and tell old stories that make you all laugh till you snort is clutch. Having the people who knew you when you had nothing or still wore jersey dresses is important because it's a grounding force.

2. THE PROFESSIONAL CREW

These are the people you've met along the way who you've bonded with in a professional setting. Work husbands and work wives fall under this category. Y'all might have met at an internship or at a job or some industry cohort group. Y'all grab coffee together or go to the bar after work. They might cover for you when you miss an important meeting or give you a heads-up about a project the company is working on that could lead to an advancement for you. These people met you in a place where you were looking to level up or get those checks and go.

Your shared experience makes these friends important, because they can look out for you on the business front. And all that time spent together means you can vent to them about work things that you might not want to bore anyone else with. They can be a key part of growth because they'll have access to insights no other groups of your friends would. That alone makes them essential.

3. THE MENTORS

Mentors are the business version of "not your little friends." They are essential because even though they aren't your peers, they can be life rafts. Mentors might take the form of a college professor who became your favorite thought leader, an old boss who championed your work and made sure you got your next position, or someone you met at a conference, had great conversation with, and now have access to. Because mentors care about your life even outside of the business (because your personal life absolutely affects your career), you confide in them. They're friends as well as guides.

Mentors are incredible, because they can unlock doors in our lives. They can make our dreams more tangible, because they are invested in our success. We need a new job? Well, they might be able to make a phone call to someone who then makes a phone call to get us the interview we need to be considered. They actively ask, "How can I help?" without necessarily expecting anything.

The domino effect mentors have is amazing. It was a mentor of mine (Barbara Allen) who nominated me for the Chicago inaugural chapter of New Leaders Council, which I got accepted for. It was there that I wrote a vision statement, three months before I got fired/laid off from my job, that allowed me to see my dreams on paper.

And many of those dreams have been realized. Barbara nominated me simply because she thought it would be good for me to have that cohort experience. My mentors have brought up my name in rooms and gotten me opportunities I wouldn't be able to get myself. They have opened locked doors.

4. THE PLAY GROUP

Your Play Group is the squad that you travel with, party with, kick it with. Y'all hang out to turn up, relieve stress, and have adventures. A lot of times, you meet this crew in college, where the union parties are plentiful, and when sweating your hair out in a too-hot club was your idea of a great night. They might have held your arms at one point as you grinded into some off-balance dude.

The Play Group is a part of your self-care routine, because they remind you that life is fun. Maybe now you're doing less weekend barhopping and more getting drunk at someone's house on a Wednesday. Still, these are the people who allow you to blow off steam without judgment. They are important, because they balance everything else.

5. THE TRUE BLUES

We've all heard that if you end up with two or three people in this category, consider yourself blessed, which is a word. The besties are an important subgroup and everyone ain't that.

The True Blues are the people who know where all the bodies are buried, because they were probably right there with the shovel next to us. We can be our truest selves with them, without pretense or angst. They've seen us at our worst but hold space for us to make it back to our best selves. They will fight for us, even without our permission. They will come to our house and open our fridge like they live there. Your mom probably asks you how they're doing once a month, and sometimes she doesn't because they've called her already. The inside jokes are aplenty, and they've seen you in the morning when you still had eye crusties.

Our True Blues aren't automatically people we've known the longest. They are people who showed up somehow, at some point, and barreled their way into our hearts. We don't know how to NOT trust them, because they've shown us over and over again that they are here to stay. Sometimes they'll disappoint us and upset us, because we are all flawed. But friendship isn't about perfection.

Each of these groups is essential to having a well-rounded village and is fundamental to our well-being. And these groups are dynamic. Just because someone started in one box doesn't mean that is where they will remain. I have a few friends I met professionally who became True Blues over time.

Also, each group plays different roles and fills a different gap. Maybe the Professional Crew isn't the one we tell about our frustration with our partners. Maybe the Play Group isn't who you want to pour on about why you want to quit your job. Maybe the True Blues don't wanna go out partying all the time. But there are people we have who fall into one or more (or all) of these categories, and if so, that is TRULY amazing. A Day One who you ended up working with who loves to kick it as much as you AND happens to be slightly older and more accomplished? What are the odds? Tiny.

You have to be okay putting people in boxes and not stressing them out to be anything but who they are. Not everyone is equally invested in our lives and well-being, even if they are our friends. If one group can't understand, another one of those groups will.

Conflicts will arise, but friendship doesn't mean zero discord. Commitment through thick and thin doesn't just apply to marriage but to friendships too. You will drop the ball and disappear from time to time because life happens to you, but one mistake or missed birthday does not mean you are disposable. Similarly, your friends will do the same. But when things arise that don't work, talk through them, even if it means a tough conversation. Sometimes you can move forward, and other times you might not be able to.

Do I have Day Ones I no longer speak to? For sure. Have I had professional friends become public enemies? A few. Do I have mentors who sometimes disappear after they feel like I've climbed higher than they can help? Absolutely. From each, I try to inspect myself for my part in the breakdown, as nothing is ever truly one-sided. And I try to figure out how I can be better the next time. It is always tempting to wanna take my friendship ball, lock the park, and go home. But if I had done that in 2006 when a close friend sent me an email to end our friendship, I wouldn't have been emotionally available to meet the friend who would later become a True Blue, who moved mountains for me at a time when I truly needed it.

That being said, there will be times when you need to let go of someone completely. How do you know who to cut loose? When the thought of this person stresses you out, it might be time to cut them off. And if this person makes you feel bad about who you are, they might need to get kicked out the community. This is different from the person who's challenging you and telling you to fix mistakes. But if they make you feel bad about who you are and they're mean to you, let them go. If you can't depend on this person in a time of crisis, you might have to step back from them, and that's okay.

I'm super loyal, so it's hard for me to cut people off. But when I have to do it, it's because I realized this person no longer wishes me well, or there's something about this person that I double-guess, which makes it hard for me to be straightforward and open. Or maybe we naturally drifted apart.

Everyone ain't gonna to come on this life journey with us, and the friends we have today will not necessarily be the friends we have tomorrow. As we get older, our friendships change. We leave some people behind.

When we fear squadding, we fear betrayal, and it's real. Do not trust EVERYONE. Sure. But "trust no one" is the quickest way to build titanium walls that no one can break through. Either we learn to let the moat down for those who are allies, or we keep the wall up, protecting ourselves from both the ones who want to see us fall, and the ones who will fight for us to keep us standing. Sure, walls keep the villains out, but they also keep the heroes out. In the process of being vigilant against the sheisters, we keep ourselves from connecting with the best people. So I take the risk. I am cautiously open, choosing to trust people until proven otherwise.

Even with all that, the friends lost, the feelings of betrayal, I am where I am today because of the FRAMILY I've been able to have. As I've risen in my career, it sometimes feels like I'm in rarefied air. It can feel lonely to step into spaces where I am the ONLY or one of two. But I walk in there on the backs of my sisters and it is an invisible security blanket.

The best-case scenario is to find friends to cleave to and rise with together. Compare notes, be sounding boards and sometimes jumping boards. If or when you fall, be buffers for each other. People can be everlasting buffoons at their worst, but at their best, they are the soft place for us to land.

So how do you do this? How do you build this community of people?

Be intentional with building a squad that will ride for you, challenge you, hold you accountable, and pick you up in the valley moments. Let the record show this doesn't mean stalking people. Please don't go out here saying Luvvie told you "be intentional," which translated to "bug people until they are tired and finally say yes to you." I didn't say that! Okay great, I've clarified.

Friendship isn't about keeping score for who is a better friend to who, or who has done the other more favors. It's about showing up as needed, to the best of your ability and capacity. It's about the action of it all. Friendship by word alone is empty and pointless. Simply be willing to show up, especially in times of need.

In order to be the friend you would want, you also need to be willing to be vulnerable. That fear we have of betrayal is legitimate, but we cannot let it keep everyone around us at arm's length. If we do, they won't know who we are, what we need, and how dope we can be. Without opening up, how can we show and receive the love we need to and from our comrades? Knowing it's a risk shouldn't stop us from being our full selves. If our friendships end, at least we know it's not because we didn't do our part.

I also believe in quality over quantity. I know they say if you have two good friends, you're lucky. Well, I feel really lucky because I definitely have more than two, but I think it's because over the years I've been able to also do work on myself to make myself a good friend. When we talk about friendship, it has to be reciprocal, right? You can't just be expecting good friendships when you're not a good friend yourself.

To be a member of a valuable squad, you gotta ditch your spirit of competition. There is a not-so-thin line between being inspired by our friends' success and being jealous of it. Are you the friend who isn't threatened by someone else's win? Are you the person who can cheer loudly because you're genuinely happy for your friend's success? If you aren't, then worry less about how to get a dope squad and more about becoming that person. Do that work.

And to have the powerhouse squad of your dreams, make sure you are leveling up yourself. I've been asked a lot how I have made such powerful friends, and folks have asked me what I did to get them. I leveled up on myself and my work and started ending up in dope rooms and getting dope opportunities that led me to meeting dope people. The key is *I* leveled up. I got better. Got more grown. Got doper. You attract who you are. I didn't force friendships.

You also have to make sure you are vouchable. What's that? Well, make it easy for your squad to be your walking Yelp. Don't make it difficult for people to recommend your presence in the room. When people say "it costs nothing" to speak someone's name up, I low-key disagree. If I'm speaking you up, it's an explicit recommendation. If you're someone who will drop the professional ball I passed to you, now my name and my judgment get tainted. My friends know they can recommend me for a paid gig and I will show up and kill! Similarly, when I speak them up in their absence, it is with confidence that they will deliver spectacularly. You are my friend, and you're not necessarily entitled to my platform, but if you're doing dope stuff, I'm going to talk about it. I'm going to use that platform because I know you won't embarrass me for putting my stamp on you. When building your friendship dream team, look for the people who believe in your work but do the work themselves too.

Our friends are part of the fabric of our lives. Pick the best people you know and hold on to them. Curate a crew of people who cheer you on, challenge you, check on you, and are committed to creating an awesome life with you. Recognize the people who are great at gassing you up, not watering you down.

Find your people. Hold them close. And know you belong somewhere. While you do that, rise together.

15

GET A NIGERIAN FRIEND

We fear the savagery.

 Nigerians are world-renowned loudmouths who happen to exist in every place on earth, roll deep, and have a reputation for cleverness. We are legion, so hear us roar.

I think everyone needs a Nigerian friend, play cousin, or auntie in their lives. They really do. In a world where fear rules our lives and we get used to cowering, we need to surround ourselves with some rowdy energy that takes up space unapologetically. That's where Nigerians come in. Not saying others aren't this, but there is a certain je ne sais quoi that allows it to be found in Naijas. We are the parliamentarians of Team No Chill. We will add color to your life. We will loan you bravado if you ever need it.

Why will your life be better for having a Nigerian who you can call friend or framily? Let me break down the reasons.

We are amazing verbal fighters. We don't even have to know how to physically fight, because the way our tongues can beat anyone down. Our opponents won't have the will to box us because we will have already destroyed them with our words. You want word soldiers and prodigious pepperers on your team, because we can take up arms for you without ever picking up a weapon or throwing a punch.

If you know enough Nigerians outside of a professional setting, you probably already know that insults are our love language and favorite pastime. It's not in wickedness either (most times), but it's because we relish the loving humbling we get to do when we slap each other with words.

You see, from childhood onward, our parents and family members have rained insults down upon us with reckless abandon. And when they weren't slandering us, they were directing their disrespect to others, so many of us learned how to assassinate people with our words very early. Plus, we learned that you can disgrace both those close to you and strangers, enough for them to clutch their pearls. This is what makes us undefeated in the art of verbal shaming. We are truly unfuckwitable.

Many of us can recall some of the tongue-lashings we got, and still remember the way they stung then. Have you ever been insulted so badly that you can't even respond? Instead, a single tear just rolls down your face, in mourning of your previously intact psyche.

Here's the thing. I'm of the Yorùbá people, and our language is deeply metaphorical. It's a highly descriptive tongue, with words for many things other languages might not have. This allows our insults to cut different. It's a sweet tongue with a spicy execution, and some of that sweetness is diluted as we attempt to translate to English. All

I know is, Yorùbá people gotta be the pioneers of the put-downs, with tongues that are Weapons of Ego Destruction.

There are two types of insults: the ones we use toward people we love and would fight for but need to humble from time to time, even in jest. And the other is for people we see as our opponents. You might clutch your pearls at these but trust me, they're our ways of greeting.

Before lunch, you might have heard that you're a useless goat, or you're daft and senseless. The one I used to hear *a lot* when I was little, with my sharp tongue: "Ẹ̀lẹ́ẹ̀kẹ́ èébú ni ẹ́." That means "cheeks full of insults." It's not my fault. It was preparation for who I am today.

But some other insults meet us in moments when we make bad decisions and they want to let us know how much they disapprove. Such as:

- "Big for nothing ijot (idiot)." All this height you have but you have no sense to match it. You're big, for no reason.

- "See your head like a four corner cabin biscuit." SpongeBob SquarePants has nothing on you.

- "Your head is so big with its five cardinal points corners. N, S, E, W, and D for Dummy point!" Because why not insult me using geography so I can learn something?

- "Ó wú bi búrẹ́dì to já sí omi." Translation: "You are swollen like bread soaked in water." This one is especially harsh if they use it to insult you AFTER you got mad from an original insult. This might cause tears.

- "If I slap you, you'll see heaven." Sooo you just wanna slap someone into other dimensions. Why do we gotta go there? The slap might not come, but the threat is enough to make me reassess my life.

We're forever roasting each other and other people's heads and mouths. Some of the insults we use make no sense, yet they still hurt like hell when you receive them. The diasporic tradition of dirty dozens is our favorite game, and we don't play fair—we play to hurt souls. Some of us are still recovering and in therapy to unlearn these insults and the hurt feelings that came with them. Chei.

The one thing that does help? When you see you're not the only one getting pepper-sprayed with slanderous words. Everyone gets it in equal measure, so you take it less personally than if you were the sole object of disgrace. It ain't just you. Silver linings, right?

It's even worse if the person we're facing is someone who has actually done something to us and we don't feel loyal to them or know them at all. Here are five of the most savage insults I've heard directed toward opponents:

- "The thunder that will strike you down is still doing push-ups." Not only do I want thunder to strike you down, but I'm also letting you know that the thunder itself is working out so it's at its strongest when it does it. SHEESH!

- "If I want to kill myself, I will climb to your level of stupidity and jump to your IQ." Fatha God! So you're just highly foolish with low levels of sense. Look at life.

- "They didn't born you or your forefathers well." Why must we go to the ancestors? What did they have to do with this? But sometimes you wanna play dirty. This is how.

- "Walking around like the unflushable toilet you are." You're full of shit and there's nothing you can do about it but offend us all.

- "You're an article with no commercial value." Chisos (Jesus) is Lord. How did we get here? Nobody's supposed to be here!

You might actually wanna learn how to fight if you have us as friends, because the way we will flout and flog people on your behalf, we might be challenged to a duel from the pure offending of it all. If the person we're beefing with hears me call them a "standard bastard" or "swaggerless buffoon," they might wanna square up, understandably.

Our insults bring different smoke to you. If reading folks for filth were an Olympic sport, Nigerians would be Hall of Famers. As your friends, we will increase your slander vocabulary, to be used sparingly, in the moments when someone has done the most with the least. We call those people aláṣejù (pronounced: ah-lah-SHAY-joo). *Aláṣejù* is a Yorùbá word that translates to "doer of too much."

You don't have to wield this weapon every day, but when you do, it will be potent clapbackery. I filter myself from my natural savagery of it all, so when people think I'm letting folks have it, they should know I am holding back, cuz I could be way worse.

Here's the thing, your Nigerian friend might insult you for sport, but no one else can. We're deeply loyal and stan those in our inner circles. You have nothing (read: everything) to fear but our mouths.

A lot of times, Nigerian group chats look like this:

PERSON 1: Good morning, useless people.

PERSON 2: You're foolish. How ah you?

PERSON 3: Head Goat in Charge, I'm fine.

PERSON 4: I saw you on Instagram looking sezzy.

PERSON 5: Eh so it's just them looking fine. Wharrabout me?

PERSON 4: Face your front. I wasn't talking to you. Big mouth.

It's all love! Can't you tell? Ha! But no one else can call us foolish or useless, because we'd squad up real quick because we took offense. Which in itself is a conundrum. How are we both unbothered and easily offended? Ask our parents. They're the royalty of incongruence. They'll hurl insults at you, but if you even LOOK like you're somehow upset, then they get upset. Similarly, they get very easily offended by the actions of others. Insults might be one love language, but taking offense is another. Remember the person who saw them at a party in 1977 but didn't greet them? They're still upset about it today, in a new millennium.

We somehow straddle the line of not taking anything personally and taking everything personally. We have learned to get words thrown at us and have them slide off our shoulders, while also taking offense to everything being done to us.

You can tell your Nigerian friend, "You ain't shit," and they might laugh because they know for sure they are from royalty (even though they might not be), and your words will do nothing to affect their elevated sense of self. But similarly, come to their house and decline their offer of food and see them feel attacked that you dared to show up in their abode without being hungry, therefore not needing the delectable goodness that is Nigerian jollof. HOW DARE YOU??

That brings me to . . . we are great because we won't let you carry your grudges by yourself. We will help. In fact, we are so good at holding a grudge that even after you drop it, we're still behind you, holding on strong. We remember who did what to you and when, even if you forgot, and we will be sucking our teeth anytime we hear their name. "Oh, so you and Jane are cool again? Did she beg you? Oh okay. Mtchew." And then we continue to side-eye. You might call us petty, but our response might be "And so?" We are Petty Wap for sure, and we know it.

That's another reason why you should get a Nigerian in your life. We've grown Teflon skin after decades of facing verbal dropkicks. We are thick-skinned and often unbothered by what others have to say about us. When you hear that you're an olódo (dummy) for breakfast, what else are people in the world gonna say to you or about you that will damage your spirit? You tell me I can't accomplish something because I'll never amount to anything? Well, it's my job to show you wrong.

On top of all of that, getchu a Nigerian friend to get the ego boost that comes with it. Why? We balance out the insults we might throw your way with ultimate cheerleading and hypeman-dom. Can't nobody gas you up like a Naija pesin, because we keep the same energy across the board. The way we celebrate you will make your head swell five times its size. At which point we will then say, "See your head like water balloon." Because: balance.

Imagine walking into a room where your friends are, and you're dressed up. And you hear "Blood of Gideon! Look at Luvvie of life. Finest of all fine babes! In fact, another one is a counterfeit because no other copies will do!" Or "Everlasting God on the throne! So you want to kill us today with beauty, àbí? You just want to scatter us and leave us nothing because you decided to bring yourself looking like the Queen of Sheba. It's not your fault, but the anointing." And sometimes, a long drawn out "WAWUUUUU" (because a simple "wow" just won't do) as they put their arms on their head for an extra measure of disbelief does the trick. You get that type of reception and I dare you to not instantly feel unfuckwitable.

My grandmother was a pro at making people feel like they walked on money. She had a friend who she would hail every time she saw her as a greeting. "AH! Ọ̀rẹ́ mí àtàtà, MARIAMU ỌMỌ BÀBÁ GOD." Translation: "My important friend, Mariam, God's child." Imagine someone greeting you by reminding you that you are heir to the Alpha and Omega. Me too, my head swells in return.

We won't let you feel humble. HUMBLE! Which kind? For what??

There is power in the gassing up that goes beyond the looks. It is an exercise in infusing confidence and courage in each other. It is a braveness drill, to get you to understand how dope you look and are, and how unstoppable you truly are. This comes in handy in the moments when you face scary things and wonder if you can make something big happen.

When you bring fear to the people who insist on making you feel like you just slayed everyone's spirits, they throw it out for you. They make the big things feel like foregone conclusions, and it's amazing to have and hear. The only thing Nigerians fear is God, Ghana jollof, and our parents' disappointment. Everything else? We can tackle it.

Growing up, our parents' expectations of us could either crush us with pressure or push us forward. A lot of us chose to be pushed forward, and that's because excellence was normalized. Doing big things in your life was the assumption, and you had no reason to do otherwise. To the point where if you got a B on the homework, they'd ask you if someone got an A. You'd of course reply with yes. And then they'd wonder what made that person different from you. What made them do better? They'd inquire with the shady "Did that person have two heads?" You'd say no and they'd sit there looking at you like the foolish person you were in the moment. Was that person better than you? *No.* So why not you?

As a seven-year-old, you might have been like, "But wait." But as an adult, I see the benefits in the train of thought. A lot of us carry that lesson with us, and we've become grown-ups who do the same, in different form, to our friends.

I have a crew of friends who are all from West Africa. If I go to that squad crew and tell them about an amazing opportunity I got in disbelief or with a hint of impostor syndrome creeping through ("OMG I can't believe it"), they set me straight: "Why not you? A whole you like this! Who else would it be? In fact, we're upset they didn't call you before this."

Why not you? That role you want to audition for. That doctorate you want to earn. That book you want to write. That stage you want to take. Why not you? Are the people who are able to do it not born on days that end with *y*? They are.

We all need the reminder that the people who have the opportunities are not somehow inherently better than us. They might have more privilege (which pushes them forward), but if the opportunity came to you and you ended up in the same room as the person with the trust fund, you gotta be doubly proud of yourself. YOU DID THAT. A whole unstoppable you!

Friends are quick to remind you of it and it is sweet. That bravado that we carry and pass out to people around us is a gift. It can be misused and become a superiority complex, but I think about how relentless Nigerians can be, and how we wear pride like a coat. It might be a coping mechanism because we come from a country where there are more than two hundred million people and everybody wants to be somebody. We say, "Naija no dey carry last" as a creed and affirmation and insistence.

Nigerians wake up and cough adversity.

You go to the market in Nigeria and the woman carrying water on her head, selling it for 500 naira ($1.30), will wonder why you dare to stand in her way as she needs to walk. She might even shame you a little for being in the wrong spot. Her head is held up high. Apologize for what? She might not have a kobo to her name, but she will also not think twice about taking up space.

Sure, our rudeness and aggression can be too much and often in the place of efficiency and good service. Like how going to a Nigerian embassy is an exercise in futility. IsweaterGawd, if you want your blood pressure to go up, go to any Nigerian embassy in hopes of getting a passport or visa in a timely (or courteous) manner. There, you will face the type of shenanigans that make you lose your hard-earned home training and any semblance of kindness.

There was a time when the Nigerian consulate in New York ended up on the news because they hadn't processed new passports in more than ten days because the air-conditioning unit had stopped working, so their equipment was overworked. But they hadn't notified anyone, so people who traveled from out of town with appointments showed up to locked doors at the Nigerian embassy.

I don't know how we dabble in excellence as a cultural value on one hand and then offer the most piss-poor of standards when it comes to receiving and giving services. Like I said, we're a complicated and convoluted people. We really do add flavor (or confusion) to your life.

Nigerians are extra AF. To be Nigerian is to be a lifelong aláṣejù, and we're not sorry about it. Our weddings are proof because Nigerians use holy matrimony as an occasion to do the utter most with the most. We have costume changes, money dances, and all the pomp and circumstance one can imagine could be part of such a moment. I swore I was not going to engage in all of that.

I was wrong.

I did all of it. In fact, I did it twice. I had two weddings in one day. The first was in the morning, from 9 a.m. to 12 p.m. That was our traditional Yorùbá wedding. In the Yorùbá traditional ceremony, the groom asks (begs) the family of his bride for her hand in marriage and he has to prove how bad he wants to marry her. He makes a promise to not just his family but hers that she will be number one in his life. His family also brings gifts to show they want to welcome her into their fold.

For our Yorùbá wedding, the clothes we wore were handmade aṣọ òkè (a.k.a. top cloth), and mine had thousands of stones sewn on it by hand. It took months to make. We had fifty people in our collective aṣọ ẹbi squad, which is the group of people who wear matching fabric and gèlè (head ties) on that day. Their fabric tells guests that they are our tribe.

Our Western ceremony was from 6 p.m. to 1 a.m. Two hundred fifty people joined us that day to celebrate our love, eat great food, and have their knees go out because of dancing too much.

My mom made sure to bring her own extra too. Part of the reason why I initially wasn't going to have a wedding carnival is that I happen to have a Nigerian mom who never asked me, "So where is your husband?" or pressured me on what I should do for a living. My mother has always trusted me with my own life, which is the ultimate compliment from a parent. She's low-key, doesn't roll with a big crew of people, and is perfectly fine in her own company. She doesn't even like going to parties. So much so that when people invite her to parties, she sometimes gets offended. "Have they seen me come to stuff like this? No. So why are they calling me?" Meanwhile, she'd probably get offended if they didn't invite her. It makes sense.

Anyhoo, when I got engaged, she was the first person we called, and she was so excited! She already knew it was happening because my boo had gone to her to ask for my hand in marriage. But the call to her made her show all of her teeth. Fast-forward six months later, and we're deep into planning the wedding. The only responsibility my mom had was picking her clothes for both weddings. All I did was give her colors to coordinate with, and all she had to do was pick the fabric her clothes would be made with. The morning colors for my family: all gold everything. Evening: She could wear whatever color she wanted. This lady ended up picking twelve different fabrics before landing on the final ones. That wasn't her most extra part, though.

A few months before the wedding, my sister turned forty and one of her friends surprised her at home with a saxophonist to play her

"Happy Birthday." We all also surprised her by showing up, so when sis came home from the spa, there were TWO surprises: Mom and saxophonist. Well, after she got the surprise of her life, she went to change because we had planned a dinner for her. The saxophonist stayed playing and my mom had her own private jam session, dancing along. She became instantly fond of him and by the time he left, he was like, "Thank you, Mommy!" How did you dance and end up with a son? I laughed so hard because it was exactly something Mama Fáloyin would have done.

A few months before my wedding, my mom comes to me and Mr. Jones.

MOM: So I want to have the saxophonist at the wedding.

ME AND BAE: *Exchange looks.*

ME: What would he do? We already have our musicians.

MOM: Well, I like him. He can sing me in when I'm introduced at the Trad [traditional wedding ceremony].

ME: Hmmm, let's talk to Akeshi about it, since she's the planner.

I didn't get a chance to talk to Akeshi because my mom had called her and let her know that she'd bought the guy's ticket from Houston. I got the call and I cackled! You know what? She hadn't asked for much else in the wedding-planning process. He could sax her and the fam in as they danced. And he could play at the cocktail hour. Why not? It would be so chill and relaxed.

The wedding day came and saxophonist did his thing at the Trad. Then he started playing Nigerian gospel turn-up songs during the cocktail hour, and it was a WRAP! The cool vibe? Who needed it? LET'S DANCE! It got so LIVE that at one point he was having a dance battle with one of my girls, Ayòdélé, where he spun and hip-thrusted. BRUH!!! People started throwing money up in the air.

There's a video from our cocktail of someone's mom (*coughs*) dropping it low to the ground as someone else's mom (*coughs*) stuffed the front of her dress with dollars while someone else stood behind them pouring money on their heads. Reception hadn't even started yet.

Long story long, my mom's extra-ness really contributed to the day and led to an overall amazing time, before the REAL turn-up happened at the reception. It was good times. The moral of the story is that I think everyone should go to a Nigerian wedding at least once in your life. It's a beautifully colorful spectacle, a feast for your eyes (and stomach), and a treat for your day. But most important, know you are worthy of being celebrated with live music even at an event that is about your daughter, like my mom.

We Nigerian people are a passionate lot, and we love us some Jesus (well, those who are Christians do). You haven't heard prayer until you've heard a Naija person pray and give God the glory. We cover everything with the blood of Jesus and we often take it above and beyond.

We take praise and worship very seriously because Christ is our bestie. This is why sometimes you don't even wanna tell your parents that something is wrong because you don't wanna be subjected to fifteen minutes of revival when you're in your Uber. All you wanna do is commute and you're on the phone tryna whisper, "AMEN." But then you hear "I DON'T HEAR YOUR AMEN!" so you shift in your seat and try not to disturb anyone within earshot.

Nigerian aunties are the prayer professionals, and they seem to have a mainline to God. If you tell someone you're cold, the prayer you might get could go like this: "May the God of holy fire SET ABLAZE any manner of snow, ice, frozen precipitation, subzero moisture in the matchless name of Jesus!" LMAO! And AMEN O! I receive it in His mighty name!

The prayers in my texts and emails and voice mails are enough to destroy a country of enemies. You just know when you say AMEN, your haters are somewhere expeditiously getting paper cuts. The prayers can get so intense that they're borderline curses.

Having Nigerians pray for you, especially in times of crisis, might have you feeling bad for whoever wronged you. I've heard someone say, "And may your enemies never prosper," and I've been like, "Wait. Should I affirm that?" Sometimes Nigerians pray so hard that you're pretty sure they've started cussing. "May your helper never sleep until they've done what they needed in your life." Ummm . . . amen? In fact, who borned you and dared you not to say a loud AMEN?!? You must want to be your own enemy of progress, blocking your own blessings.

We do Old Testament flood-the-earth appeals to Christ. There's even a Yorùbá song called "Mommy O" that praises moms and prays for their longevity on this Earth. All is well, until the line in it that prays that anyone who wishes your mom a short life will be run over by a trailer. It escalates so quickly!

We pray heaven DOWN! Even in worship, we're intense. When a church is called Mountain of Fire, you should know they ain't there to play bald-headed games about their supplication. They're the ones who might pray something like "The same way a bird flies and doesn't collide with anything, may your destiny's airplane never collide with anything." Wow, what a vision!

I f you're reading this, maybe you already have a Nigerian friend. Or maybe you don't. Maybe you're thinking: "I mean I did go to school with some Nigerians, are we friends?" To that I ask, has their mom cooked for you? No? Then you're probably not friends. It's okay. It's not too late for you.

How do you make Nigerian friends? How do you find a shady and bold Naija to squad up with in this scary world, so y'all can take it on with sharp tongue in tow? I have a few tips.

GO TO A COLLEGE LIBRARY

If you go to any school library, you are sure to find at least one Nigerian there, nose buried in books. They're studying to be a nurse, doctor, lawyer, engineer, whether they like it or not. You hear "Go and face your books" all your life and you do just that when you get to undergrad, cuz you don't want the lambasting that will come if you don't. It's as simple as that.

GO WHERE AFROBEATS IS BEING PLAYED

If you're walking by somewhere and you hear some Afrobeats booming, there is a West African there, especially a Nigerian. The drumbeat, the ample opportunity for lyrics, the vibes—we're all about it. Dip in there and join us as we drop it low and let our bodies move to the beat. And when you join us, we'll gas you up and the story can go from there. In fact, seek out the Afrobeats Night at any club and you're good. But that's easy. You knew that, right?

Also, you can buy a pair of white loafers. I feel like 83 percent of the white shoes that exist in the world are owned by African men. Facts only (by facts, I mean I completely made that up). You will not meet a Nigerian man who does not own a pair of white loafers of some sort. I don't know why they had a meeting and agreed this was their uniform. Bless it.

DECLARE ALLEGIANCE TO
NIGERIAN JOLLOF

Jollof is a tomato-based rice dish that is the West African version of basically every yellow rice. And because we love to center ourselves, let's compare it to other dishes. Paella is Spanish jollof. Fried rice is

Chinese jollof. Jambalaya is Creole jollof. You get me. It is a necessity in the Nigerian diet, in all its spicy and flavorful goodness.

Jollof was not created in Nigeria; the Senegalese were the pioneers. But we are deeply passionate about the fact that we think our jollof is the best. Because: Nigerians. We are in a never-ending jollof war with our Gold Coast cousins, the Ghanaians, and we know the truth: Naija jollof carries first. (I love that even if you wanna argue with me right now, I've already put it in this book, so you can argue with your reflection.)

Anyway, to get a Nigerian friend for life, a shortcut is to denounce Ghana jollof. You must talk about how it doesn't have enough peppeh and how it doesn't measure up. It doesn't matter whether you mean it or not. Them the rules. I don't make them; I pass them along. You can't be neutral in this war. You gotta pick a team.

I know you know a Nigerian (we're everywhere). Cultivate a real relationship with them. Get a Naija auntie who can pray the Holy Trinity down. Get a Naija friend who will gas you up, insult you, and then have a dance battle with you at the same time.

Your life will never be the same.

16

FUCK FEAR

We fear FEAR.

 Fear is a hater. Fear will have you sitting down when you should be standing up. Fear will have you not saying that thing that is necessary when you need to. Fear will talk you out of your purpose so quick that your destiny gets whiplash.

Fear is real, primitive, and innate. It's one of the most natural emotions. To not have any fear is actually a physiological disorder called Urbach-Wiethe disease, and it happens when the brain's amygdala is damaged. True story.

We are not supposed to be walking around fearlessly. Our angst is a biological necessity because it keeps us safe from doing dumbass things without safety nets.

To be afraid is to be human. But I think that's assuring: It's really cool to know that we're all out here walking around with varying levels of "WTF is this?" happening at any given time. Some of us have learned to hide it better or handle it so it doesn't overtake us. Some people make choices to move past their doubts, knowing it might not work out, but they will try anyway, while others can point to pivotal moments when they have let fear be their main decision factor. But we all feel it.

I wrote this book because I want to always be the type of person who overcomes her doubts. But in my life, I have been the type of person who let fear dictate her decisions more times than I can count. My journey to where I am today was longer than it could have been because I let fear stop me from owning my purpose and my passion and my profession for a long time. And it wasn't until I made the decision to push past those scary moments that I started seeing my life move forward in ways that blew my mind.

The choice to fight fear is not like joining some lifelong club that once you're in, you can't get out. Nah. It's a moment-by-moment, day-by-day decision. The biggest scaredy-cat in the world can decide to do something brave at any moment. It might be as small as ordering a doughnut they've never had. Or as big as proposing to the love of their life. Or as audacious as going skydiving because their friend asked them.

We are all fighting battles with the world, systems, ourselves. Battles that are easy to lose. It's so much easier to keep doing what feels comfortable. What feels safe. But then we might look up one day and realize that we've safety-netted ourselves into lives that feel like cages. Cages can get comfortable, but comfort is overrated. Being quiet is comfortable. Keeping things the way they've been is comfortable. But all comfort does is maintain the status quo.

What forces us to live comfortable lives that might not serve us?

What forces the people in our lives to shrink? It is partly caused by our fears and other people's angst layered on top of each other.

Do we realize how often we pass on our fears to other people? Do we realize how much we impose the things we are afraid of on the people we love and care about every single day? I know exactly why people are afraid of choosing the path that is unfamiliar, of experiencing things and being free. We are constantly telling people to be scared.

I took a trip to Mexico one year and posted on social media, casually, about loving how I was getting the opportunity to eat mangoes every single day, because they are my favorite fruit. I got so many comments from people who were warning me that I would end up lying prostrate to the toilet throne, because when they ate mangoes, they had the runs. Meanwhile, it was day six and I was perfectly okay, and continued to be. The same thing happened when before the trip I told people I was going to another country and was told to "watch out for kidnappers." Or when I said I was sitting outside and someone warned me about how the mosquitoes were going to make a meal out of me. Mind you, at no point was I asking people for advice. I was simply sharing what I was doing, and I was instantly met with tales of misfortune.

I get it. The world is scary. Shit happens. But we lead our lives with so much fear. We're so busy bracing for constant impact that we stay right where we are, too afraid to move, because that monster we think is around the corner will jump out.

Sometimes this anxiety comes from our loved ones. The generational curses we talk about breaking can be limitations that those we love have habitually placed on us. The weapons that have formed might actually be from our families and friends, who meant well but ended up using ammunition of apprehension on us. Breaking cycles can mean unlearning what those closest to us have taught us.

How free would we be if we weren't being tethered down by other people's anxieties, doubts, and insecurities? How high could we fly if people weren't pulling at our ankles to keep us grounded to earth because that's where they are?

You deserve to be free of other people's weight. You deserve to be unbuckled from other people's doubts. You carry enough of your own. We all deserve to walk light.

When people try to drop their bags of fears at our feet, let us drop-kick the bag back to them. We don't want it. I'm not holding your doubts. I'm not making space in MY life for YOUR angst. I will not sleep under a blanket of your dread. It's not mine to carry. No thank you.

Sure, we can live lives where we are minimally afraid because we've covered ourselves in bubble wrap and don't take any risks, but THAT life is boring. That life is wasted. That life is a version of fluorescent beige. Your gravestone will be all, "They were here." Dassit. Dassall. You'll get to heaven and God will roll His/Her/Their eyes at you. All this breath, all this movement, all this BEING. And you wasted it being the person version of a flavorless rice cake. What will you have done that you were proud of?

When I'm dead and gone, I want to have left a mark. It's like in the movie *Coco*. We only truly die when our names no longer pass off someone's tongue. I want to be missed. I want my absence felt. I want my contributions to be bigger than my small stature. I want this world to be better because I was here. And if I'm moving with fear and doubt and anxiety first, I'm standing in no gaps, writing in fluff, speaking in whispers.

I am not fearless. But I've learned to start pushing past fear because oftentimes, the fear itself is scarier than whatever is on the other side. It's like being afraid to walk through a dark hallway. If you close your eyes and run through it, you'll be okay. And you'll look back and say, "That wasn't that bad."

For me, fighting fear is facing freedom. We owe it to ourselves to say FUCK FEAR, and we owe it to the people who look up to us, or surround us, or love us.

We owe it to ourselves to lighten our load and drop dead weight. Drop it all. The friends who don't really have your back. The partner who makes you feel worthless. The job that makes you tired of waking up. The trauma that makes you self-sabotage. The self-doubt that makes you think you're not good enough.

We owe it to ourselves to climb the mountain that feels too tall.

The world isn't going to get less scary. We might never get braver. I'm basically lowering my expectations. That's why I say we need to acknowledge that and get on with the shits. We must keep doing the things that scare us, knowing that what is right is often the opposite of what is easy.

Get on with it, and start by forgiving yourself for not having the courage to do something you wished you had in the past. Forgive yourself for not speaking up in moments that might have called for it. Forgive yourself for the mistakes you've made that now feel avoidable. You did your best with the information you had and understood at the time.

Everyone who has done major things has started with one step. It wasn't that they looked up one day and it was all done for them. (Well, except for some white dudes. Because Daddy and nepotism are the best security blankets.) Most people who did major things or changed the world got the idea and one day decided to take one step, followed by another, followed by another. Rome wasn't built in a day, but the bricks they laid to build it had to begin on some day.

Those dreams we have the audacity to dream? They can't stay on the "wish list" pile forever. Well, they can, but then what was the point? We actually have to DO.

So, in case anyone needs encouragement to BE, SAY, DO, here it is, because really cool things can be waiting for you on the other side of fear. The big things we are so afraid of doing because they seem too ginormous for us, we must do. Even if we do them poorly. Ask that scary question. Write that book. Learn that language. Check off the bucket list. Travel to 150 countries. Start that major business. Purge your shoe closet (*looks at myself*). Run that marathon. (This is not my ministry and I still think marathons are conspiracies. Of who? I'm not sure.) Go on that audition. Make that move.

Do all that shit. Or do none of that, if that's what you're compelled to do. But that thing that you keep thinking about but you keep stopping because you're afraid? DO THAT THING.

In the moments when I want to run back to what's comfortable or I dare to cower in the face of doubt, I think about Olúfúnmiláyọ̀ Juliana Fáloyin, my guardian angel and my prototype of a professional troublemaker. That God-loving, favor-finding, whole-face-smiling unicorn of a woman. I think about her, as a teenager, starting her life from scratch by herself at the age of eighteen. I reflect on the woman who doctors told wouldn't speak again when she had a stroke. I can't help but muse on my muse who moved through the world boldly confident that God and her faith were bigger than any fear.

I carry and will continue to carry my grandmother with me everywhere I go. Every day, I look down at my right hand, at the gold filigree ring I never take off. It's the one Grandma gave me one day when I saw her wearing it and instantly squealed how much I loved it. Without hesitation, she took the ring off and handed it to me. It's funny that it adorns the middle finger of my dominant hand. It works.

A professional troublemaker is someone who is committed to being authentically themselves while speaking the truth and doing some scary shit. Here is to us, daring to live boldly. I owe it to Mama Fáloyin, my favorite troublemaker, to do this. When fear tries to stop me, I need to put on my pants, say a little prayer of strength, and dance for twenty minutes to celebrate my insistence to conquer doubt.

Fear is a hater, a liar, and a cheat. To be FEARLESS is to not commit to doing LESS because of our fears. We owe ourselves fearlessness, and we can start now.

EPILOGUE

COURAGE IN THE TIME OF FEAR

In the middle of writing this book, the coronavirus (COVID-19) pandemic began. It wasn't enough for me to be working on my most vulnerable piece of writing yet, which in itself scared me to pieces. Then the world had to throw other wrenches in the mix and gift us with a never-before-seen deadly virus that flipped everything upside down. There's also murder hornets and human-sized bats we gotta worry about. And any other animal that is native to Australia. This is a lot of scary shit to deal with.

To have to write this book about tackling fear, in the midst of this chaos, was a test for me to see if I can do and be who I say I am when it is especially difficult. Hundreds of thousands of people have died from this virus and there are still those who are thinking, "I'm not going to stop this from letting me live my life." They have somehow convinced themselves that there is nothing to fear, even as science and data and common sense grabs their face (from six feet away) with the warnings.

In this instance, I believe they are being wildly foolish. This is when fear serves its ORIGINAL purpose: to keep us from acutely endangering our lives and the lives of those in the world. When we are staring down the barrel of a gun whose bullets are a virus that is highly contagious and killing people at rates in multiples of the seasonal flu, fear is valid and necessary. This anxiety is based on facts. If we do not have it, we are likely to put the people in our community, even those we don't know, in jeopardy. We are likely to put ourselves in harm's way.

Now compare that dread with the uneasiness you get when you have to speak up in a meeting. Or the jitters you get when you have to tell your parents you don't actually want to be a lawyer but a photographer instead. Or the worry you have because you don't want to dream too big because of the potential disappointment. Those fears now seem trite, don't they? Probably not, because they are legitimate also. But next to any kind of physical or medical threat—whether it be a virus, a treacherous political climate where Satan's minion got the nuclear codes, or when you're stopped by the police and you're Black and you're not sure if the dude in blue is going to see your brown as a weapon—the trepidation we have in our everyday lives can feel silly.

If life has taught us anything, it's that it's full of uncertainty. And that's some scary shit. Right now, I don't know how this pandemic will unfold, how many lives it will ultimately steal, or how long we will be inside, unable to touch those we love (outside of those under our roofs). The only thing certain right now is that nothing is certain. The unknown is disquieting, and it's easy to give in to anxiety.

What we can do when we are in uncharted waters is to know we are doing our part. I might be indoors, but I'm not hiding from the world or the work that got me here. I am using my fear to put pen to paper, because writing a "Fear-Fighter Manual" during a time of rampant unease is almost poetic. It's like God sent me a dare and I'm being charged to rise to the occasion. It's meta AF.

Some people have needed to rest during what is happening. I couldn't, because book deadlines with advances are real. Plus my editor and agent are bold women who ain't afraid to call me to the carpet. But more important, in a global crisis, I felt helpless to do much more than the work I am purposed to do: WRITE. I'm staying home and staying out of the way of the essential workers. And I'm writing because that is my catharsis.

Times of crisis and chaos present us with the opportunity to do the best work of our lives. People use words that they pull from the depths of their spirits. People paint with strokes that they summon from their souls. People sing notes that come from the cosmos. People innovate. We must keep doing that.

Another thing we can do when we're in uncharted waters: Ask what we can learn from this. What is this experience trying to teach us? How are we supposed to change because of it?

Right now, I am hoping we learn to be kinder and more generous to each other. I hope we give each other a bit more grace.

I also hope that we begin to really understand that everybody's pain is our business. Because it can become our pain very quickly. You can't just be like, "That house is burning? Well, that ain't got nothing to do with me." Because the fire can spread to your house very quickly. We have to understand that if we can put out their smoke, then it doesn't become our fire. Let me repeat: The quicker we can put out their fire, the less likely it is to become ours.

Everybody's problem is our problem too. When we see people being discriminated against, and we keep quiet and think it has nothing to do with us, we're off base. You don't think you're next? I extrapolate situations to see how they can come and affect me very quickly. I know that if something bad happens to someone else, it can happen to me too.

These crisis moments call for us to elevate whoever we are. To change, grow, mature, evolve. If we do not, we're going to keep getting the same expensive and heart-wrenching lessons. We need to ask ourselves what we should be learning from all this.

What would my grandmother say right now if she were alive? How would she deal with these times? She would pray over Bible passages during her three-hour 3 a.m. vigils. She would tell me to pray. She would have called the whole family with the Bible passages she thought we should read for protection (Psalms 91 and 121 were her faves). Her assurance would calm my spirit, and even though she might not be in front of me, I'd see her smile. I would know that there was a prayer warrior advocating on my behalf in the middle of a worldwide storm. I would probably sleep better because Mama Fáloyin and Jesus had a conference call where my name came up.

In her absence, I'm trying to fill my own gap.

That being said, I still have to do my part and not let the idea of faith keep me from being fearful. Because to use my Christianity as armor would be to invalidate what is material. Toxic positivity is real, and some people hide behind religion to escape real life and real circumstances. And it's dangerous.

What's toxic positivity? It is the idea that you should always have a positive response to every situation, no matter how severe the circumstance is. The intent behind it is admirable: that we should find the good in everything, in an attempt to keep our eyes on happy. But the results can be harmful.

Sure, constantly wallowing in negativity is not healthy. However, what makes this positivity toxic is that it discredits feelings and makes people feel weak for not being able to plaster a smile on their faces at all times. It is a way to sidestep dealing properly with our lives. You know what toxic positivity often is? Denial. Avoidance. Evasion of reality. It is why we must acknowledge that fear is legit, and it is natural.

Everything does not have an immediate upswing or feel-good to it, and that's okay. Life can be a cruel hellcat sometimes and we can face shit that will knock the wind out of us. What we often do is pull our Jesus card and skip over the part where we actually deal with facts. What we should do is feel our feelings, take the time, and then move forward.

Christians are champs at toxic positivity. We excel at it because we have been taught that faith and fear cannot coexist. We've been Instagram-graphicked to pieces about how there is no way we can believe in God yet still be anxious. But it is an oversimplification of scripture and a flattening of what is normal human experience. Even people who aren't religious or spiritual have received the message that to be courageous is to be fearless. So add that to the God guilt that we tie to fear, and we have the perfect storm of people feeling inferior for daring to be apprehensive. It's an oppressive state of affairs and I'm judging us HARD.

People die and folks will retort, "Well, at least they're with God now." Or "Everything happens for a reason. It's part of the plan." Which, okay cool. Glad we believe that. But when we invoke those words when someone is feeling pain that is as physical as it is emotional, it says that whatever their feelings are should be soothed by the platitudes of looking at the upside. It isolates and others them in their pain.

I'm here to tell you that you can be a Christian or spiritual or a monk and still worry. You can be connected to a higher power and still be anxious. You are not doing spirituality wrong by still having the nerve to be worried. Worry is a part of life. The goal is that we don't let the doubt render us catatonic with defeat. You can be scared, but move forward and live. That's what matters.

There are times when we will be anxious because we have a valid reason to be.

Some of us are legit scared, if not for ourselves then for the people we love or for society at large. Listen, I'm afraid half the time. Fear is here. It is present. I acknowledge that I feel this thing, that it is scary and uncomfortable, and I go forward anyway.

This is why I'm writing this book. The goal isn't to not feel negative emotions; it's that we don't let them consume us. Whether you're a deacon or a heathen, I don't want you to feel you are failing at life because you are not always on Hashtag Gratitude mode. Worrying doesn't mean you don't trust God. It doesn't mean you're weak. It means you're human.

Fear is there and it is natural. It will always be present. And yet we must still keep going. We can't afford to let fear, whether big or small, legitimate or contrived, numb us.

Here I am, writing through it, writing to it, and writing from it. It shall be well. Someway.

SLAY THE DRAGON

The Truth-Telling Guide

 There are very few universal truths, but one of them is that humans are wired to yearn for belonging. Another is that rice is the elixir of life. (I'm not arguing. This is my book so I do what I want. HA!) But really, we all want to exist in the comfort of acceptance from those around us.

Which is why telling the truth, which can disrupt the harmony of agreement in a room, can be scary.

We fear REJECTION. We fear PUNISHMENT. We fear HURTING FEELINGS.

But I'm of the same mind as Oprah, who once said, "Speaking your truth is the most powerful tool we all have." Chances are, like her, you wanna become someone who is able to make change happen with your words. You want to be bold in the face of fear, to speak up or do something difficult. You wanna be someone who elevates any room they're in with integrity.

That's EXACTLY what a professional troublemaker does, and it's why being one is important. Professional troublemaking is disruption for good, and you can start today. Whether you've let fear block you from speaking up in the past, or you've had a hard time using your voice consistently, it's not too late to develop the habit.

Sharp tools are vital, but they are also dangerous when used recklessly. Truth-telling is no different. That is why I'm writing this guide. I hope it gives you the exact guidance you need to wield your honesty sword carefully and confidently.

Shout-out to those of us with sharp tongues, who know we can slice people left and right with our words. We, especially, gotta know how to not cause chaos with our mouths.

Telling the truth is HARD, y'all. Consistent candor is not common, and when I asked my audience what part of speaking up was scariest for them, I saw some common themes. Let's go through them.

FEAR OF REJECTION

You might have a friend, partner, or family member you need to say something to, but you're scared to damage the relationship. You're worried that your vulnerability might turn into you losing a valued member of your life village. You're afraid they'll walk away from you because people do not like to be challenged or opposed. And oftentimes, if we're having tough conversations with them, it's because we want them to atone for something they've done or to adjust a habit they have. Shout-out to those of us with abandonment issues. (It's me. I am "those of us.")

There are three things you should consider if you're struggling with a fear of rejection:

1. **Your feelings are valid.** You feel how you feel and that's just how it is. I can sometimes try to convince myself that my feelings aren't hurt because I don't wanna have to have the tough conversation. It would be easier if I was just FINE with what was said or done to me. But that never works, because you cannot logic away heart hurt. At best, you can swallow it down and compartmentalize, or even repress. But your feelings are still here, in the emotional fetal position. Meanwhile, this person has no clue you're trapped in a glass case of negative emotions, spurred on by them. Which is why . . .

B. **Not telling them is not a great option,** because your silence can become resentment. You're sulking somewhere, angry and hurt, while the other person is living their best life, oblivious to the pain they've caused you. All it does is allow this feeling to fester. Who wins? NOBODY. Not you, because your spirit is bothered. And not them, because they don't know the truth of what they broke, and therefore they cannot fix it. Resentment is poisonous.

iii. **You owe them a chance to fix it.** Getting the courage to speak up to a loved one is a gift because you are giving them the chance to show up for you when they've disappointed you. We are all flawed, and even when we try our best, we will fall short. We will do something unknowingly that hurts someone we love. But when we are faced with the silent treatment, as a result of us being HUMAN, we are being punished, without due process.

And if they double down on their foolishness, showing that they knowingly hurt you . . . well, then, you have a data point you can use to make a decision. "Is this person treating me with care? Should I give them continued access to me?" Quickly, your fear of rejection might turn into your making a decision to be the one rejecting a friend, partner, or kinfolk who is not good for your spirit. If they reject your truth or are callous about your feelings, maybe they aren't your people.

The truth will get you the answer you need, either way. If someone cuts you off because you voiced a thoughtful truth, it's more about them than you. And it hurts like hell to think about losing someone you care about, but some goodbyes are necessary. Grieve what you had, and let them go (easier said than done but ultimately, you will have to do it).

FEAR OF PUNISHMENT

When it comes to telling the truth or speaking up, punishment is a real and acute fear. What if we face retaliation (emotional, physical, financial)? The world, after all, is full of petty and vindictive people.

You might have a boss who makes the work environment difficult for you and others, and you're afraid of what could happen if you speak up. You might hear "NO," and that itself feels like punishment, even though most NOs won't kill you. If the person wields power over you, retribution is possible when we use our voices, so I absolutely understand this.

But here's the thing: What if that punishment never comes? What if we stop ourselves from doing or saying what's right and what could change things for the better because we are afraid of a phantom consequence that won't happen? We'll talk about these possibilities (in detail) shortly.

FEAR OF HURTING FEELINGS

You aren't afraid you'll be cut off or punished but you hate the idea of hurting the feelings of someone you care about. Your intentions are good, you love them deeply, and being the catalyst for their pain gives you a stomachache. I get it.

The same things to consider about the fear of rejection are the same things to consider here. But also keep in mind that you're navigating a fear of discomfort too. We don't want the weird feelings that come with loving confrontations (an oxymoron, mayhaps?). But hurt feelings are temporary, and honestly, they are a requirement. Hopefully, the person whose feelings are hurt sees it as a growth opportunity.

Above all, I want you to know that you are not responsible for other people's feelings. You are not the chaperone to other people's reactions, because all you control is YOU. How they take it is completely out of your hands. As a type-A control freak, this is something I still struggle with. It's tempting to wanna supervise someone else's emotions, but it is truly an exhaustive mission that often fails. Save yourself from the headache.

FEAR OF GETTING IT WRONG

You don't wanna get it wrong, either the situation or your delivery. You don't wanna be judged, humiliated, or misunderstood. You are unsure about your viewpoint, or whether you can convey it properly. Those fears might keep you from speaking up. Understood and duly noted.

But here's what I want you to know: there is no REAL "getting it right" because anyone can take anything from what you said. Even the RIGHT tone can be subjective.

Take the pressure off yourself. Your delivery doesn't have to be perfect. Give yourself permission to be imperfect upfront and to wield vulnerability in the moment of truth. And if you're afraid of getting it wrong, SAY THAT out loud. The truth is sincerity, after all. That includes you being honest about the discomfort of your moment of courage. For example: "Hey, it's kinda tough for me to say this." Or "Okay, so I'm a little nervous but I'll say this anyway." This candor shows you're human, humble, and tuned in to the fact that what you have to say has you on high alert. But also note that your discomfort does not invalidate your feelings. Your fear does not nullify the point. And in the right room, in front of the right people, it will probably be received with the heart you intended.

It's okay to get it wrong too, because if you decide later on that you didn't like the words you used, or your tone, you can once again choose honesty and tell the person, "I messed up. I'm sorry." An apology is always on the table. Integrity is always worthy.

Note: If you cussed someone CLEAN TF out and showed your entire ass, then that's another story. There are times that apologies won't heal the damage, but that's a whole chapter for another time. There are justifications for making the choice to not just BURN the bridge but BLOW IT UP. But if that's the choice you make, you gotta deal with the consequences.

FEAR OF BAD TIMING

Is there a perfect time to drop truth bombs on folks? In the past, you might have wanted to speak up but stayed silent because you weren't sure if it was the anointed and appointed time for your voice to rise above the wackness. And then afterward, maybe you ruminated on it in the shower and kicked yourself because you felt like you missed the right time.

Well, let me say that the truth can be early but it ain't never too late. The truth might drag its feet but when it shows up, we're all better for it. If you missed what you thought was the right time, you can return to the person like, "Hey, that conversation we had the other day? I gave it more thought and I wanna revisit it." Or "I know I didn't say anything last week but it's been on my mind and I wanted to circle back with you."

We have to give ourselves permission to fuck up. Humaning is hard, and our constant need to GET IT RIGHT gets us stuck. Our pressure to have it together actually makes us fall apart in more ways than we realize.

And I know you're wondering, "Is there a time NOT to speak up? Is there a way I can know that now's the time to ZIP IT UP and be quiet?"

There are three specific times you can clam up:

A. You are flooded and overwhelmed. Something was said or done that has you feeling so emotional that your thoughts are cloudy and your impulses (not logic) take over. When I get especially triggered and angry (or hurt), I might start to cry. The tears aren't because I'm sad but it's like my feelings balled up, rammed themselves behind my eyeballs, and then poured out in water form.

In those moments, the TRUTH should take a backseat because I am liable to lack EVERY FILTER and lose my whole sensible shit. Which serves no one, and would not be productive to anybody. These are the times when fifteen seconds of words can destroy ten years of kinship. In those times, I just gotta STFU and feel my big feelings instead of opening my mouth and throwing word grenades.

You can still be honest, though and say "I am angry. I would rather not speak right now."

Let the truth wait for when you are back in control of your body and your words.

2. You are on the receiving end of a loving critique. Someone you love is telling you about something you have done or said that rubbed them the wrong way. Now, there are two sides to every story, and what might be happening might not even really be your fault. Or it might be a projection of their shit. I know, girl; it's happened to me too. But your job at that point is to LISTEN. This ain't the time to tell them that they're also raggedy and that they borrowed money from you and didn't return it. That's the TRUTH, but when used in that exact second, it is defensiveness. If you throw their truth back at them to make yourself the hero, you're indicating to the other person that they can't be psychologically safe with you. Instead, tell them, "I hear you. Let me reflect on this and get back to you. But I am listening."

And then come back and make your case. Maybe in telling them you missed their birthday party because you were actually upset at how inconsiderate they've been, you'll realize, "Aw, shit. I should have been honest with them first." We are all walking around scared and creating cycles of resentment that could have been handled if we made the choice to be courageous.

However, there is definitely a time to tell truth to go to hell and that is if:

iii. **You will be in danger.** If what you have to say will lead to your physical harm, please choose silence to avoid violence. Protect yourself at all costs because your survival is of the utmost importance. I will never advocate for you to use your voice if it will lead to your life being taken, harm upon your body, or destruction of your basic needs. Sometimes, the truth can antagonize people, and if that person is Satan's mentee, it won't go well.

Remember that time in college when you went to the club and your girl was there with someone else's boyfriend and his girlfriend showed up? Well, the truth is the dude your girl was dealing with was a trifling summabitch, and when the girlfriend showed up, she had all the right to fight him (and maybe even your homegirl) but you kept your mouth shut because if you poured gas on the mess, y'all would be on fire . . . and you can't fight. So let's not. Like that. Just *shhh*. Because sis looked like she had hands and would wipe the floor with all of us.

I think about how women often have to be quiet, as WE are antagonized, purely for our physical safety. Like when we're walking down the street and get catcalled. How many of us have been followed when we speak the basic truth of "I don't want to give you my number?" How many of us have had to LIE and say "I have a man" just for the guy to back off? How many times have we had to give our number because we fear that if we don't, we could be assaulted? How many people have done all of that and have STILL been abused, attacked, or even killed?

We do what we must to stay alive in this land mine of a world, and sometimes that means we know the time isn't right to say something, or sometimes that means we have to outright lie.

These aren't the only three scenarios we can choose to be quiet, but they are three that are good times to exercise the STFU coupon code of truth.

Fear is real. And using your voice in challenging moments is ripe with anxiety and doubt. We're afraid to rock the boat. We're afraid to disrupt harmony. We're afraid to distance ourselves from others. We are afraid of the power we wield with the truth. We're afraid of being the troublemaker.

In the absence of fear, there can be no courage. Because if something is easy, it's probably not brave. If it were easy, everyone would do it. It is a choice to be outspoken when silence would be more comfortable, and that is brave. Truth-telling is not a universal habit, and I want us to choose courage more often. To help in this valiant quest, I present my Step-by-Step Guide to Truth-telling. What do you do in the moment, in the meeting, at the dinner table? How can thoughtful honesty unfold in a room? What do you do when you are afraid of what could come from it? Let's get into it.

"THE WAY TO RIGHT WRONGS IS TO TURN THE LIGHT OF TRUTH UPON THEM."

—Ida B. Wells

STEP 1: ASSESS THE SITUATION

Someone said or did something, and shifted the space and the energy of the room. Something ain't right and you know it. You feel it!

Start by identifying what went wrong. What about the situation is off?

Was it a coworker's bad idea that if left unchecked could lead to major backlash for the company? Was it a racist joke that your uncle just made at the dinner table?

Was it an unkind and underhanded statement your friend made?

What about this situation didn't curl all the way over?

STEP 2: ACKNOWLEDGE THE FEAR
TO YOURSELF

You want to take action and not let this moment pass but you're afraid. Well, good. Fear is a red flag that something isn't sitting well and you are now out of your comfort zone. It's also a sign that you're human.

Acknowledge to yourself the fear that's popping up. Name it and claim it. Which of the five fears I identified earlier is it? Is it a fear of rejection or punishment or hurting feelings or getting it wrong or bad timing?

When you think about taking action and about being honest in this situation, what scares you most?

STEP 3: PRIORITIZE
THE BEST-CASE SCENARIO

We are anxious about speaking up because we are afraid of the negative consequences that may follow. This is when that fear of punishment often takes over. We are afraid of failing or being punished or being rejected. And those fears can keep us tight-lipped—not once, not twice, but throughout our lives—until we realize one day that we no longer know HOW to use our voices to speak up during tough times.

Truth-telling is a muscle. But we've spent years (or even decades) fearing the worst-case scenarios that could come with that authenticity, and in the process, that muscle has atrophied. I understand. Now, I want you to face this fear head-on, consider what is actually likely, and weigh your options more.

Take quick stock of what the possible consequences for speaking up are, and make sure to include the best-case scenarios, not only the worst-case scenarios.

I recognize this could be a new way of thinking for a lot of us. We're so afraid of what could go wrong that we rarely imagine what could happen if it actually goes right. We'll sit in the meeting afraid of being fired so we don't challenge the terrible campaign idea. We'll shut up, as if challenging our uncle's bad joke means we'll be excommunicated from the family. We will remain silent as our friend disrespects someone else, afraid that our objections mean we lose good faith with all our friends. We build up our fears to become dragons in our heads and then allow these dragons to stop us from getting to the other side.

We're so worried about what could go wrong, we've eliminated the possibility of our best-case scenario happening. We're choosing the NO automatically when the YES could be game changing.

Instead of eliminating the best-case scenario, prioritize it.

When confronted with a truth-telling situation, get really real with yourself. This process might be quickly done in your head in the moment or you might wanna think through and write it down over a few minutes or days (if super serious, even a month). I've done that.

Ask yourself:

What is the best-case scenario? What is the worst-case scenario?

What could go right? What could go wrong?

What if they tell me YES? What happens if the answer is NO?

What does SUCCESS look like in this case? What does FAILURE look like?

Let's look at how these questions play out with a specific scenario. You're in your annual review and you really want to ask your boss for a raise because you feel you've earned it. But you're afraid of the NO that might come, or you're afraid you'll get fired for even asking.

In that case, getting real with yourself and examining all the possible scenarios might look like:

BEST-CASE SCENARIO	WORST-CASE SCENARIO
What is the best-case scenario? What could go right? What if the answer is YES? What does SUCCESS look like? **BEST CASE:** Boss says YES and gives me a 20 percent raise. Would mean I can get a bigger apartment and help my aging parents with bills. Makes me feel less pressured, less financially strained, and happier overall. **AMAZING BEST CASE:** Boss says YES and gives me a 20 percent raise AND a promotion. It completely changes my tax bracket and my financial standing. For the first time in my life, I don't need two jobs to pay bills and I am now able to go on my first vacation in a long while.	What is the worst-case scenario? What could go wrong? What if the answer is NO? What does FAILURE look like? **WORST CASE:** Boss says NO. I stay at the level I'm at. I lose nothing but gain some hurt feelings. **APOCALYPTIC WORST CASE:** Boss says NO. FIRES me for asking. I lose my paycheck, and I'm unable to get a new job. I lose my house after falling behind on my mortgage and my life goes to complete shambles.

Read this and reflect on what's actually at stake. Assess the reality of the situation and act, knowing you are clear on what could actually happen if you use your voice.

Sure, that apocalyptic worst case is scary. But one thing we should ask ourselves when we're afraid of the hellish worst-case scenario: Is it LIKELY to happen? Like . . . of all scenarios, is that one the most possible? Many times, the answer is NO. A lot of things would need to go wrong for you to be fired for asking a question or challenging an idea in a meeting.

The next thing to ask: If that apocalyptic worst-case scenario happens, are your basic needs on the line?

One thing you might consider, if you can manage it, is having a "Fuck-You Fund." That is a pot of money somewhere (maybe earmarked in your savings account) that allows you to tap out of jobs that don't serve you at any time you want. It allows you to leave situations (or relationships) that are no longer for you. In case people piss you off, your Fuck-You Fund will buy you time as you figure out what's next. You ever met someone with an FYF? The coworker who mumbles, "I don't need this goofy-ass job"? They're speaking from the privilege of the FYF. That's a form of freedom in itself, and I STAN. If you need tips on getting financially sound, pick up my girl Tiffany Aliche's book *Get Good with Money*. If your mouth gets you in trouble, let your bank account have your back.

Next, ask yourself: Is my survival and the survival of others at stake?

Many of us are sitting in ivory towers, where the fear of punishment in our heads is overstated. I think about Black and Brown people whose voices and courage have caused them to be hurt or incarcerated or even killed. They aren't sitting in a cushy meeting on Zoom, afraid of not being invited to the team happy hour if they object to a shallow campaign. They are on the frontlines, telling the truth about racism, white supremacy, queerphobia, and more. They're laying their lives on the line because the best-case scenario of their voice and work is that systems of oppressions are overhauled to no longer marginalize people based on how much melanin is in their skin, who they worship, or who they love. Their best-case scenario is transformative change in our world, while their worst-case scenario is losing their livelihoods AND their actual lives.

Yet, they persist. They have weighed all these things, and even though they are often placed in real danger (physical or otherwise), they move forward anyway. THIS is truly courage. The rest of us might not be called to do that work, but we can at least put our fears into perspective.

Run through the scenarios exercise and you'll often find that you might have added a bit of color to what could happen as a result of you using your voice. You have invited that dragon you created to sit on your couch and have tea.

If you decide to move ahead and take action, there might be consequences, yes. But by choosing not to take action and choosing to stay where you are, you're actually choosing failure in advance.

If the worst-case scenario is likely AND would put you in danger, by all means SAVE YOURSELF.

But if it's likely and there is no real danger to you, ask yourself: What is keeping me quiet? Can I deal with whatever that scenario is?

If worst-case scenario is NOT likely, then the stakes are probably not that high.

Move forward with speaking up now, knowing that you are prioritizing the best-case scenario for the betterment of the room.

STEP 4: ASK THEM A QUESTION

Now that you know you're going to challenge this thing, start by developing a deeper understanding of the situation. This accomplishes two things: It affirms or denies your interpretation of the event, giving you that deeper understanding. It also allows the other person to reflect, which can lead to a change of heart OR a double down. Both are useful.

When you ask a question, the person has to engage with their own words, thoughts, and actions more. And if the person repeats their wrong (be it a wrong idea, wrong belief, or wrong action), then you can govern yourself accordingly.

As I shared earlier, if what happened was an insensitive joke or comment, ask the speaker earnestly, "What do you mean by that?" Your curiosity will have them either explaining their crassness or they will stop in their tracks, hopefully, apologizing because they recognize how out of line they were. If they gleefully explain it, well now you have information you can do a lot with.

Asking a question also buys you time as you gather your thoughts and further process what just happened.

PERSON: HA! You know how those people's food smells terrible?

YOU: *straight face* You mean Nigerians? How do their food smell?

What you just established there is the fact that you are willing and ready to challenge foolishness in your midst. It tells the other person that you aren't willing to brush off tactlessness, and they can find themselves in holes they dug.

STEP 5: ASK YOURSELF THE THREE QUESTIONS

When you've taken the time to zoom out and assess the situation you find yourself in and then have considered the consequences—weighing the best-case and worst-case scenarios—you're almost ready to speak the truth in hard situations.

I talked about this in chapter 6 (Speak the Truth), but it is worth repeating: When it's time to say the hard things, I ask myself these three questions to check in with myself:

Do you mean it? Why?

Can you defend it? How?

Can you say it thoughtfully? How?

When you've answered these questions, and the answer to all three is yes, the fear may still be present, but you go forth anyway. You'll have a plan for when the time comes to speak up and you'll no longer have to worry about feeling stuck or frustrated with yourself for not doing it.

Telling people around you thoughtful truths is a form of love. It says

"I care enough to hold you accountable. I care enough to move past my comfort zone to meet you and watch your back." It says "I want you to win so here I am, doing my best to support you with consideration."

This checkpoint does not guarantee people will receive it. Remember earlier, when I said your job is not to control folks' reactions? You are not Professor Xavier from X-Men or the Scarlet Witch. Your job is to honor yourself and be the person who makes you proud at the end of every day.

STEP 6: SLAY THE DRAGON: SAY IT THE BEST WAY YOU KNOW HOW

Soooo you're ready to say this thing. It's time to slay the fear dragon you created (one that's probably bigger than the actual issue in front of you).

Say the thing that is difficult even though you might be uncomfortable when you do it. Depending on who's in front of you, you can even admit that part: "This is really hard for me to say but I think it's important." "I don't like tough conversations but this one feels necessary." "I feel like I'm going against the group, but I want to honor myself here."

Be proud you did it scared. Take a deep breath. Chin high. I'm really proud of you. Keep doing it SCARED.

STEP 7: DO IT ALL AGAIN

There will be countless opportunities for us to speak truth, use our voices, and slay fear dragons. If you missed the chance last time, don't beat yourself up. Just commit to doing better next time, because there will always be a next time. And in case you did miss the chance, remember you can circle back and let the truth be heard, even if you are responding to something from days prior.

Relationships can reach a deeper understanding after tough conversations. Friendships can become more meaningful. You might prove your leadership qualities at your job and save your company from public embarrassment.

Similarly, relationships can break up after being challenged. Friendships can end. Jobs can be lost.

Telling the truth doesn't come with guarantees. It doesn't always make you the HERO. History is littered with disrespected truth-tellers who we later revere because hindsight is 20/20.

But history was also built by the troublemakers who insisted on doing this hard thing for the greater good over and over again. The world we live in exists, as good as it is, because of the disruptors who constantly slayed dragons, even though they didn't know what would meet them afterward.

To honor ourselves more, we need to rise up to the challenge of questioning those we know, love, or care about. The ones in our community (professionally and personally) are the ones we can reach. When we are at the table, let's not walk away lamenting what we could have done or said. Let's walk away knowing, "Well I did my part." If my silence will not make me proud, and if my inaction will convict me, I know that I have to tell the thoughtful truth. Because ultimately, the judge that matters most is me.

Courage is a habit. There isn't a truth-teller gene or personality trait. It is a choice that people make day in and day out to show up, to be uncomfortable, and to use their words with integrity. You can start making that choice now and the next time you are presented with the option. And then do it again. And do it again. VOILÀ, you too are a truth-teller. It's a commitment to yourself, to those around you, and to the world that you will be the person who uses their words to make the spaces they're in better.

Slay the dragon, friends. Use your voice. Speak the truth. Not just when it's difficult—especially when it's difficult.

The Steps to Truth-Telling

Step 1: Assess the situation

Step 2: Acknowledge the fear to yourself

Step 3: Prioritize the best-case scenario

Step 4: Ask them a question

Step 5: Ask yourself the three questions

Step 6: Slay the dragon: say it the best way you know how

Step 7: Do it all again

All my love to
Fúnmiláyọ̀ Fáloyin

Acknowledgments

TURN ALL THE WAY UP! When I finished my first book, *I'm Judging You*, I felt like I climbed a mountain. With this book, I feel like I did it again, with better shoes and a warmer coat. And almost got knocked off a couple times but pushed against the wind and got to the top anyway, making the view even sweeter.

Shout-out to meeee, cuz I DID THAT! Sometimes stopping to smell the roses looks like high-fiving yourself, and this book is something that feels revel worthy. Also, people write books and forget how to act. I am people.

My life truly is a testimony of God's grace, and this is yet another thing I've done that I hope makes Her/Him/Them proud. I am constantly shown that my steps are ordered by forces greater than me, and for that I am thankful.

Grandma, I know you're still working on my behalf and fighting for me from Beyond. Thank you. I hope you love this.

It took a village for this book to come together. Thanks to my agent,

Kristyn Keene Benton, who sent me a set of dominoes when it was time for me to start writing. She used my own words ("be the domino") to remind me of what my mission was, and her deep belief in my work pushed me forward. She also didn't side-eye me anytime I called her with some random idea.

Thanks to the team at Penguin Random House for believing in this book, this message, and my voice! Props to Meg Leder, my editor, who championed this book and made my words sing!

To the man I married, Carnell: thank you for playing many roles, as best friend, husband, and anchor. You see me in ways I'm sometimes not audacious enough to see myself. You don't let me have limits because you see stardust all over me. I remember when I finished this book and said, "Wow. This is the best thing I've ever written." You replied with, "I'm so proud of you, and it should be. You're the best YOU you've ever been." And my heart grinned like a Cheshire cat because words of affirmation are my top love language, and you get me. And I thanked God, once again, for blessing me with a life partner who affirms my very being. Mr. Jones, you're dope AF.

I am surrounded by love and people who prove that there is GREAT-NESS in the world, in the form of soft places to land. Shoutout to my family. I thank God for my mom. I am the daughter of Oluyemisi, who is the daughter of Fúnmiláyọ̀, who is the daughter of Celena. From her, I've learned generosity and the art of stunting when it is necessary. She is love in walking form.

I gotta shout-out my big sister, Kofo. You are the cheerleader of life, gist partner, dance partner, matron of honor, sometimes twin. Your heart is gold and you deserve all the good things life has to offer. Thanks for the grandma stories I forgot too. Whew, we got some of our funny from that lady.

So many thank-yous to my aunt, Bunmi B. She's the one I called over and over again to tell me more stories of Grandma and verify my facts, and she provided the oríkì. She's a quiet storm, a woman of integrity, and a joy bringer. Thank you for always picking up my calls, being the family historian, and for that laugh that brightens up a room.

Our family is a true tribe unto itself: Dele, Morayo, Rolake, Wonuola, Folarin. I'd fight for y'all but you already know this.

I surround myself with people who don't allow me to be raggedy, and for that I am thankful. I even pay someone to hold me accountable to being less trash. I must thank my late, great therapist, Dr. Patterson, who passed away two months before *Professional Troublemaker* dropped into the world. I thank her for helping me grow up. I have more of that to do, and the legacy of work she leaves behind will live loudly in me as I show up as the most vulnerable and true version of me. Dr. P has changed my life and I won't ever forget her. Shout-out to Aliya S. King, my friend, mentor, and first person who read this entire manuscript in full and ran her editing comb through it. She is also great for snatching my eyebrows with truth, and her edits for this book elevated my words.

LOVE to my FRAMILY (friends who become family) for peer-pressuring me into greatness and being everlasting dream enablers. Boz, Justina, Yvonne, Cynthia, Tiffany, Eunique, Felicia, Jessica, Tahira, Myleik, Maaden, Seun. They're the ones I call when something feels BIG, almost too big, and they always remind me that "If not you, then who?" Y'all push me onward and upward, constantly loaning me power whenever I'm lacking. Thank you, and I love y'all!!!

ALL THE LOVE to the citizens of LuvvNation, the most thoughtful, funny, chill-deficient play cousins on the interwebs. Building a safe space in a dumpster-fire world is one of the best things I could have done, and when people tell me my audience is amazing, I grin. Why? Because if they're a reflection of me, then they are proof that there is ample goodness in this world. LuvvCousins are the best!

Thank YOU, dear reader, for taking the time with my work. You and I officially go together. To have people find value in my work is such an honor. For that, lemme bless you with some prayers. May you never stub your toe on the side of the bed in the middle of the night. May you always season your food perfectly. May your pot of rice be perfectly cooked always. Amen.

This section could be a tome in itself, and there are so many more people who are significant to me who are not named here. You are probably one. Abeg don't be upset if I didn't name you. I had a word count to adhere to (see how I'm just throwing my publisher under the bus—HA!). But for real, thank you to everyone who sees, reads, buys, shares, and takes in my work.

Thank YOU for seeing me.

Luvvie